MW00565519

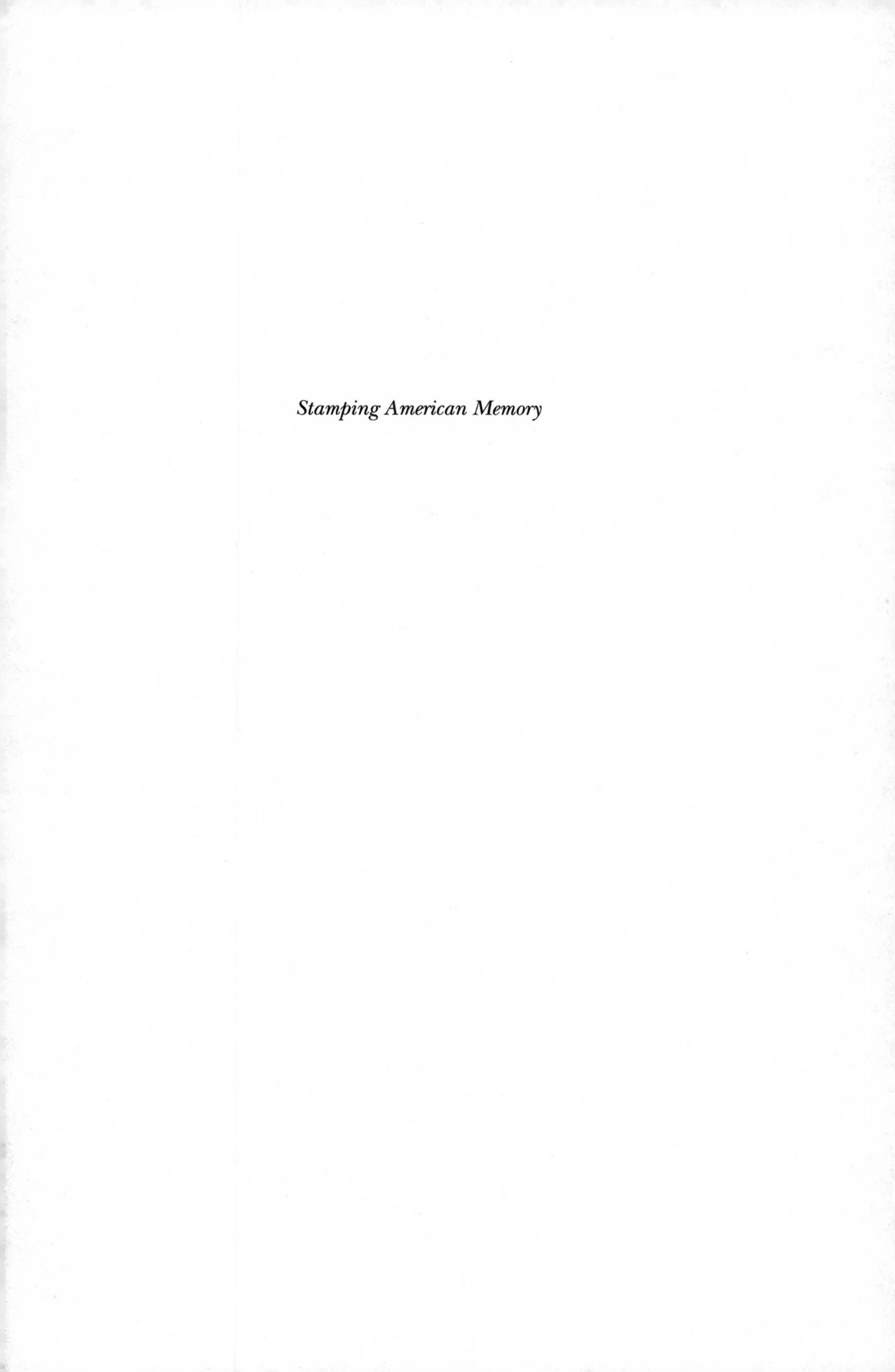

Stamping American Memory

DIGITAL HUMANITIES

Series Editors:
Julie Thompson Klein, Wayne State University
Tara McPherson, University of Southern California
Paul Conway, University of Michigan

Stamping American Memory: Collectors, Citizens, and the Post
Sheila A. Brennan

Big Digital Humanities: Imagining a Meeting Place for the Humanities and the Digital
Patrik Svensson

Ethical Programs: Hospitality and the Rhetorics of Software
James J. Brown Jr.

Digital Rhetoric: Theory, Method, Practice
Douglas Eyman

Web Writing: Why and How for Liberal Arts Teaching and Learning
Jack Dougherty and Tennyson O'Donnell, Editors

Interdisciplining Digital Humanities: Boundary Work in an Emerging Field
Julie Thompson Klein

Pastplay: Teaching and Learning History with Technology
Kevin Kee, Editor

Writing History in the Digital Age
Jack Dougherty and Kristen Nawrotzki, Editors

Hacking the Academy: New Approaches to Scholarship and Teaching from Digital Humanities
Daniel J. Cohen and Tom Scheinfeldt, Editors

Teaching History in the Digital Age
T. Mills Kelly

Manifesto for the Humanities: Transforming Doctoral Education in Good Enough Times
Sidonie Smith

DIGITALCULTUREBOOKS, an imprint of the University of Michigan Press, is dedicated to publishing work in new media studies and the emerging field of digital humanities.

Stamping American Memory

Collectors, Citizens, and the Post

SHEILA A. BRENNAN

University of Michigan Press
Ann Arbor

Published in the United States of America by the
University of Michigan Press
Manufactured in the United States of America
Printed on acid-free paper
First published June 2018

A CIP catalog record for this book is available from the British Library.

Library of Congress Cataloging-in-Publication data has been applied for.

LCCN 2017059437
LC record available at https://lccn.loc.gov/2017059437

ISBN 978-0-472-13086-3 (hardcover : alk. paper)
ISBN 978-0-472-12394-0 (e-book)
ISBN 978-0-472-90084-8 (Open Access ebook edition)

http://dx.doi.org/10.3998/mpub.9847183

Cover credit: Pilgrim Tercentenary, two cents, 1920 (*left*) and National Recovery Act issue, 1933 (*right*). Courtesy Smithsonian National Postal Museum Collection.

For Ian

Acknowledgments

During my first year at Bates College, I selected a work study job at the campus post office where I sorted and delivered mail, weighed packages to be sent across country and abroad, and generated money orders. I worked there for four years and never once considered researching stamps or the postal service. And yet it became formative in my professional and personal development. Similarly, I always collected things at different stages of my life, but never stamps. It wasn't until I started working at a museum that I began to see how different objects came into museum collections and how one person's personal fascination with certain things transformed everyday objects into artifacts through the process of accessioning. This experience triggered my curiosity about the areas of collecting practices, memory studies, and material culture. During graduate school, when a family stamp collection arrived, I realized that I had a starting point for a bigger project.

I intended to write a synthetic history of collecting in the United States, but after some research found an enormous number of philatelic sources that scholars barely touched. My adviser at the time, the late Roy Rosenzweig, encouraged me to follow those sources and to focus on stamps and stamp collecting. I worried that the topic would be too narrow and, frankly, that I would grow bored. I never expected to discover that stamp collecting was so engrained in American culture in the early twentieth century that it was the subject of hundreds of popular press articles and radio shows and used by department stores to promote sales. Or that the topic and practice figured into movie scripts like *Charade,* fiction like *The Crying of Lot 49*, or one-liners delivered by Groucho Marx in *Duck Soup.* Stamps and stamp collecting mattered, and I found good stories that connected collectors, noncollectors, and the US government in dialogues over the subjects of commemorative stamps because people cared about how those subjects represented the United States as a nation and an ideal.

The ideas embedded in this book and digital monograph were shaped, influenced, and supported by many people during its formation. I started this research under Roy's guidance. At many times throughout this project, I wished for his counsel. I was lucky to have learned from him as my teacher and adviser, boss and mentor. I came to the PhD program at George Mason University because of him, and I remained to work at the place now named for him, the Roy Rosenzweig Center for History and New Media.

A major part of Roy's legacy is the ethics he embedded in the work and the staff at the Center. The commitment to openness—to new ideas, collaborations, open-source software, open-access publishing—permeates our work there and work my colleagues and I do outside of the Center. The free, online version of Roy and Dan Cohen's 2005 book, *Digital History: A Guide to Gathering, Preserving, and Presenting the Past on the Web,* motivated me to seek out publishers who would be amenable to a hybrid publication that includes a free, open-access, digital version. This is what led me to the University of Michigan Press and its Digital Culture Books division. The Press was one of the first academic publishers to invite scholars to experiment with form, review, and collaboration in digital formats. I am grateful to the Press and the Humanities, Arts, Science, Technology Collaborative (HASTAC) for creating opportunities that encourage junior scholars to publish digitally and for awarding me a Digital Humanities Publication Prize in 2012 to create *Stamping American Memory* as a hybrid publication.

I never intended to publish a print monograph. I wanted to create a long-form, open-access, digital project that invited commentary and underwent an open peer review process that might grow in a digital space into something far beyond my own ideas and sources. Developing, designing, and shepherding digital work, however, is challenging.

What I developed resides at stampingamericanmemory.org, and, here is the print monograph. The print form retains some elements of the digital, because I wrote and revised with online readers in mind. The digital version contains more images and more discreet sections, but the ideas and the sources remain the same, and I hope you as the reader find this style works in print.

As I waded into the options for publishing *Stamping American Memory* digitally, I sought and received guidance from colleagues and friends who themselves successfully pushed back on traditional publishing formats and shared lessons they learned, including Kathleen Fitzpatrick, Dan Cohen, Tom Scheinfeldt, and Jack Dougherty. I am also grateful for those who generously volunteered their time to review this work during the open peer review process, who received no compensation but did so because they were interested this work and in participating in this type of review. Many thanks go to Denise Meringolo, Clarissa Ceglio, Ivan Greenberg, and Alyssa Anderson.

My research relies heavily on sources maintained locally and shared digitally from the Smithsonian National Postal Museum. The Postal Museum was one of the first history museums in the United States to launch a collections database filled with deep descriptive metadata and images. *Arago: People, Postage & Post* has been critically important to my work, and the images found in my digital and print publication draw heavily from sources in *Arago* I examined closely on my computer screen at home, and returned to over and over. This type of openness exemplifies how sharing collections online furthers scholarly research. The Postal Museum's librarians and curators are responsive and helpful. This is also true of the staff at the American Philatelic Society, all of whom are genuinely pleased when researchers approach them about accessing records, objects, and special collections.

I feel lucky to be part of George Mason University's history department, which values and supports digital history scholarship. Throughout the project's development, I relied on feedback, advice, and support from my dissertation adviser, Alison Landsberg, and committee member Michael O'Malley, as well other members of the faculty, especially Christopher Hamner, Mills Kelly, Lincoln Mullen, and Rosemarie Zagarri. My GMU classmates saw this project develop and helped me to sort out problematic pieces over many years and cheered me on along the way: Bill Carpenter, Katja Hering, Chris Hughes, Jenny Landsbury,

Steve Saltzgiver, Kevin Shupe, and Rob Townsend. Susan Smulyan at Brown University has been a mentor and friend for twenty years who always offers the advice I need, rather than telling me what I want to hear. *Stamping American Memory* is better because of all of you.

Since 2005, I have worked with many smart people at the Center for History and New Media who embody Roy's vision. You all challenge me, make me smarter, and indulge my desire to discuss details about food and popular culture at the dev table in between our work sprints and meetings. I am grateful for the lasting friendships developed over these years, and for the opportunities to collaborate and consult on many important digital projects. The Center is a unique place, particularly for its legacy of hiring and preparing individuals to do digital humanities work across it many forms. This is evident in the list of innovators and leaders who now count as Center alumni. From that list, there are a few individuals in particular, Sharon Leon, Lisa Rhody, and Joan Troyano, who have supported me through the ups and downs of this project and other personal challenges in countless ways. Thank you.

To my family and dear friends whom I do not see nearly as often as I would like, thanks for providing me with endless happy distractions via Facebook, emoji-filled texts, and kind notes. I am grateful to be part of a large family, fictive and consanguinal, filled with strong women. My mom, Ann Brennan, in particular, continues to push through difficult challenges during her life with an enviable amount of inner strength. Thank you for leading by example. My brother Marty and I are doing all right, because of you. I look forward to celebrating the end of this project with you both, Jada, and Ian.

To Ian, who pushes me to be more observant and creative than I am on my own and encourages me to step away from my laptop, I look forward to discovering more new things with you, and to the next big thing.

Contents

Introduction

> Much of the revelation was to come through the stamp collection Pierce had left, his substitute often for her—thousands of little colored windows into deep vistas of space and time . . . No suspicion at all that it might have something to tell her . . . what after all could the mute stamps have told her . . .
>
> —Thomas Pynchon, *The Crying of Lot 49*

Scholars, like Thomas Pynchon's character Oedipa Maas, often overlook stamps and the practice of stamp collecting, missing how those "deep vistas of space and time" imprint visions of the past on the cultural memory of those who viewed them.[1] Throughout his novella, Pynchon hints of an uncovered complexity and influence of the US postal service not only for communication, but also as a central institution for circulating, managing, and shaping visual meanings of nation on stamps.

Millions of Americans collected stamps at one point in their lives between the 1880s and 1940, yet, despite its popularity, stamp collecting has not been examined closely by scholars. Many historians often overlook all aspects of postal operations and their influence on American culture. Traditionally, the study of stamps has been the domain of collectors and enthusiasts who immerse themselves in learning the details of stamp design and production, and do not uncover the cultural contexts in which those stamps were produced. Stamps are not mere instruments of postal operations, but rather, objects deeply embedded in culture, with complicated stories to tell. Stamps are designed to be symbolic, and we should interpret them as such. Pynchon's text stages both the importance of the postal service as an index to national life and the value of looking more closely at stamp-collecting practices. *Stamping American Memory: Collectors, Citizens, and the Post* bridges this gap between historians, collectors, and enthusiasts.

This study follows Pynchon's trail by demonstrating how American commemorative postage stamps hold meanings beyond their mute images, images that illustrate how Americans and their government commented on the past and the present. To investigate the meaning of the stamps, I look at the institution producing them and the ways in which people chose to collect, save, discuss, and display their stamps. Stamp collecting emerged in the United States as an activity independent of the postal service. This changed once the US Post Office Department (USPOD) recognized this community of collectors and printed limited-issue commemoratives designed to be saved. Those stamps were rarely redeemed for postal delivery, giving commemoratives the potential to increase the gross income earned by an agency constantly struggling to balance its budget. By selecting scenes and figures from the American past for printing on commemorative stamps, the USPOD emerged in the early twentieth century as one of the most active federal agencies engaged in public history making prior to the New Deal. *Stamping American Memory* makes that history visible, while also investigating the relationships and intersections among stamp collectors (philatelists), noncollecting citizens, and the postal service. These relationships shape concepts of nationalism, consumption, and memory making in early twentieth-century America.

This study begins after the American Civil War, approximately thirty years after the postal revolution began in Great Britain. In 1840, the British developed a system for prepaying postage based on the weight of a letter rather than on the distance it traveled. The stamp served as a physical representation of paid postage, bearing the head of reigning monarch Queen Victoria. This system emerged from the needs of the sprawling British Empire, where a very small letter might travel thousands of miles and across oceans to reach its destination within British territory. European and North and South American nations followed the new British model and also adopted the prepaid postage system in the mid-nineteenth century. A few individuals found these colored bits of paper curious and fascinating, and began casually collecting and trading stamps among associates without the acknowledgment or support of government postal services.[2]

Since governments created stamps to serve the needs of empires, it is not surprising that collecting stamps mimicked imperialistic tendencies, but on a much smaller scale. Stamps often acted as official and visual press releases to the world announcing the establishment of a newly independent nation, the ascension of a new monarch, or the election of a national leader. All stamps contained identifying signs to indicate the country of origin in words and/or symbols, the denomination in native currency, and a design that included color, typography, and imagery. These variables combined into designs that represented the dominant ideologies of one nation or empire on behalf of it citizens, and were offered for the community of collectors around the world to interpret. For colonies, protectorates, and occupied territories, that vision most often was controlled by the ruling authorities, who focused imagery on the beauty and exoticism of place to de-emphasize questions of sovereignty. Stamps stand as symbols for nations as distinct political and ideological entities, so collectors easily used national or imperial distinction as a consistent way to classify and arrange stamps.[3]

Beginning in the late nineteenth century, collectors who amassed and traded stamps organized them by country or colony neatly in albums. Scholars of collecting assert that the act of assembling collections creates something new even when collectors follow conventions for organizing these objects.[4] A stamp collector built his or her own small empire when collecting stamps from around the world or when collecting stamps from specific countries. The earliest US commemorative stamps celebrated conquests of empires while promoting American-run world's fairs from the 1890s to 1910s. When saving the "stepping stones" of American history, produced by the postal service, collectors read in their albums a constructed narrative of American exceptionalism.[5] Fittingly, the practice of collecting stamps grew in popularity in the United States as America's role increased economically, politically, and militarily around the world.

The development of stamp collecting from the 1880s through the 1930s not only mirrored the transformation of the United States into an international political power, but also mirrored the transition of the United States into a consumer society. Russell Belk posited that collecting by non-elites occurs only in consumer societies, when nonessential objects are bought, traded, and consumed in ways similar to other material goods.[6] Stamp collecting became popular at a time when mass-produced items were readily available and Americans increased the amount of money spent on nonessential household items, even if discretionary spending for most remained modest. Stamps, in general, were not expensive, and individuals obtained free stamps in product packaging, through trading duplicates, or from friends' and neighbors' mail. Collecting stamps held broad and varied appeal: for some it was purely aesthetics; others were intrigued by subject matter, the potential value, or the methods of production; while some simply enjoyed the thrill of the hunt. Collecting as a practice was not a new phenomenon in the time period I examine. Collecting for fun, however, became increasingly accessible and acceptable to Americans with some means, as the culture of consumerism was shaped by merchant capitalists, private and federal institutions, and advertising agencies from the 1880s through the 1930s.[7]

Part of this consumer culture was a new and powerful advertising industry. Advertisements sold consumer goods by referencing the American past and invoking national symbols to associate purchasing a product with patriotism and good citizenship. Simultaneously, the Post Office Department printed and sold its own products that invoked national symbols and referenced the American past. These stamps served dually as prepaid postage and as a consumer collectible. Commercial advertising strategies framed consumption as an essential component of American identity and citizenship. Purchasing consumer goods, as constructed by advertisers, had the power to unite Americans through what Charles McGovern defines as "material nationalism." To advertisers, Americanness was found in things, and the language of those things promoted social harmony and assimilation while simultaneously erasing the presence of people of color or ethnic minorities.[8]

Similarly, the USPOD sought to unite Americans by selling a selective and triumphalist vision of the American past that erased contributions by people of color and obscured the legal foundations of oppression and inequality. This vision embodied the contradictions of civic and racial nationalisms as defined by Gary Gerstle.[9] While promoting the principle that all Americans enjoyed economic opportunity and political equality, commemoratives obscured complicated narratives that masked the legal and economic barriers preventing the achievement of full citizenship rights for anyone categorized as nonwhite. History presented on stamps functioned to tell its citizens, *This is your story, be proud*, even when it did not reflect the diverse and brutal realities of American history. Through its commemoratives, the USPOD emerged as a powerful institution that legitimized particular narratives about the national past, explaining why different groups lobbied so strenuously for their images and events to appear on commemorative stamps.

Carrying federal authority, commemorative stamps functioned as a type of souvenir to the American past, and, when saved, it became a miniature memorial. Susan Stewart sees a souvenir as an object that offers an incomplete vision of an event or place that it represents, thus requiring a new narrative that displaces the authentic experience.[10] Souvenirs are bought by tourists. Marita Sturken's assertion that Americans occupy the role of "tourist" when relating to their history is also useful in this context. Tourists experience history as a "mediated and reenacted experience," much like tourists who visit sites where they do not live. As tourists, people approach their visit to the past from a detached, innocent, and uncritical position. Souvenirs, produced to make money from tourists, imprint specific images of sites on the memory of persons keeping the trinket that also simplify complex realities of history.[11] By nature of their size and the imagery represented on these miniature memorials, stamps served as federally produced souvenirs that encouraged a tourist-like engagement with the history represented on stamps printed in the early twentieth century.

Purchasing a commemorative stamp, unlike buying a souvenir, did not represent a real visit to the past, but provided a gateway for millions of collectors and citizens to create and share a cultural memory of that event. Small in size, stamps were more accessible than memory sites, such as museums, archives, and monuments. These sites have power as nation-building tools. Much like structural memorials built in public spaces, one vision of the past dominates the stamp's imagery and often screens out other perspectives.[12]

As scholars of memory and memorialization have shown, the institutionalization of memory in a society serves the needs of a nation or community at a given time. Often, the messages projected through museum and monument designs are contentious. John Bodnar sees these struggles as the result of clash between an official and vernacular culture. The voices of official culture want to present the past in patriotic ways to emphasize ideals and achievements rather than in ways that engage complex realities. In contrast, the voices of vernacular culture represent the varied interests of diverse groups, reflecting personal experiences emerging from smaller communities.[13] Stamps provided official narratives generated by the USPOD, and by the 1920s commemoratives were the products of negotiations among collectors, noncollectors, and postal officials. Conflicts arose when the postal service chose to print commemorative stamps resulting from vernacular petitioning to honor a local anniversary or hero. Once selected for printing, local stories were elevated to national ones memorialized on a stamp. These stamps carried unmatched official legitimacy lent by their designation as a government issue. The same designation stripped away any complexity of that original narrative. Once circulated and saved, the images became "entangled" between history and memory, and embedded as the cultural memory of all those who viewed the stamp.[14]

Stamping American Memory is a cultural history that builds on the scholarship of postal history, nationalism, consumption, collecting, material culture, and memory and memoralization. I begin in the first chapter, "Building Philatelic Communities," by tracing how stamp collecting emerged as a hobby in the United States in the late nineteenth century during the age of imperialism and the era of American progressivism. Collecting objects other than fine arts grew in popularity, and philatelists began distinguishing themselves from casual collectors by forming exclusive clubs that mimicked professional associations, defined standards of practice, and published journals.

"Learning to Read Stamps" looks at how noncollecting citizens learned that stamps contained symbols and that stamps could be used for other purposes beyond mailing a letter. This accessibility and visual appeal of stamps invited different groups to use stamps as pedagogical tools for teaching about nation, imperialism, capitalism, and gender. Postal officials began to notice these collectors, and I explore that relationship in "Federal Participation in Philately." Merchant-capitalist, department store founder and owner, and postmaster general John Wanamaker recognized that collectors were consumers, and he pushed the Department to print its first commemorative stamp series, celebrating the World's Columbian Exposition in 1892. That success prompted the Department to print other world's fair stamps, participate in public exhibitions, and open the Philatelic Agency to serve collectors. During this process, the USPOD began to see collectors as consumers with money to spend, even if it was only two cents at a time. The Department expanded its already close relationship with Americans by encouraging them to purchase and save commemoratives as patriotic souvenirs, and the USPOD became an active participant in collecting culture and public history making.

Aware of the power infused into stamps, citizens, collectors, and postal officials engaged in negotiations over stamp subjects, which I discuss in "Shaping National Identity with Commemoratives in the 1920s and 1930s." Postal officials designed commemoratives to showcase the uniqueness of the American past and to represent all Americans. The faces on stamps, however, were overwhelmingly male and racially white, while scenes celebrated Western European immigration, conquests of native peoples, technological conquest of lands, and military heroism.

"Representing Unity and Equality in New Deal Stamps" closely examines how President Franklin Delano Roosevelt used the commemorative stamp program to build popular support for his federal initiatives and to project national unity during the Great Depression and on the eve of World War II. Seeking evidence of his verbal commitments to uplift the conditions of all Americans during his presidency, petitioners sought FDR's approval for commemoratives that celebrated achievements of women and African Americans, which also acknowledged the remaining legal barriers to achieving full political equality. Roosevelt understood that the visual language of stamps carried great political power and that those messages would be distributed widely to millions of Americans.

While reading *Stamping American Memory*, readers will see, I hope, that stamp collecting was not just an insignificant hobby practiced by a few obsessed individuals. Rather, that collecting provides a way to examine how millions of individuals and the federal government participated in a conversation about national life in early twentieth-century America. As a collectible, stamps transformed into miniature memorials through the act of being saved. This study draws upon sources known to historians and to philatelists separately that haven't been adequately brought together in one piece of scholarly work.

Brief History of Collecting in the United States

Collecting is a centuries-old practice most often associated with European royalty until the revolutionary era of the late eighteenth and early nineteenth centuries and the emergence of capitalism, particularly in the United States. During the early Republic, prominent individuals such as Thomas Jefferson and Charles Wilson Peale collected a variety of natural, technological, and art objects as interest in collecting slowly increased in the United States. Some sought to complete autograph sets containing the signatures of each signer of the Declaration of Independence, while others pursued art, coins, and books. Many collectors retained their collections privately, while others wanted to connect with like-minded individuals and founded clubs in the mid-nineteenth century.[15]

Those interested in learning more about art and who lacked the money to purchase original pieces on their own joined the American Art Union (AAU), one of the earliest collecting clubs in the United States. From 1839 to 1853, the AAU's dues supported American artists and each year gave members an engraved print created from paintings by artists including Thomas Cole, Asher Durand, and George Caleb Bingham. Additionally, AAU members had an opportunity to obtain original art through an annual lottery system. In 1852, the New York Supreme Court, however, declared the art lottery to be illegal and forced the AAU to dissolve and auction off its remaining holdings. At its peak, the AAU's rolls grew to include nearly 19,000 members across the United States.[16]

Others interested in coins might have joined the American Numismatic Society (ANS), established in 1858 to pursue and study ancient coins. The ANS positioned itself as a national organization that brought together local numismatic associations established in cities across the United States and encouraged the formation of new groups. Wealthy New York bibliophiles established the Grolier Club in 1884 to discuss their book collections and to dabble occasionally in poster collecting.[17]

Many others collected privately without belonging to clubs. This was particularly true for women and children, who collected a variety of free or found objects, from butterflies to buttons to trade and prayer cards. In the 1870s and 1880s, colorfully printed and mass-produced chromolithographic trade cards appeared in consumer product packaging to encourage brand loyalty among consumers. The advent of advertising trade cards also signaled a deliberate move on the part of consumer capitalists to produce items for the purpose of collecting and preservation that encouraged spending to broaden a collection. At the same time, churches and religious societies saw the popularity of advertising cards and printed their own versions that included biblical figures and passages or prayers. Some practicing Christians enjoyed collecting prayer cards because doing so offered a material connection to their faith and also functioned to identify them as part of a larger religious community. Some of these private or home-based collections made by men, women, and children landed in scrapbooks, while others were merely thrown away.[18]

With the growth of collecting in the middle and late nineteenth century, collectors of all types of objects were labeled as being afflicted with "the collecting mania." Evidence as early as 1812 in French publications referred to collectors as developing a mania for pursuing autographs and historical letters. This language does not resurface until the 1860s. According to one assessment in 1868, a stamp-collecting mania appeared in the United States and affected young people, while the mania for collecting pictures and coins mainly affected adults.[19] Many newspaper articles referenced the "collecting mania" and a "mania for collections," while it was occasionally discussed in popular literature.[20]

Generally, manias were associated specifically with women at a time when many health professionals believed the female physiology made them more susceptible to mental disorders. Popular discussions positioned the mania in opposition to the scientific ideal as both concepts were being developed and shaped by cultural, gender, and class-based stereotypes. Women identified as middle class or of means who shoplifted merchandise from department stores were not common criminals, but instead were afflicted with kleptomania, which left them physically unable to resist goods that passed before them.[21]

The "collecting mania" or "mania for collections" was applied to both men and women collectors who could not help their desire to acquire more objects. To prevent the mania from setting in, a variety of articles warned readers against collecting objects of any kind by the 1880s and 1890s. Something that started innocently as a childhood activity, according to one observer, might progress to an adult "disease" or to the early stages of dementia, leading one to an asylum. While stamp collecting appeared to onlookers in the nineteenth century as "merely a form of mild insanity or monomania," for some "enthusiastic collectors, it became the principal interest of their lives." By the 1920s, as collecting grew in popularity, more adults accepted it as a suitable leisure activity and found that collecting offered individuals "the surest remedies against the tedium and monotony of life."[22] In the early twentieth century, more Americans grew interested in collecting, and public opinions of collectors began to change, as we will see, due in part to the growing legions of stamp collectors.

Building Philatelic Communities

> "Well, I declare! You stamp collectors beat my understanding!"
> "Well, I suppose to one who is not interested in philately, stamp collecting seems like a queer business."
> "It isn't a business—it's a disease."
> —"The Prevailing Malady," 1895

Stamp collecting started as an obscure leisure-time activity in the 1860s and 1870s, but quickly emerged as a popular and more structured pursuit by the 1880s in the United States and internationally. Identifying themselves as philatelists, stamp collectors created a large community in the late nineteenth century that extended well into the twentieth through the establishment of clubs and the success of a wide-reaching philatelic press. Defining themselves as experts, these collectors wished to bring respectability to a leisure activity that they enjoyed and that others ridiculed. Clubs established the study of stamps as a serious discipline, defined by their own as scientific, and created a professionalized feeling about the hobby through club meetings and publications that mimicked academic journals. As new groups of philatelists formed and dissolved, hierarchies also emerged in the philatelic world as clubs restricted membership based on race and gender, and "philatelists" distinguished themselves from mere "collectors." Philatelists also debated among themselves about the practices of philately, and whether it led its followers down a path of knowledge and enlightenment or a path toward materialism and greed. Philatelists formed a national network that helped to legitimize their activities, influenced businesses to pay attention to them in consumerist ways, and expanded the hobby to attract a broader audience as it grew in popularity. Through the process of selecting, saving, and preserving stamps, collectors and philatelists established relationships with their favorite objects. Importantly, the US Post Office Department noticed those connections by the 1890s and intentionally printing colorful stamps that told stories, historical narratives about America's past.

Early Stamp Collecting

People began collecting stamps in Great Britain and France soon after the postage revolution in the 1840s, and the practice spread to the United States. The first dealers in the United States, George Hussey, James Brennan, J. M. Chute, John W. Kline, and Ferdinand Marie Trifet, were found in New York and Boston in the late 1850s and early 1860s. To promote a serious aspect of studying and collecting stamps, Georges Herpin coined the term "philately" in 1864, drawing on the Greek root *philos,* meaning fond of, and *atelia,* meaning exemption from tax or tax receipt. Early collectors in Great Britain focused on the colors and subjects of stamps. In contrast, French collectors began examining the elements of stamp production, including the variation of shade, paper, watermarks, and perforations, with less concern for the subjects. As a handful of international businessmen joined casual enthusiasts in analyzing stamps for their subjects and their production qualities, stamp collectors slowly became "philatelists."[1]

The earliest stamp collectors earned reputations as "cranks" who were afflicted with a disease, often referred to as the "collecting mania," a perception that continued for decades after the hobby emerged in the 1870s and 1880s. Many collectors felt the need to justify why collecting stamps was not "a queer business" and battled accusations that they were engaged in a childish folly by insisting it was a worthy pursuit.[2] Wealthy Americans and nouveau riche industrial capitalists collected fine art, yet their behavior rarely was equated with a mania.[3] Economically stable Americans of more modest means also learned to collect things in the nineteenth century, and stamps became one of the most popularly collected items. Collecting stamps appealed to many different audiences, and grew in popularity in part because of the ways that this budding hobby community organized in the United States during the 1870s, 1880s, and 1890s.

Philatelists began to connect with other collectors, and by the 1880s, the first American stamp association had been established. Predating technical hobby clubs created after World War II, philatelic societies formed a national network of clubs in the nineteenth century to help legitimize their activities, to explain their hobby to a broader audience, and to increase the popularity of the practice.[4]

By the early twentieth century, a stamp-collecting culture emerged as collectors established communities by forming membership clubs, published and circulated hundreds of philatelic papers, and encouraged others to collect. These communities sought to define themselves by a set of practices and behaviors that distinguished members as "philatelists" and constructed philately as a type of scientific pursuit. Comprised predominantly of white male members of financial means, members wanted to attract new collectors to philatelic clubs, but they also constructed barriers and rules that reinforced exclusivity of the privileged represented by their paying members.[5]

Other collectors never joined clubs but participated in the philatelic culture through the circulation of stamp literature and exposure through mainstream media collecting columns and stories about new commemorative releases. These institutional structures helped to shape how philatelists and collectors viewed themselves and how they practiced their hobby. This community became influential as the hobby grew in popularity and in the ways that philatelists shaped stamp production in the United States through the early twentieth century.

Who Collected Stamps?

Quantifying collectors and analyzing their demographics is difficult, because most individuals collected privately, outside of formalized clubs. Kings, queens, lords, czars, and American politicians put a public face on philately in late nineteenth- and early twentieth-century periodicals, but most American collectors were not famous or worthy of headlines. They worked in a variety of occupations and lived in both rural and urban areas. *Rogers' American Philatelic Blue Book of 1893* indicated that late nineteenth-century stamp collecting was truly a pursuit of young adults who worked in a variety of occupations. The *Blue Book* listed more farmers than doctors and more clerks than bankers, and showed that skilled workers such as electricians, carpenters, blacksmiths, quarrymen, patternmakers, and coal miners publicly identified themselves as stamp collectors. More than half of the 2,000 respondents did not belong to a philatelic association, but they must have occasionally read a philatelic paper to know about Rogers's free listings in this directory.[6]

Directories, like *Rogers' Blue Book* and others printed by prominent philatelic publisher Mekeel's, showed that collectors lived in big cities and small towns across the United States. Most collectors listed themselves by their last name and first initials, making gender speculation difficult, but the occupations listed indicate that most probably were male. Rogers compiled his directory to grow membership in the American Philatelic Association, of which he was a member. *Rogers' Blue Book* provided some excellent information about collectors not found in other directories of collectors (such as *Mekeel's*), particularly age, occupation, and affiliations. Out of the 2,000 collectors listed, only 1,718 were American collectors, and only 54 identified themselves solely as dealers. Not surprisingly, *Rogers'* did not ask about the race or gender for the listings.[7]

Circulating addresses also gave collectors the opportunity to build communities and foster connections across geographies via the mail system by writing to others seeking to trade or buy stamps. By the 1890s, stamp collecting was an established pastime shared by many men working in white- and blue-collar occupations across the country who had a few extra dollars and hours to spend on a hobby, and some of them joined newly forming philatelic clubs.

Women Collectors

For a hobby that men appeared to dominate, at least publicly, it is intriguing that women played a formative role in shaping the mythology of early philately. One philatelic writer claimed that the first gatherings of stamp collectors in Paris in the 1860s were hosted and attended by women who exchanged their duplicate stamps on Sunday afternoons in the Tuileries Gardens. When the postage system was still new in Britain, women collected stamps featuring the profile of reigning monarch Queen Victoria. In the 1880s, women's magazines such as *Godey's Lady's Book* and *Ladies' Home Journal* proposed that stamp collecting was an appropriate activity for women. Because it was an indoor amusement, "restful" and "quieting after the mind has been busily occupied with duties," it was viewed as a proper way for middle-class women to spend their leisure time. Women were well suited to the pastime because it involved creativity—when arranging a collection—that capitalized on their "natural artistic tastes." *Godey's* instructed women how to decorate tables with stamps, and *Ladies' Home Journal* taught women how to throw a "fad party" that included a stamp-collecting hunt.[8] This style of collecting and using stamps by women was seen by some club philatelists, as noted by one in 1919, as lacking "the great principles of philately."[9] Those principles emerged with the establishment of a network of philatelic clubs in the 1870s, 1880s, and 1890s that guided members to organize and analyze stamps in particular ways.

Club philatelists, for example, never advocated decorating with stamps, but rather urged collectors to protect and save stamps carefully in albums. Since collecting and presenting stamps in decorative ways were not valued by philatelists, most material evidence of those pieces was not saved. Nonetheless, articles in women's magazines exposed women to the hobby even when they were not accepted into many philatelic clubs in the late nineteenth and early twentieth centuries.

Nonclub Collectors Influenced by Popular Media

The popular press also exposed the diverse American public to information about stamp collecting and increased interest that led to broader adoption of the hobby. Whether observers were extolling the values of collecting, perpetuating the idea that anyone could find a rare stamp in a box of old letters, or framing stamp collecting as a "mania," stamp collecting was in the news. The presence of stamp-collecting articles in American newspapers and magazines was not overwhelming, but the numbers of articles increased greatly from the 1870s to the 1930s, marking a sharp growth in exposure never shared by similar hobbies, including coin collecting.

By searching the contents of the historical newspaper databases, it is possible to see an overall increase in numbers of articles referring to philately and stamp collecting in the 1890s, and then again in the 1920s and 1930s. Articles first appearing in larger-market papers, such as the *New York Times* and *Washington Post*, were often reprinted in smaller-market papers. The fewest total articles appeared in the African American press, meaning there was less casual exposure to philately than to readers of the major dailies.[10]

As early as the 1870s, youth magazines promoted stamp collecting as an appropriate and educational activity for young people. *St. Nicholas* was among the first nonphilatelic publications to devote valuable copy space to promoting stamp collecting. It published numerous articles on stamp collecting that offered primers to teach child readers about stamps from different nations and the practices of collecting. *St. Nicholas* began a trend that many other periodicals would soon follow. In 1910, the *Christian Science Monitor* began publishing regular articles on stamps for young readers, and *The Youth's Companion* started a stamp-collecting column in 1919.[11]

This trend spread to the dailies as well. In the late 1920s, the *Los Angeles Times* printed a regular hobby column that often included articles on stamps; the *Chicago Daily Tribune* began a Sunday stamp column in 1932; and the *Washington Post* added the "Stamp Album" to its "Junior Post" section for young readers in 1934. The *New York Sun* even bought ads in the *Chicago Tribune* inviting its readers to subscribe to the *Sun's* Saturday paper specifically to read its special stamp-collecting section. In 1936, the *Philatelic Almanac* listed 150 papers supporting stamp departments that generated regular articles or columns.[12]

With the emergence of commercial broadcasting in the 1920s, listeners not only tuned in to hear musicians and comedy acts, but also listened to stamp-collecting programs. Newspapers listed daily programming from their home city and from other regions; shows ran from fifteen minutes to a half hour. *Mekeel's* tracked philatelic radio programming and listed nine regular shows in 1932 broadcast from stations in Illinois, Georgia, North Carolina, Pennsylvania, New York, and New Jersey. By 1936, more than sixty stations broadcasted philatelic shows. Those who listened regularly were exposed to stamp-collecting practices and "the drama of the postage stamp."[13]

As philatelic information spread in different media, stamp collecting attracted new practitioners and appealed to the interests of different people. Magazines, newspapers, and radio programs brought some activities that had been exclusive to philatelic clubs and publications out into a public realm. For collectors who did not belong to a club, especially for those excluded from clubs, this exposure increased their philatelic knowledge and allowed them to connect with the philatelic community through the media.

Organizing into Clubs

Philatelic clubs and associations defined the practices of philately and helped to legitimize stamp collecting as a leisure-time activity. The formation of philatelic associations mirrored some of the processes undertaken by newly forming professional associations that demanded their members uphold certain standards and practices. These societies, as almost exclusively all white, all male, and all admitted through sponsorship, demonstrated the exclusivity common to late nineteenth-century clubs. These collectors were part of a "consuming brotherhood" that emerged in the late nineteenth century. Spending money on dues and stamps was similar to how members of fraternal orders and elite dinner clubs consumed: purchasing costumes, paraphernalia, or cigars.[14] Stamp societies created standards for normative collecting behaviors that lent legitimacy to their practice so outside observers would see purchasing stamps and collecting paraphernalia as nonfrivolous and worthy expenditures.

Together with these new organizations, stamp collectors internationally distinguished themselves from other collectors by constructing their hobby as a scientific and rational pursuit. In contrast with those afflicted with a collecting mania, philatelists claimed to practice a rational leisure-time activity they broadly defined as a "science" because their collecting work involved researching through observation, classification, and arrangement. The language of science permeated many aspects of everyday in the late nineteenth century. Definitions of science and who qualified to be called scientists was also highly contested. As Progressive Era social scientists worked to create a science of the sociohistorical world, philatelists tried to utilize scientific practices by studying the world of stamps with support of their newly created associations.[15]

The idea that philately could be scientific may also have been rooted in nineteenth-century European philosophical ideas about writing history. This type of historical inquiry was promoted by the newly formed American Historical Association and was taught in graduate programs training professional historians. Collecting documents for careful study and comparison helped historians draw conclusions about historical "facts" that led to supposedly objective histories.[16] Although not seeking to answer historical questions, philatelists studied stamps as primary documents. Such research equated to scientific study in the minds of some. One British publication asserted, "If minute observation, research, dexterity, taste, judgment, and patience are sufficient to lift a pursuit from a hobby to a science then assuredly Philately is a science."[17]

Philatelic associations and individual philatelists perpetuated the idea that the collection and study of stamps was a scientific practice, even if they did not explicitly explain why. In one British book on philately, Arthur Palethorpe simply declared that "philately now ranks as a science," equating the practices of philately with that of a serious discipline. A philatelist classified a stamp by country of origin, year issued, denomination, paper type, paper perforations, printing process, and subject. Careful observation of the ink or perforations of a stamp might lead a collector to find differences or perhaps a mistake. Because stamps were mass-produced, any differences within a sheet or printing were considered to have more value than the monetary amount assigned to that stamp.[18] Stamp journals printed by philatelic associations described and defined philately as scientific. The editors of the *American Journal of Philately* commented that their readers enjoyed debating "in the field of our sciences," while the *Northwestern Philatelist* billed itself as "a monthly magazine devoted to the sciences of philately."[19] Whether thinking about philately as scientific history or using the term "science" to gesture to individuals engaging in research and study of stamp design and production, incorporating this rhetoric was prevalent in stamp literature.

Collectors found support in the new philatelic associations and societies, as some hid their collecting habits from the hobby's critics. Eva Earl, a contributor to *Pennsylvania Philatelist*, acknowledged that in 1894 it was "customary to laugh at the devotees to stamp collecting—all the world laughs."[20] Vindication of this push to recognize philately as a disciplined pursuit came in 1907 when King Edward VII of Britain declared stamp collectors to be "scientists" and philately to be a "science," as he elevated the London Philatelic Society to status of "Royal" by officially incorporating the Society with a royal charter. Most likely influenced by his son, who amassed a large collection of stamps, the king observed the prince researching and attending to his collection. Prior to the king's proclamation, philatelists in the United States delighted in the establishment of a Section of Philately in the Brooklyn Institute of Arts and Sciences devoted to the study and promotion of stamp collecting in 1898. The Institute hosted lectures and meetings where collectors could bring their stamps for "study and comparison" for the purpose of making meetings "profitable and interesting." More than a quarter century later, the Maryland Academy of Sciences elevated philately from a subsection of its history department to become its own department, placing philately, once again, "among the sciences."[21]

Defining their hobby as a science also offered philatelists an opportunity to achieve an expertise in the small bits of paper they collected, traded, or bought through stamp clubs and associations. Club founders and members were stamp dealers, who bought and sold stamps for a living, and casual collectors, who bought, traded, or sold their stamps during their free time. Informal meetings of collectors were not new, but when those collectors formed associations, they organized in a more systematic way. The first permanent organization in the world was the London Philatelic Group in 1869, now known as the Royal Philatelic Society. The American Philatelic Association (APA) formed in 1886, and its founders encouraged local affiliates to gather wherever "six philatelists can be brought together." As a national society, the APA would connect smaller groups meeting across the country in the pursuit of philatelic knowledge.[22]

American Philatelic Association

In the 1886, the newly created American Philatelic Association desired to build a network of regional collecting clubs that together formed an internationally significant organization that rhetorically fit with late nineteenth-century concepts of American exceptionalism. The founding members of the APA were not isolated from the transitions of American business and leisure life near the end of the nineteenth century. A breakdown of local autonomy in small "island communities" began in the 1870s as hierarchical needs of industrial life took hold in the United States.[23] In a similar way, the APA sought to join island communities of stamp collectors to form an infrastructure that supported and nationalized the hobby. The founders believed that the adage "In union there is strength" applied to stamp-collecting communities. Bringing national recognition to the hobby, the APA promised to promote philately "as worthy and rational" because "it should be regarded in the same light as are the generally recognized specialties that have worked their way from obscurity to the positions they now apply."[24] Signifying similarities with newly forming professional associations, these founding members suggested stamp collecting could emerge from obscurity with a formal organization leading the way. By establishing a society of like-minded individuals, philatelists hoped to spread the word about stamp collecting to a national audience.

On September 14, 1886, the APA held their first meeting to draw up by-laws and a constitution, elect officers, and establish membership and affiliation rules. The small group chose John K. Tiffany, an attorney from St. Louis, Missouri, to be the APA's first president. By-laws detailed best practices for obtaining stamps and discouraged counterfeiting. According to the preamble of their constitution, the APA would help members learn more about philately, cultivate friendship among philatelists, and encourage an international bond with "similar societies" in other countries.[25] Philately had a strong international component for all collectors, since most collected and studied stamps printed in countries other than their own. Additionally, the APA believed that connecting with groups outside of the United States would raise the stature of this association and make the APA the premiere national philatelic organization. The overall mission of the APA sought to legitimize and publicize the practice of stamp collecting.

Less concerned, rhetorically, with excluding unaffiliated stamp collectors, the APA's constitution encouraged people to join. Technically, "any stamp collector" could apply to the secretary of the APA for membership. Current members considered a candidate's background for one month before voting to accept or reject petitioners. This procedure was in place to ensure no known counterfeiters applied. Yet if a candidate was not sponsored by another member, chances were high that the application for membership would be denied. This practice mimicked how other exclusive social clubs operated in an attempt to keep out undesirables, namely women and people of color. For an annual fee of two dollars, APA members received the *American Philatelist* journal, gained access to the APA library, and enjoyed the community of collectors for buying and trading varieties. While embracing all stamp collectors, the APA firmly and publicly rejected those dealing in or making counterfeit stamps.[26] By denying membership to known counterfeiters, the APA reassured members that the stamps they dealt or traded were government-issued stamps.

While partaking in social gatherings was one aspect of club life, leadership in the APA encouraged a serious study of stamps as part of membership. The second president, Charles Karuth, asked members in 1899 what the APA had done for the "advancement of the science of philately." Karuth saw its membership comprising mostly collectors and not philatelists, as he carefully distinguished between the "mere amassment of stamps" and the study of philately. So as not to be viewed as "stamp cranks" and to distance themselves from schoolboys who swapped stamps, APA members were encouraged to engage in the valuable and scientific side of philately. If they did this, Karuth believed, philatelists would be "recognized as gentlemen who had chosen a valuable branch of study."[27] Karuth's plea illustrated how the APA sometimes functioned like a professional association as it distinguished between professionals and amateurs. At the same time, Karuth's comments also demonstrated a growing tension among club philatelists who wanted to encourage more individuals to collect stamps, but only within strictures established by clubs.

Philatelists represented their pursuit with an allegorical figure, "Philatelia," the goddess of philately, who engaged in rigorous study of stamps. Philatelia symbolized their pursuit and may have acted as a guide for those pursuing philatelic knowledge. The APA adopted the image of Philatelia for its seal in 1887 and it is still used today. In the seal, Philatelia holds a stamp album in her left hand while she places a stamp into it with her right. As a figurative deity, she sits on a globe that makes her appear larger than the physical world that she sits upon while

Fig. 1. Seal of the American Philatelic Association (Image courtesy of the American Philatelic Society)

tending to the stamps kept in her album. Her position suggests that she can control the world on which she sits, gesturing that collecting stamps is symbolically similar to the imperialistic logics that justify how one country believes others are available to be collected and controlled. She is focused on her stamp album, appearing studious and unaware of others, and is not welcoming or open as she faces away from observers. Her focus on the album and its stamps offers a model for all philatelists who described themselves as "prostrate admirers and worshippers" and "all in love with one female—the Goddess Philatelia."[28]

Similar to female figures incorporated into other seals and artworks, Philatelia represented the ideals of the APA. Personified representations of America and Columbia, as well as other ideals and virtues, took female forms with which many Americans were no doubt familiar. Iconography similar to Philatelia appeared on public murals in the 1890s, with painted women representing justice, patriotism, and the disciplines of science in the Library of Congress. Imagery represented a real political and cultural conflict, because some of the principles personified by women were not legally available to them at the turn of the century, including rights to participate in democracy, to make economic choices, and to be protected equally under the law. Similar to these female mural icons, Philatelia celebrated activities that took place predominantly in a male world and was beloved by men.[29] Women collected stamps privately, but were not welcomed in most philatelic clubs. Philatelia, like other female idyllic icons, had limited symbolic powers to represent equality for American women at the turn of the century.

As the APA and other philatelic groups sought to expand their memberships, they still did not welcome women or people of color. Evidence of white women collecting stamps does not explain why many were turned away from pursuing memberships in stamp societies. First, formal organizations were exclusive and remained that way for many years, and some club names implied they were not for women or girls. The Sons of Philatelia and the Philatelic Sons of America were founded in the 1890s to encourage philately among young people, but sounded like male-only fraternal organizations. Records indicate, however, that a few female collectors belonged to these organizations, but their numbers remained small.[30]

With some club names sounding like a fraternal organization, many male collectors believed that philately was in fact a brotherhood—even transforming them into a brotherhood of Renaissance men. Knowledgeable in many subjects, including history, astronomy, geography, and languages, philatelists portrayed themselves as cosmopolitan men of the world. "We Collectors are brothers, comrades, citizens of a great, progressing, ever-widening Brotherhood."[31] This concept of brotherhood was grounded in ideas learned from experience with fraternal organizations and dinner clubs, and perhaps in saloons, where men socialized in their leisure time. Philatelic club kinship was referred to as "a Freemasonry among Stamp Collectors," where a fellow collector was "always warmly welcomed."[32] Likening the bonds formed to Freemasonry solidified philatelic clubs—in their minds—as a white-male-only domain, while participation in the hobby was not.

Clubs protected the brotherhood by controlling who earned memberships, making philatelic clubs almost exclusively male and white. In the 1880s, a few women applied to join the Staten Island Philatelic Society but never enrolled as members. Rolls from the APA indicate that there were five female members in 1889, but women never became a strong portion of national stamp-collecting societies. By 1915, 3 percent of the Southern Philatelic Association's membership were women. Most women, it appears, gave up on applying to clubs created in the late nineteenth century. By the mid-1920s, some women turned to newer and smaller stamp societies where the membership rules were less stringent. Even as late as 1990, one of the most exclusive clubs still did not allow female members.[33]

These clubs were not welcoming for people of color, either. Surprisingly, as African Americans established fraternal, religious, and social clubs on their own terms, stamp collecting appears almost absent from their leisure-time clubs.[34] And yet an African American publisher, who later became the assistant registrar to the US Treasury, reconstituted the Washington Philatelic Society (WPS) in 1905 together with white Washingtonians and became the club's first president. Cyrus Field Adams was a well-known businessman as editor and publisher of *The Appeal* who used his position at the paper and in various advocacy organizations to argue for political and economic rights of African Americans. He also loved to collect stamps and amassed a collection of over 6,000 when he served as the Washington Philatelic Society president. His presence in a white-dominated, "exclusive" club displeased some philatelists from other societies. Rumors were generated that spread through African American newspapers, and even in the *New York Times*, that Mr. Adams was passing as white, and to protect his identity denied an African American philatelist membership in the WPS. Adams had in fact voted for the applicant, whose membership was denied by a majority of the other members. These accusations demonstrate that Adams was an outlier as a collector in both the philatelic and African American communities.[35] The comics and jokes printed in philatelic magazines remind us that while philatelists were uniquely engaged within their hobby's community, they were not isolated from broader American social and cultural behaviors and discourse where racial stereotyping and racism was common.

As philatelic societies grew and established their membership criteria, they also carved out identities for their organizations and collectors. From its beginnings, the APA set forth to build a strong national philatelic organization in the United States designed to compete with British and continental European nations that had already formed their own national philatelic clubs.[36] To be on par with other national association, the APA articulated a vision in a few key ways.

First, the APA's desire to lead in philatelic pursuits came in the form of a vision. *The Philatelist's Dream*, an illustration printed in 1906, demonstrated how the APA could be a leading stamp society in the world.[37]

Fig. 2. "The Philatelist's Dream," illustration (Image courtesy of the American Philatelic Society)

In the *Dream*, a vision emerges from a philatelist's cigar smoke rings while he sits at his desk with his stamp album open. The first smoke ring approximates the APA's seal, with Philatelia sitting on a globe studying her album. In the next ring, Philatelia turns toward the viewer, with her album on the floor, and stretches as if she has awakened from a dream. The third ring is empty, as if Philatelia left the APA's seal. She appears above the three rings holding the globe and stamp album in her arms as she extends her right arm in an action of leadership and movement. Boys, men, and at least one woman follow the APA's Philatelia as she leads them west across the image.

The APA's image represents a striking similarity to late nineteenth-century art representing American destiny and progress, as the APA envisioned itself as a leader in the philatelic world. *The Philatelist's Dream* is reminiscent of the 1872 painting *American Progress* by John Gast, which was distributed widely and sold in lithograph form.

Fig. 3. "American Progress," chromolithograph, published by George Coffut, 1872 (Prints and Photographs Division, Library of Congress)

The female figure wears the "Star of Empire" and floats above people leading them and approving of their westward movement as settlers from the East proceed west across the painting. Settlers push out herds of buffalo and Native Americans, with trains, stage coaches, and ships bringing more settlers to complete the conquering of peoples and lands. The female figure carries a book in hand, not unlike Philatelia's album, symbolizing knowledge and learning. This awakening of the APA's Philatelia suggests that club philatelists internalized a vision of America as a unique place with a distinctive history, extending that exceptionalism to their philatelic association. Through this imagery we see that some club philatelists equated studying and collecting stamps with the cultural of imperialism. As the United States continued to conquer North America and islands in the Pacific and Caribbean, American stamp collectors became leaders in conquering the world in their philatelic knowledge and also in the ways that they amassed nations, stamp by stamp.

The second part of the APA's exceptionalist vision included an organizational theme song first presented at the 1906 annual meeting.

"Rah! For the American Philatelic Association"

Verse 1: Listen now! Ye nations all,
To our Philatelic song,
That shall tell the story of the A.P.A.;
The Association great,
Of a Nation big and strong,
Which for enterprise most surely leads the way.
Chorus: "Rah! "Rah! "Rah! For the A.P.A.;
It's the pride of the U.S.;
For it holds in loving thrall
Stamp collectors great and small,
And throughout the world its power is manifest.
Verse 2: From Atlantic's rugged coast
To Pacific's Golden Gate,
And from Southland's gulf to shining northern lakes,
Are the mighty bounds from which,
Representing every state,
A.P.A. its worthy membership takes.

Verse 3: And its members, they are true
To Philately's good cause,
Making A.P.A. their ever-guiding star;
For it is a tie that binds,
By its strong but simple laws
That most wonderful and wise in nature are.
Verse 4: So, we hear from Europe's marts,
Round the world to Isles of Spice,
Hearty commendations given A.P.A.;
And the nations each declare,
"We would give a handsome price
Could we learn the art of building in such way."[38]

Similar to the *Dream*, these lyrics demonstrated that members enthusiastically believed that the APA would provide a leading example in the international philatelic world and amply represent the "big and strong" United States. This organization of white male philatelists paired evenly with American foreign policy that constructed a narrative of masculine progress and "manifest" destiny that justified occupations and invasions of sovereign nations.[39] Rhetorically, the APA constructed itself to be as strong, and perhaps as masculine, as the United States had become in the geopolitical landscape. The lyrics call out to the world's philatelists to notice the APA's strength, which comes from its members—"great and small," "representing every state." For its members, the APA stands as the "ever-guiding star," which is almost equivalent to Gast's "Star of Empire," leading philatelists to gain new philatelic knowledge, and also to become a leader in philately. Much like the *Dream*, the lyrics indicate how APA members internalized the idea of American exceptionalism—of the United States as a nation and with regard to APA. The APA certainly was not the only club with members hailing from all states, but its members believed that it stood for ideals of America and that persons trading and collecting stamps in marts in Europe and Asia recognized the APA's strength as an organization.

The Philatelist's Dream and theme song added to a grand vision the APA's members held for the organization as it expanded and faced competition from other organizations. The last components of this vision came in 1908 when the APA changed its name to the American Philatelic Society (APS) and increased the frequency of publishing its journal. The name change made the APS sound similar to the well-established Royal Philatelic Society, and possibly distanced it from professional associations that it initially mimicked. The APS started publishing its journal, *American Philatelist*, quarterly rather than yearly, and American Philatelist began soliciting and printing articles that focused on the study and history of stamps rather than merely publishing the minutes and speeches from the annual conventions. Members were constantly encouraged to recruit acquaintances, and membership nearly tripled from 574 in 1895 to over 1,500 in 1908.[40] As many other stamp clubs formed, the APS relied on its members to help connect smaller clubs to the APS through affiliations. The network of philatelic clubs grew across the country together with an active philatelic press that spread the word about stamp collecting to interested readers while simultaneously recruiting new members.

Stamp Papers

Philatelic clubs formalized communities of collectors by defining practices and limiting memberships, but a much larger community grew around stamps through the flourishing philatelic print culture made possible by the postal system. Beginning in the late nineteenth century, this print culture facilitated the growth of an imagined, and most likely more diverse, community of stamp collectors and philatelists stretching across state and national borders.[41]

Stamp papers emerged after the Civil War and disseminated information about the practices and vocabulary of the hobby to collectors at all levels of interest and investment. The first serial, *Stamp Collector's Record*, published by S. A. Taylor, began in Albany, New York, in December 1864 and continued until October 1876, and the number of publications grew exponentially. Between 1864 and 1906, over 900 stamp papers were published in the United States alone. While Americans created the largest number of stamp papers during this time, hundreds of other publications circulated from Great Britain, France, Germany, Canada, Argentina, Egypt, Spain, Turkey, and Venezuela. Some publications published serious studies of stamps, watermarks, or articles about the countries that produced specific stamps, while other papers were the work of one person sitting at home writing a newsletter.[42] A drop in American periodical postage rates, from two cents per pound in 1874 to one penny per pound in 1885, encouraged this flurry of circulation in all types of periodicals.[43]

Some papers attempted to generate business for dealers, while others were small outlets for local philatelic clubs. Dealers such as Scott Stamp and Coin Company Limited and C. H. Mekeel Stamp Company became publishers, printing papers to encourage philately and to stimulate the market for stamps and collecting paraphernalia. *Mekeel's* became the first weekly newspaper in 1891 and reported philatelic news from around the world by publishing notes from clubs, announcing new issues, and hosting stamp exchanges. Like most periodicals of the day, *Mekeel's* also sold advertising space. Few in-depth articles could be found in its tabloid-style pages, but it maintained its hold as the definitive newspaper for collectors from 1891 to the present. *Philatelic West* began in 1895 as the journal of the Nebraska Philatelic Society and quickly grew from a regional to national publication by 1902, when it became the official organ of more than ten collecting associations. Its publishers boasted of the largest paid subscription list of any American philatelic monthly.[44] Millions of Americans learned philatelic practices and connected with fellow collectors through these publications.

Many individuals contributed to this print culture even if their papers were short-lived. One teenager, known later in life for his fiction, started *Stamp Collector* in his Syracuse, New York, home. L. Frank Baum printed at least four issues of this serial between 1872 and 1873. During the 1870s—"the golden age of amateur publishing"—it was not uncommon for boys, more so than for girls, to create publications using the Novelty Toy Printing Press and to distribute them locally or to mail them to interested young readers around the country.[45] Baum was no doubt familiar with these and other stamp-related papers as he created his own.

While young printers delighted in their creations, some adults cringed at the abundance of amateur publishers. One adult writer found no "earthly use" for amateur papers he claimed were produced by boys with "limited knowledge" of stamps that "only bring ridicule upon collecting from outsiders" and disgust from "advanced" collectors.[46] If forming stamp clubs and publishing journals helped to legitimize the hobby of stamp collecting, the interest generated by younger collector-publishers was viewed by some as a distraction rather than as a boom to stamp collecting. Even the smallest and shortest-lived papers show us that there was great enthusiasm for participating in a public discussion about stamps and the practice of collecting them.

Philatelic publications were so prolific by 1892 that they became the subject of disparaging articles. Harry Franklin Kantner of the *Pennsylvania Philatelist* declared that the "philatelic writer" was "one of the most potent factors in the Philatelic field," fighting for the progression of the hobby. To fully express his concerns, he wrote a poem entitled "The Philatelic Publisher's Soliloquy." This parody mocked the dilemma facing an amateur publisher who invested his own money and time "to clip news by the sweat of his classic brow," gather postal statistics, and "revamp old philatelic articles that delight none." The soliloquy borrowed from Hamlet:

> To publish or not to publish,—that is the question.—
> Whether 'tis better to announce a new philatelic journal;
> The fulfiller of a long, long felt want
> Or to give up these grand ideas of gaining popularity
> And never issue the wished for journal?[47]

Kantner's disapproval of the proliferation of stamp papers continued the following year when he decried "the 'stamp fever' [that] had become the 'publishing fever.'" His article actively discouraged "all ambitious young men" from starting new papers. In December 1894, the *Weekly Philatelic Era* rejoiced that an "exceedingly small number" of new philatelic papers appeared that season, which was much more pleasant than the "obnoxious" mushroomed growth of past years. An author for *Philatelic West* desired to start his own paper in the 1890s and reflected how fortunate he was that he did not burden himself and the "already long suffering philatelic public" with such a venture.[48] These collective comments demonstrated that while some stamp associations openly encouraged all to collect stamps, not everyone agreed that all collectors should participate in the philatelic print culture, or even the broader community of philatelists, equally. Within the philatelic community, philatelists drew lines among their own.

Applying a hierarchical framework to stamp papers and journalists was in keeping with the post–Civil War tendency to distinguish between high- and lowbrow activities.[49] Even as stamp collectors tried to construct a cultural space for themselves as learned individuals through clubs and readership of journals, some proposed fracturing within their own ranks. Kantner proposed instituting hierarchical labels for philatelic publications. He categorized papers into four classes: professional, semiprofessional, amateur, and price-list journal. He classified his own journal, *Pennsylvania Philatelist*, as semiprofessional because it was less "scientific" but more literary than the "professional" *American Journal of Philately*. Kantner criticized smaller "amateur" papers that merely reprinted stories from larger journals and did not produce original articles. Quite aware of philatelists' place within the greater American culture, Kantner commented that it was "not only a progressive age in general affairs but also in philatelic matters."[50] Philatelists used the structure of a club, like that of a professional association, to promote standards of practice. Many stamp collectors believed in American exceptionalism in all matters, including philatelic. One way to ensure that American philatelists contributed to a global print culture was to classify papers by their content and discourage just anyone from starting his or her own paper. As a group, stamp collectors were earning an expertise in their collections, but some philatelic writers, like Kantner, felt that even enthusiastic philatelists needed to respect the hierarchy and defer to the expertise of others.

Despite complaints by vocal writers such as Kantner, the journals lived on and connected thousands of collectors each year. Like professional journals, most philatelic publications kept members abreast of the field and facilitated communication among societies. Articles featured news of first issues of American and international stamps, explanations of different types of stamps, philatelic literature reviews, and letters from readers.[51] A handful of papers, like *Weekly Philatelic Era*, offered subscribers a free exchange notice to facilitate the commerce of stamps among the community that was enabled by the postal service. Beyond articles, most papers accepted advertisements from dealers in stamps and collecting ephemera. Such items advertised included albums and specialized tools for handling stamps. Merchants engaged with hierarchical rhetoric and might call out to "serious collectors" in an advertisement.[52] Not only were collectors defining themselves in ways typical of the period, but in reading about their hobby they were also bombarded with advertising by dealers and manufacturers selling accessories, including magnifying glasses, hinges, and tongs. A cottage industry grew up around philatelists. By reading these papers, collectors educated themselves in the minutiae of philately.

Connecting and corresponding with other collectors was an important part of the culture, and philatelic publications helped collectors connect with others to buy, sell, and exchange stamps. One did not need to belong to a club in order to acquire more stamps and participate actively in the hobby. Around the time that C. H. Mekeel began his *Weekly Stamp News*, he also printed a directory containing names and addresses of collectors and dealers who paid one dollar to be listed. Five thousand collectors responded in 1891, which increased to nine thousand by 1897, and each entry described the person's collecting specialties, such as specific countries, and sometimes mentioned the languages in which they corresponded. The listings demonstrate global connections of collectors. Not only were collectors living outside of United States represented, but many American philatelists wanted to connect with foreign collectors and dealers. For example, Leon Lambert of St. Paul, Minnesota, desired to "correspond in English, French, Spanish, Portuguese, Italian, and Dutch to exchange on the basis of any catalogue. Sample copies of foreign papers desired." Charles Townsend of Akron, Ohio, called out to collectors "in all part of the world, particularly those in Mexico, Central and South America, and the Islands in the West Indies." And dealers from Peru, Britain, Austria, Switzerland, Italy, and France bought ad space in this directory.[53] Not only were stamp collectors and dealers supporting the governments who produced stamps by purchasing them, they were also supporting the postal system by conducting transactions through the mail. Stamp papers and directories provided contact information to allow collectors and dealers to conduct transactions and facilitate the practices of collecting on their own.

Collectors also used their philatelic papers to discuss what they liked about collecting. Some journals, like the *Philatelic West*, offered regular testimonials, and others published philatelic poetry that expressed the joys of stamp collecting or of reading a particular paper. In the *Philatelic West*, "Modern Maud Muller" skipped past her lover to get to the post office in a blizzard to retrieve the latest copy of her *Philatelic West* magazine, which she loved more dearly than her man: "And when to his heart her form he pressed, / There was something nearer to her heart—THE WEST."[54] This light-hearted poem, penned by a man in 1901, jested that the *Philatelic West* was so good that a "modern" woman would not be swayed by matters of the heart and would put aside her love interests to read her favorite stamp paper. The poem also represented an enthusiastic female collector, an audience some publications tried to develop.

Readers of philatelic journals often heard from editors that they needed to recruit more members of their society or subscribers to the paper. Verna Weston Hanway encouraged philatelists to enlist at least one more collector and proposed starting philatelic societies in the public schools.[55] One tactic was to recruit women as subscribers to stamp papers even if they were not members of a philatelic society. Some women read philatelic papers like *Philatelic West*, whose editors recognized its readership. As early as 1905, the *West* offered readers a "Woman-Collectors' Department" authored by Hanway. In her column, she encouraged women to collect and wrote various articles on stamps, curios, and books. She urged busy women to engage in a healthy hobby to relieve them from the turmoil of their days that they might find pleasure in their collections. She tried to recruit women by writing in the pages of the *West* that women were genetically predisposed to be collectors because curiosity was "an essentially feminine attribute."[56] *Pennsylvania Philatelist* and *Philatelic West* were the first papers that really identified a need to attract female readers and society members. Of course, since these papers were businesses, attracting any and all new readers or members was a key to their long-term success.

As philatelists discussed and defended their hobby, it is undeniable that stamp papers played an important role in the growth and shape of philately. Though some collectors and journalists did not like the proliferation of philatelic literature, one cartoon printed in *A. C. Roessler's Stamp News* captured the reason for the paper's existence. In panel 1, the first man says to the other, "I don't subscribe to stamp papers—they cost too much." In the second panel, the other man holds the first one down, beating him, saying, "Without papers your hobby would be dead in a year, you poor it."[57] *A. C. Roessler's* also needed to justify its existence and remind its readers to send in their subscription payments. But the cartoon deftly illustrates that the print culture acted as the glue that connected stamp collectors from around the world and made stamp collecting a popular pursuit. Papers offered subscribers opportunities to acquire more stamps, to learn about different varieties, to best care for their collections, and to create an imagined community. Although many small American stamp papers disappeared or merged with other publications by the early 1900s, many still thrived and supported the growing numbers of stamp collectors into the twentieth century.

Forcing Order within Stamp Albums

Philatelic clubs and papers played an important role by setting and circulating standards for stamp-collecting practices, including ways to properly care for and maintain a stamp collection. Novices learned that philatelists did not keep stamps in cigar boxes or decorate furniture with stamps, as some women's magazines encouraged. Rather, philatelists ordered the world of stamps in their albums. Albums protected stamps from deteriorating, and in subtle ways marked gender differences between collectors. By setting standards of collecting and modeling that behavior, club collectors, who were overwhelmingly male, distinguished themselves as philatelists, while others who collected stamps were mere collectors.

To begin training collectors in the proper way to care for and maintain a collection, some philatelic literature offered primers on collecting for novices. Young readers learned how to start collecting with the *ABC of Stamp Collecting*. Philatelists admonished novices to care for their collections properly, because "nothing detracts more from the interest and value of any collection, than a slovenly, careless and dirty arrangement."[58] This only matters, of course, if an individual collected for the purpose of reselling stamps or participating in a public exhibition.

Keeping stamps in albums offered collectors a neat and orderly space to organize and display their stamps. The first albums appeared in France in the 1860s as publishers began printing albums in Europe and the United States. Early albums were organized visually by geography: first by continent, then region within the continent, and last by country. Later albums listed countries alphabetically, including colonial headings such as "German East Africa" or "British Guyana."[59] Albums forced an organizational structure, by country and denomination, but also provided blank pages for an individual to augment an album with issues not represented in the pages or to collect in a personal scheme.

Albums also protected stamps from human and environmental damage and separated stamps designated as collectors' items from stamps purchased to mail a letter. While some albums were custom-made, say for British royalty, most were commercially produced by publishers or dealers and sold by stamp and novelty shop owners.[60]

An album offered the collector an apparatus to classify and display stamps from different countries, empires, and colonies, giving the appearance that collectors held the world in their albums. For example, Scott's "International" and "Imperial" albums offered spaces to hold collections of all varieties of postage stamps printed, while Mekeel's created albums for specialists in Mexican or American stamps from North and South America. Order was dictated in an album so that the collector placed stamps from a specific geographical location in a specific place. When flipping through an "International" album, one found maps of continents and regions that represented national borders but not states or provinces within each country. In the map pages, we find North and Central America first, and then localities follow in alphabetical order after the stamps of the United States.[61] Selling to American customers, it is not surprising that Scott's privileged the US map and American stamps within this international album. American exceptionalist narratives were prevalent in commemoratives, as will be discussed later, and these ideas were present in American album design as well.

Philatelists bought and traded countries, represented in stamps, and then ordered the world in their albums. This process was influenced by an imperialistic view of the world where imperial powers fought over lands, natural resources, and peoples in an effort to gain an economic and political edge. An individual stamp collector chose which countries to collect and then made an effort to achieve that goal. As a virtual representation of the globe, an album offered collectors the opportunity to show off their stamps and glimpse the holdings of others with an eye toward acquiring those countries as well. Collectors occasionally spoke of their collections in this imperialistic way. Verna Hanway described how many philatelists fondly laid their eyes upon a valuable stamp sitting in an album with the "pride of a conqueror."[62] One could create a miniature empire within one's own collections held in albums.

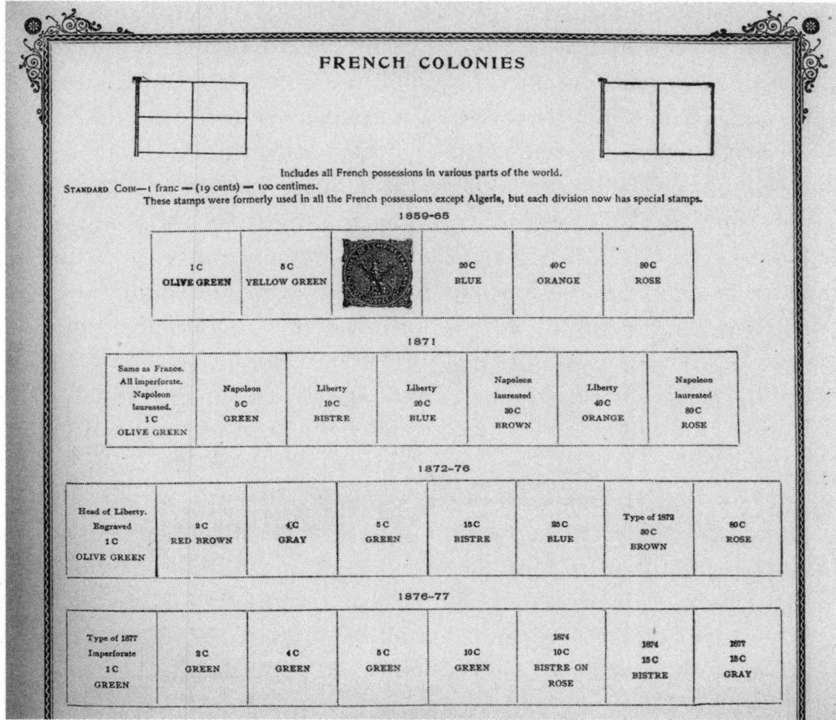

FRENCH COLONIES

Includes all French possessions in various parts of the world.
STANDARD COIN—1 franc — (19 cents) — 100 centimes.
These stamps were formerly used in all the French possessions except Algeria, but each division now has special stamps.

1859-65

1C OLIVE GREEN	5C YELLOW GREEN		20C BLUE	40C ORANGE	80C ROSE

1871

Same as France. All imperforate. Napoleon laureated. 1C OLIVE GREEN	Napoleon 5C GREEN	Liberty 10C BISTRE	Liberty 20C BLUE	Napoleon laureated 30C BROWN	Liberty 40C ORANGE	Napoleon laureated 80C ROSE

1872-76

Head of Liberty. Engraved 1C OLIVE GREEN	2C RED BROWN	4C GRAY	5C GREEN	15C BISTRE	25C BLUE	Type of 1872 30C BROWN	80C ROSE

1876-77

Type of 1877 Imperforate 1C GREEN	2C GREEN	4C GREEN	5C GREEN	10C GREEN	1874 10C BISTRE ON ROSE	1874 15C BISTRE	1877 15C GRAY

Fig. 4. Page from Scott's International Postage Stamp Album, 1912 (Author's collection, author's photo)

As albums imposed order in a collection, they also acted a tool to encourage consumption by highlighting the empty spaces. An empty space meant there was still a stamp left to buy. Dealers often published albums and reminded consumers that albums provided "a valuable and necessary aid in providing for a collection," while also selling stamps to help fill those albums.[63] Albums also reflected how well collectors cared for their stamps, and philatelists judged one another based on the condition and size of a collection kept inside. Philatelists spent much of their time carefully placing stamps in their appropriate slots within an album. This also meant each time they opened an album, empty spaces stared back. These albums represented checklists, of sorts, that guided a collector when making future purchases or trades.

Empty spaces motivated many collectors to fill them, and went unseen when one kept stamps in a box. Some collectors saved money to buy an expensive stamp or two that might complete a set, or that might give them something desirable to someone else for future bartering. Albums forced order, while also encouraging consumption.

Albums also facilitated looking at stamps in certain ways that made them appear like souvenirs from an international shopping spree. Physically visiting a foreign country was not necessary for acquiring stamps as souvenirs because an individual acquired stamps through dealers or exchanges, or from fellow collectors at club meetings. Souvenirs offered an incomplete vision of an authentic place or experience that allows the consumer or recipient to create a personal narrative surrounding that new object, which delighted some collectors.[64] H. R. Habicht found great romance in the idea that a French Napoleon stamp "witnessed" the commune in Paris and then was carried to South Africa with its new British owner only to be auctioned off after the Boer War to someone who would later donate it to the Berlin Postal Museum.[65] Stamps gave people like Habicht an opportunity to connect with the past and create their own memories of events or places that they had never experienced. Stamps, then, held a transformative power for some philatelists who created memories for stamps and sometimes projected themselves into the stamp's past life.

Verna Hanway romanticized about the stories hiding in the pages of an album. Engaging in a collection was an intimate experience that involved the collector's personal context of memory. For Hanway, remembering "the old days" was one of the pleasures of a collection:

> But you and I fellow collectors, hold its memory as something tender and sacred. Others, materialists, may deem it a madness, but if this be madness, "there is a pleasure in being mad, which none but madmen know."[66]

Stamps told stories to Hanway. Her album brought her closer to those stories and the personal memories she associated, or created, with stamps. She distinguished collecting stamps from a practice merely for the sake of acquisition. Mining these personal relationships forged through stamps is difficult for historians who can only see stamps carefully placed in an ordered album, but cannot read the metanarrative present for the collector.

Fig. 5. Page from homemade stamp album, ca. 1917 (Author's photo, album courtesy of Cheryl Ganz)

Gathering evidence of different ways that people collected and illustrated their own narratives through their stamps proves difficult because philatelic standards do not recognize collecting conventions falling outside of standard album keeping. Handmade albums or decorative stamp pieces are often discarded because the philatelic community places little or no value on them. For example, the album pictured in figure 5 is worthless in the eyes of auctioneers today. Someone made this album using a local department store catalog and reinforced it with cardboard. The collector gummed—without the hinges typically used with a philatelic album—inexpensive stamps and stamp-shaped stickers to each page in colorful patterns over the illustrations of women modeling the new winter line of coats. Created during World War I, the album displays a red cross in stamps that may have been a way that this person remembered those wounded in war. Stamp papers discouraged this type of decoration with stamps and particularly discouraged gumming stamps directly to paper.[67] This collection fell outside of philatelic practice enforced by its community. Other examples of women collectors may not have been saved, given that the album would have had no monetary value.

Order and classification in albums minimized aesthetic and creative reasons for collecting stamps, which also enforced gender differences between male club philatelists and independent female collectors. Philatelists tried to distinguish themselves as experts in stamp knowledge, and they acquired that knowledge through careful classification and study of stamps as placed in their albums. This meant most disapproved of other ways that people collected and used stamps, particularly in decorating, such as when *Godey's Lady's Book* in 1888 printed instructions for creating a postage stamp table. Women readers learned how to gum rare stamps to the top of a small wooden white table and then to glaze over the stamps with a smooth veneer. In 1905, an American woman made a dress that was completely covered with patterns created from over 30,000 stamps. William O. Sawyer papered a twelve-foot square room with over 20,000 US postage stamps in 1921. Responding to the latter, *Philatelic West* exclaimed, "Oh the affront to philately!" This style of collecting or amassing stamps for the sake of decorating or using stamps in art projects was never recommended in philatelic journals.[68] Once used in a decorative way, stamps could not be resold. The value of saving stamps might be considered lost on a decorative project.

Decorating with stamps was more often associated with women than men, which begins to address one of the more puzzling pieces of this history of stamp collecting: how men came to dominate this hobby. Steven Gelber proposes that a commodification of stamps took hold in the 1860s when the earliest collectors began trading stamps and amassing sets. Gelber argues that since stamps represented payment and were classified by country, year, and denomination, those sets possessed "real market value." Sets were meant to be completed. Male philatelists developed a market model of collecting that they taught to other club philatelists through gatherings and the philatelic press. This model militated against female participation and made stamp collecting feel like a business endeavor and not a hobby. Stamp dealers set up shops in business districts, such as in Manhattan's financial district on Nassau Street, furthering the connection between the male world of business and philatelic practices.[69] Caring for a collection in albums not only enforced the idea that stamps needed to be classified properly, but that stamps comprised sets and the sets were meant to be filled. In order to complete one set, you might have to break up another, so one protected stamps in case one wanted to sell or trade them. Collectors who decorated with their stamps were not participating in the market model, nor were they studying their stamps carefully for their watermarks or perforation. They collected stamps for fun and because they enjoyed the aesthetics.

There was a constant tug within the philatelic world between those who believed they were "true" philatelists interested in the education and enjoyment of the hobby and unconcerned with making money, and those who collected stamps to sell and trade in the hopes of earning money.[70] As the hobby attracted more followers, the marketability of a stamp collection grabbed the attention of many. The hope of getting rich from finding rare, old stamps in an attic or in a relative's trunk persisted, even when a majority of collectors never got rich from their stamps.

Even as white men controlled philatelic clubs and influences common practices, white women still collected and were urged to participate. Verna Hanaway and others urged women to collect because stamps seemed to naturally fit in with women's interests. Even though Eva Earl found life as female philatelist challenging, she still encouraged other women to participate in this hobby. Noting that stamp collecting was quite usual for "our brothers," it often was discouraged in girls. She began her collection with duplicates she received from her brother, and then Earl "caught the fever." She became more curious than ever about the pastime that she described as one of the "most seductive of pursuits." Schooled in the market model, so to speak, Earl worried that she might not be able to continue collecting because "we girls have little or no money," unlike "you men, you have every thing."[71] Even as Earl wrote publicly about her experiences, she was quite aware that she did not have many sisters in philately in 1894. Clifford Kissinger observed that the numbers of female philatelists were quite small and that they were rarely heard from in the philatelic press. His solution was that women needed more encouragement from "the sterner sex," urging married male collectors to encourage their wives to begin their own albums. Kissinger insisted that "our hobby must appear favorably to the feminine taste" because of the "pleasing colors of many of stamps" and "handsome designs." Speaking to a mostly male audience, he urged men to "encourage the ladies—we need their presence, and should gladly welcome them to the ranks, and accord them that recognition to which they are entitled."[72] Women definitely collected stamps, but often did not identify as philatelists. The scope of their participation in the hobby is difficult to gauge from the 1880s through the 1920s, because they were excluded from most collecting clubs and were not frequent contributors to stamp papers. Material evidence of their collecting practices and habits most likely were thrown away, much like what almost happened to the handmade album shown in figure 5.

Stamp collectors and philatelists built an international community in the late nineteenth century by formalizing the practices related to saving, circulating, and discussing their favorite objects through clubs and the circulation of hundreds of stamp papers. Importantly, the US Post Office Department noticed those connections. By the 1890s, the USPOD began a commemorative stamp program, knowing there was a ready audience of collectors and individuals interested in saving stamps and the meanings associated with those objects. Philatelists were specialists who wanted to spread the word about their leisure-time pursuit. Noncollectors viewed stamps as payment for mailing a letter, and would need to learn to see stamps as something else, as something embedded with meaning and value.

Learning to Read Stamps

O Mary found a little stamp,
A rarity, conceded.
In fact 'twas just the very one
Her dear old daddy needed.
It also chanced, this wondrous stamp,
That Mary did discover a
Rare Patriotic Cover.
Now, Mary knowing that her dad
Liked stamps found in a garret,
Made haste to yank from envelope
Said stamp, as well as tear it.
And thus she brought it to her dad
In ecstasy to show him,
But, from his look of seething rage,
She found she didn't know him.
A fortune he had won and lost
Through his beloved daughter,
Because to leave old stamp intact
He ne'er before had taught her.
And thou, O stamp-collecting sire,
Take this advice from me:
While in their youth, and ere too late,
Teach kids Philately.

—G. M. McCracken, "Poor Mary," 1933

One might expect to find this jokingly didactic poem about the need to teach children about philately in a philatelic paper, yet this appeared in the *Washington Post* in 1933. By the 1930s, literacy in stamp collecting grew far beyond groups of philatelists and individual collectors, as stamp collecting permeated public culture. From the 1880s to the 1930s, Americans slowly learned to see postage stamps as something other than purely a sticker that represented prepayment for mailing a letter. In the poem above, Mary noticed the stamp on the "Rare Patriotic Cover," because she had been trained to identify it as something special and worth saving. Like Mary, Americans of all ages knew that people collected stamps for a variety of reasons. Starting in the late nineteenth century, stamps appeared as consumer collectibles inside cigarette packages that rewarded customers for purchasing one item with the gift of another. American newspapers, magazines, and eventually radio exposed their audiences to articles, columns, and programs about stamps and collecting, circulating the idea that stamps—whether found in packaging or on purchased intentionally—were educational. Club philatelists shaped those discussions by publishing primers on collecting, giving lectures, volunteering with after-school groups, and holding public exhibitions of their collections that encouraged close reading of imagery and signs engraved on stamps.

Different groups adopted the practices of reading stamps and their imagery for a variety of reasons. Stamps' accessibility in price and in visual appeal made them attractive pedagogical tools for teaching geography and empire; visualizing religious missionary work; encouraging orderly and structured play, and engaging with the marketplace. These efforts to educate students and adults overlapped over a period of fifty years, as different generations of Americans learned the practices of collecting.

Stamps as Consumer Collectibles

As philatelists exposed noncollectors to their hobby in the 1880s, Americans began to view stamps as something other than postage. Collecting, in general, became increasingly accessible and acceptable to Americans as the culture of consumerism developed and was shaped by merchant capitalists, private and federal institutions, and advertising agencies from the 1880s to the 1930s.[1] In the 1880s, stamp publishers and tobacco companies printed chromolithographic trade cards and free postage stamps to advertise their products and attract customers. Many dry-goods companies capitalized on new chromolithography

Fig. 6. Scott's International Stamp Album trade card, late nineteenth century (Author's collection, author's photo)

technology and customized cards branded with the company's name and products. These trade cards were a popular collectible in their own right because they came free in packaging and contained attractively colored images that belonged to sets, meant to be completed. Many children, particularly girls, collected and kept cards in scrapbooks, an activity that prepared girls especially to become keen and brand-conscious shoppers for their future households.[2] Trade cards that advertised stamp albums associated stamps and related materials as consumer products to male and female consumers.

Some trade cards advertised for stamp dealers and publishers, while others contained stamps and encouraged the collecting of the cards and the stamps. Scott's Stamp and Coin Company used stock cards to advertise its most popular album. In figure 6, we see the Scott's imprint labels on the large clothing box, visually equating it with consumable woman's clothing, and possibly expensive French clothing. Charles A. Townsend, a dealer in Akron, Ohio, stamped his name and address on the front of a series of famous persons cards, including President Buchanan and actress Pauline Markham. On the reverse side,

Townsend printed a shortened price list of stamps he held in stock at the time.[3] Stamp dealers and publishers promoted their business in ways very similar to how other consumer goods merchants and manufacturers advertised their products in the late nineteenth century.

Rival tobacco companies competed for adult customers in the late nineteenth century by offering card sets with illustrations of presidents, baseball players, animals, and fish. In an effort to attract more customers into trying their cigarettes, W. Duke and Sons offered smokers a series of trade cards relating to postal matters that included a "genuine foreign postage stamp" in every box. On the back of the cards, Duke told customers that these stamps were not only for "the beginner," but also for the "owner of a large collection," who would find stamps "such as he could never find before."[4] Duke recognized that trade cards weren't the only mass-printed items to be collected; so were stamps. Advertisers identified an emerging philatelic culture among men of certain economic means and hoped some of them might consider trying a Duke cigarette if they were already inclined to smoke and collect.

To encourage saving stamps accumulated from buying cigarettes, the Duke Company recruited a trusted name in philately, J. Walter Scott, to produce a beautifully designed album to hold the complete set of stamps available to Duke's cigarette customers. Scott, who advertised his own albums, endorsed this album as a legitimate philatelic product—something that club philatelists would easily recognize. In a letter printed on the album's inside cover, Scott stated that Duke's generosity in giving away stamps on cigarette cards "made this album a necessity." Many who had "never seen a foreign stamp before have now become eager collectors." An album was a necessity if one adhered to principles of philately that clubs and dealers promoted. The album forced an order so that new collectors learned to arrange the free stamps by country. Duke's album represented a complete set of stamps to be distributed in cigarette boxes, which was not as large as Scott's "International" albums that represented all known varieties produced and circulated in the world at a given time. Stamps offered their consumers an "educational advantage" because, according to Scott, stamps led people directly to the study of history and geography, and this album cried out to be filled and encouraged consumers to smoke more cigarettes.[5] As stamp collecting grew and clubs began to form, Duke Tobacco and Scott Stamp and Coin merged their capitalist interest to sell cigarettes and promoted stamp collecting as a consumer activity in the 1880s.[6] With stamps readily available for certain groups, philatelists revealed what philately could teach collectors.

What Philately Teaches

In 1899, well-known stamp dealer and philatelic writer John N. Luff explained to a crowd gathered at the Brooklyn Institute of Arts and Sciences' newly established Section of Philately what he believed that philately taught its followers. Philately, he asserted, opened up a wide field of research:

> It trains our powers of observation, enlarges our perceptions, broadens our view, and adds to our knowledge of history, art, languages, geography, botany, mythology and many kindred branches of learning.
>
> The mechanical part of stamp making may be studied with much profit and entertainment. Considered in all its aspects, philately is even more instructive than matrimony.
>
> It teaches even the unwilling and the careless. In the effort to fill these spaces in their albums they must learn what varieties they are lacking and in what these differ from other and similar varieties.[7]

Luff and other philatelists believed that learning of some kind was inevitable when collecting stamps, even for those unaware of the process. That learning began, according to Luff, first by looking at a postage stamp. He highlighted for the audience the different design elements and then encouraged them to analyze the physicality of the stamp, including the paper, perforations, and gum. The process of observation, he explained, led stamp collectors to read meaning into stamps, because a stamp was designed deliberately and required interpretation. Luff's lecture was widely distributed in print form in the early twentieth century, and fellow collectors pointed to this book as an excellent primer for introducing stamp collecting to new audiences.

Collecting, then, made stamps good vehicles for teaching different skills or literacies. Knowledge of current events and political geography, for example, was often cited as a benefit from philately. In 1894, one collector wrote that "stamp-collecting brings the situation of every important nation of the earth again and again through life to the mind of the collector." Referencing the rapidly changing political landscape in south and central Africa amid the "scramble" by colonizing European empires, philatelists saw themselves as more involved than the average person in current events, because they followed international political developments in newspapers to keep up on new stamp issues. Newly issued stamps often revealed new governing bodies over previously sovereign territories. In those cases, imperial governments not only constructed and enforced new territorial boundaries with infrastructure and military posts, but also through printing postage stamps that constructed new identities for people living in regions who weren't necessarily culturally connected.[8] These colonial identities circulated on stamps and became the identity that collectors and stamp spectators associated with people living in those territories. The needs of empire led to the creation of postage stamps in the 1840s, and sometimes empire was very visible on stamps themselves.

Collecting during this period of intense competition for power and sovereignty in Africa and Asia was exciting for philatelists, because it meant new international stamps were regularly available for purchase or exchange. The mainstream and philatelic press constantly informed readers about newly issued foreign stamps that held power to teach collectors about other countries. As debates and fears over immigration to the United States in the late nineteenth and early twentieth centuries ensued, using stamps to expose adults and children to foreign lands and cultures frequently framed the discourse. In 1910, one Washington and Lee professor praised stamp collecting for teaching geography, the expansiveness of British and other European empires, and different systems of money.[9] The *Christian Science Monitor*, which took an early interest in stamp collecting by sponsoring regular columns, consistently extolled the values of learning with stamps for keeping children in touch with events around the world and "political and social history." Parents and children might examine a series of stamps that traced changes in governance, which contributed to the popular belief that stamp collecting taught geography, politics, and history. Collapsing empires, "belligerent nations" occupying territory, and newly independent states all represented the changing geopolitical landscape during and following World War I.[10]

Alternatively, stamp collecting offered potential to generate greater cultural exchanges. With a large and growing immigrant population in the United States, some groups could have connected an interest related to stamp collecting, learning about Italy, for example, to a native-born Italian immigrant. Collecting was about the stamps and nations, however, and not necessarily about understanding the individuals or cultural history of the stamp's originating locale. A collector seeking Chinese stamps in the 1880s might also fully support the Chinese Exclusionary Act. Collectors enjoyed gleaning small tidbits of information about a country from a stamp, which was just another product—or souvenir—from nations, empires, and colonies.

Some collectors described the experience of viewing stamps as being transported virtually to another nation. Images of foreign rulers, holidays, and landscapes carried one teenage girl to that country in her mind. She learned "everything that you would like to know about in any country" from its stamps. Anne Zulioff imagined the journey her stamps took from a printing press onto a precious letter, and then to land into her stamp album.[11] In this example, small colored bits of paper acted as an agent activating the imagination. Adults and children learned to look at and read stamps as cultural objects embedded with meaning. That meaning, of course, was subjective and personal. The history and culture Zulioff described was imagined. Teaching that global politics and cultures could be understood through the imagery and rhetoric of stamps encouraged understanding the world in over-simplified ways.

For many educators, using stamps to teach elementary school children geography and global politics was logical. Stamps were colorful, accessible, and led to discovering basic facts about foreign countries. Additionally, educators incorporated stamps into their classroom, because they believed they were capitalizing on a child's "collecting instinct."

A Collecting Instinct

At the turn of the century, some educators integrated stamp-collecting practices into their classrooms because child psychologists urged them to take advantage of a child's instinct and desire to collect. Some popular writing about collecting described the activity as childish, given that children seemed to enjoy collecting and saving many different types of natural and manufactured objects. Noted psychologist Granville Stanley Hall and his students from Clark University pioneered the field of child psychology and researched behavior at different stages of childhood development, including collecting.

Psychologist Caroline Burk researched the question: is there a collecting instinct in children? After surveying over 1,200 children in two California cities, Burk published her findings in 1900. She found that 90 percent of the children surveyed collected something and most kept between three and four collections at a given time. Girls kept a slightly higher number of collections than boys. Stamp collections were very common with boys and girls. Burk determined that the desire to collect began as early as three years old and intensified from ages eight to ten. Influence of friends, family, and fads motivated most youngsters to collect specific types of things, and stamps were no exception. Through her findings, Burk saw potential pedagogical uses for collecting.[12]

Burk's study was quite influential. School psychology textbooks included sections on understanding the collecting instinct in children, citing Burk's findings. Textbook authors, some psychologists themselves, championed collecting in classrooms. Specific pursuits, like stamp collecting, fostered "the scientific attitude of the mind" by encouraging classification, organization, and arrangement. It was argued that this instinct led students to organize historical events in chronological order and recognize national heroes.[13] Not only did many educators believe that a collecting instinct existed, but that the practice of collecting stamps taught students how to read and interpret the signs embedded in the designs.

Additional research that followed in the late 1920s and early 1930s challenged Burk's findings by proposing that collecting habits reflected social environments and could be indicative of problematic behaviors. In contrast to Burk, psychologists Harvey C. Lehman and Paul A. Witty found that only 10 percent of children collected anything in Kansas towns and cities during 1925. Lehman and Witty's data illuminated gender, regional, and demographic differences, and they concluded that collecting might be a fad and not an instinct inherent to all children. By the 1930s, Lehman and Witty's research reflected anxiety about the population shifts to urban areas, as they found rural children were more likely to maintain collections than their urban counterparts. Unlike advocates of the playground movement who prized an idealized vision of rural play that associations attempted to replicate in large towns and cities, Lehman and Witty believed their data provided some evidence that the isolation of rural living promoted individualism that adversely prepared young Americans for modern life. Alluding to notions that American farmers were uncooperative politically, Lehman and Witty maintained that farmers' children needed to learn cooperation and socialization—skills the urban-based psychologists assumed these children lacked—through participation in team activities at school.[14] Strikingly, given that Witty and Lehman's later research occurred during the Great Depression, they never examined economic factors (individual family income or locality averages) as influencing collecting habits. Data about the collecting activities of children were instead analyzed to speculate if and how childhood play predicted political behavior in adulthood.

Witty and Lehman's research indicated a declining interest in collecting among children of all ages in the 1930s, yet we know that the sales of stamps, media attention, and philatelic activities in schools and during extracurricular groups actually increased throughout the 1930s. Burk's study in 1900 had already laid the groundwork for stamp collecting to be viewed as an acceptable classroom and extracurricular activity.

Philately in the Classroom and Extracurricular Activities

At the turn of the century, Burk's research coupled with encouragement from philatelists for teachers to incorporate stamp collecting into classroom activities. Stamps appealed to educators because of their availability, color, and imagery, printed around the world. Teachers in New York public schools encouraged their students to collect stamps as early as 1885, because, as teachers remarked, their students learned facts about foreign countries as easily as they learned the rules of marbles. A principal in Chicago observed that all of his best students collected stamps and that stamp collecting led to improved academic achievement in high school. Teaching geography with stamps continued for decades, and sometimes journalists teased that "Hobbies Solve Teachers' Problems Nowadays."[15]

In addition to solving problems teachers faced in their classrooms, stamps were adopted as pedagogical tools to help students learn about geopolitical boundaries and difference from the 1880s through the 1930s. Some philatelists viewed international stamps as visual press releases of changes in governance and believed in the power of a stamp to relay that information: "Upon the simple postage stamp can be studied the rise, decline, and fall of empires, kingdoms, and republics."[16] Stamps illustrated who was in power, but stamps alone could not challenge readers to investigate complicated stories behind the changes in empires, kingdoms, and republics, or why empires expanded. Teachers could, however, ask students to look at a stamp and then find its country of origin on a map. Mary Branch's poem offered anecdotal evidence that stamp collecting successfully taught world geography.

Three months ago he did not know
His lesson in geography;
Though he could spell and read quite well,
And cipher, too, he could not tell
The least thing in topography.
But what a change! How passing strange!
This stamp-collecting passion
Has roused his zeal, for woe or weal,
And lists of names he now can reel
Off in amazing fashion.
. . . And now he longs for more Hong Kongs,
A Rampour, a Mauritius,
Greece, Borneo, Fernando Po,–
And how much else no one can know;
But be, kind fates, propitious.[17]

The type of knowledge gleaned from stamps reflected a style of history and geography commonly taught in schools in the late nineteenth and early twentieth centuries that rewarded rote memorization of facts such as political leaders or world capitals. Philatelists taught that to understand and classify stamps properly, collectors must know "where each stamp-issuing country is located, and by what government it is ruled." Mary Branch observed that students learned basic information about a country from its stamps. Students learned to read stamps as representing nations and highlighted geopolitical differences among them.

As it grew in popularity, stamp collecting appeared as an extracurricular activity sponsored by youth-focused organizations. In the early twentieth century, adult progressive reformers developed recreation programs to keep idle children busy with what they saw as productive activities, and they taught recreation coordinators that collecting stamps qualified as healthy indoor play, because it kept children busy and discouraged delinquency.[18]

The After School Club embodied many of those sentiments. Much like the Boy Scouts of America, also founded in the 1910s, the American Institute of Child Life's (AICL) After School Club sought to fill all nonschool hours with wholesome activities and acted as a "correspondence recreation center." The After School Club's handbook recommended different activities by age group, and listed collecting stamps and other objects as an appropriate activity for seven- to fourteen-year-olds. Young collectors worked toward earning "degrees" after studying and learning from their objects. The club also offered traveling collections of minerals, fossils, and stamps. Ultimately, the objective of this club was to make "young people wholesomely happy and to help build them into efficient and useful citizens."[19] The AICL and its board of leading scholars and researchers in the welfare and education of children, including child psychologist G. Stanley Hall, recommended stamp collecting as a wholesome activity that would shape young collectors into better citizens.

Upon further investigation, we see that the AICL's mission to nurture young citizens was intertwined with emerging scientific fields studying and defining phases of childhood. In the 1910s, the AICL proclaimed its concern with the welfare of children and was affiliated with many organizations "concerned with childhood." Mothers who joined the AICL received complimentary memberships to all affiliated groups, including the new Eugenics Record Office in Cold Spring Harbor, New York; the YMCA; the US Children's Bureau; and the Audubon Society, among others. Curiously the Eugenics Record Office (ERO) received a prominent position at the top of the list. The ERO collected family trait histories, and its director H. H. Laughlin advocated for eugenics-based immigration legislation and policies restricting reproduction of the "unfit." The eugenics movement enjoyed many supporters in the early twentieth century, including progressive reformers, who sought to improve the American population through a variety of means.[20]

It is difficult to know how these affiliations developed, but it is possible to see how collecting stamps appealed to the AICL. Collecting and arranging stamps requires an ordering of the world relying on identification of differences among nations and defining people by politically determined geographic borders. Stamps are tools that unify a nation or empire by imposing postal infrastructure and through the visual imagery designed to erase cultural diversity. Collecting practices, however, encourage identification of differences between nations represented on stamps that are enforced in albums. Viewing visual representations of nations in stamps offers an opportunity to teach young people about the perceived scientific differences and racial hierarchies among peoples of the world. Stamp albums provide spaces to order the world that also respected and enforced boundaries. According to philatelic practice, a stamp fit exactly into a space designated for it and did not belong anywhere else. Philatelists organized stamps according to a world order as proscribed by stamp-producing powers. This, of course, does not mean philatelists supported eugenics merely because they collected stamps. But it allows us to see that stamp collecting appealed to many different groups. For another group, the world's stamps symbolized a gateway to spiritual duty and fulfillment.

The Women's Missionary Union of the Southern Baptist Convention encouraged stamp collecting to inspire young people to become missionaries. Their publication for children, *World Comrades*, started a stamp column in 1934 written by "Bob the Stamper." He introduced readers to foreign stamps so that those nations would "become a call to the heralds of the Great Commission." One column told the story of a man who linked his Bible studies with the family's stamp album by writing a scriptural passage "to fit the stamps" on each page of the album. Each time anyone flipped through the album, the marginalia reminded the reader about the Bible and faith. One reviewer praised the magazine for capitalizing on the collecting instincts of children "in the interest of Bible study and the spread of Christ's Kingdom throughout the earth."[21]

The Women's Missionary Union believed that stamps possessed power to motivate young people to volunteer for Christianizing missions across the globe. If the stamps of each nation represented a path for pursuing the "Great Commission," then an album represented work to be done and the hope of salvation. Identifying nations, territories, or colonies imposed a different order on the world, and helped Southern Baptists visualize the scope of their missionary work. Southern Baptists, like other groups, found meaning in stamps beyond their face value. Bob the Stamper used stamps to teach young people about the potential for uniting the world in the name of Christianity, and the album provided motivation and a path for accomplishing this goal.

Progressive reformers and educators preoccupied themselves with preventing idleness in children because, in their minds, idleness led to delinquency and vice. Stamp collecting was "something to do" and kept youths "out of all sorts of mischief and very often bad company." This sentiment motivated some philatelists to work with young people by starting clubs in YMCAs and places like the Boys Hotel for homeless boys in Kansas City, Missouri. Some saw this as "missionary work for the hobby," knowing that "every new collector adds to the stability of stamp collecting." Collectors donated old stamps, albums, and literature for the benefit of the boys and girls. Dealers also prepared stamp packets that contained a variety of common and inexpensive stamps for beginning collectors, sometimes referred to as the "boy trade" even though boys and girls received these packs.[22]

In 1929, one philatelist reported that 10,000 new stamp-collecting after-school clubs had formed that year in American schools—many with the help of APS members. The Oakland Philatelic Society, for example, organized fifty school stamp clubs from 1931 to 1932. In Los Angeles, philatelists organized fourteen Playground clubs by 1933. Both in Oakland and in Los Angeles, California clubs sponsored competitive exhibitions where adult club philatelists judged and awarded ribbons to the winning students, such as from the Lincoln Heights playground in 1931. Dealers, particularly in the late 1920s and 1930s, actively engaged in this "missionary work" to groom new young collectors (and their parents) who one day might become customers.[23]

Collecting with Boy Scouts

The business side of collecting was rarely addressed in schools or in most extracurricular activities, but it was an important element to earning a Boy Scout merit badge introduced in 1931. By adding this badge, the Boy Scouts of America (BSA) acknowledged stamp collecting as an activity worthy of building character in young men. Prior to making the badge official, stamp collecting and the Scouts already enjoyed a close relationship. In 1926, the "Lone Scout" program provided boys living in rural areas—too sparse for troops—an opportunity to participate in Scouting by organizing stamp-collecting clubs. More than 100,000 boys registered for the Lone Scout program. With assistance from members of the American Philatelic Society, the BSA crafted requirements for the badge. Scoutmaster and APS member William Hoffman asked fellow members to offer their expertise to local Scout councils across the country and to volunteer as "Expert Examiners." In contrast, the Girl Scouts of America did not offer a stamp-collecting badge until the 1960s.[24]

Stamp collecting in the Scouts was so popular and enjoyed such favor with practicing philatelists that the BSA created a Boy Scout Stamp Club that met in Washington, DC. It was run by a philatelist who belonged to several societies and who guided them through the stages of earning their badge and in general collecting practices. By one estimate, nearly 25 percent of DC-area Scouts in 1934, approximately 750 boys, collected stamps and participated in this club.[25]

To help boys pursuing the stamp-collecting badge, the BSA printed a philately guidebook. Earning the stamp-collecting merit badge required that a Scout be committed to collecting and required assistance from a philatelic club member to achieve each of these milestones based in philatelic practice:

1. Own and exhibit a collection of 500 or more well-conditioned stamps, collected by the Scout;
2. Exhibit 10 varieties of stamps, including air mail, envelope, surcharged imperforate, perforate, postage due, pre-cancelled, flat plate, rotary press, telegraph, revenue and registration;
3. Exhibit and explain the following classes and stamps and names one country of issue: postage, commemorative, special delivery, postal packet, express, split or bisected, postmasters' provisionals, and private proprietary;
4. Exhibit and explain cancellations and their relation to the value of a stamp;

5. Explain the principal characteristics of stamps viz: class of paper, watermarks, separations, impressions.
6. Exhibit the following issues of U.S. stamps: 10 different commemorative, present postage, present envelope; 2 different memorial, 1 flat plate, 1 rotary press, 10 different official or departmental and 4 different air mail stamps;
7. Demonstrate ability to "catalog" accurately 5 stamps provided by the Examiner;
8. Explain in full the "condition" of a stamp, and how the exact value of a stamp is determined.[26]

The creation of this badge expressed the BSA's confidence that stamp collecting helped boys as they matured into young men, and that collecting related to a "boy's vocational outlook." Boys needed to collect and properly organize and describe a variety of stamps and were required to explain how the value of a stamp was determined. These young collectors learned about the stamp market through Scouting. By the 1930s, more badges related to experiencing and experimenting with vocations, such as blacksmithing, carpentry, cotton farming, or salesmanship.[27] With the exception of dealers and a few novelty shop owners, stamp collecting was a hobby, even as it was categorized a vocational badge. As an avocation, the practice of philately might earn someone extra money if the collector cared for and amassed a variety of rare stamps. Stamp collecting forced an ordered classification of stamps and taught these boys that stamps could be worth an amount of money different from the value printed on the stamp. With the guidance from a local philatelist, a Scout was prepared to sell and trade his stamps.

Practices introduced to Scouts mirrored capitalist activity of the marketplace. Following this market model could make collecting profitable, and Scouts were required to discuss how a stamp was revalued in the philatelic market to earn their badge.[28] Explaining the design on stamps was not required for this badge, even though we see that reading images is the primary approach to teaching about stamps normalized by philatelic clubs. Mentoring a Scout to sell and exchange stamps might serve him well "as the boy grows to manhood."[29] Shaped primarily by a national philatelic association, the process for earning a stamp badge socialized Scouts in philatelic culture as much as it taught practices. In this very direct way, the BSA and the APS groomed boys in the all-male Scouting network to become philatelists, another homosocial network of adults.

These examples typify the connections philatelic clubs made with nonphilatelists and how philatelists worked to increase the general public's exposure to stamp collecting. Their involvement in extracurricular activities varied. Stamps' availability and accessibility made them easily translatable as pedagogical tools for individuals and groups to use as they wished. Philatelists pushed back, in some ways, through the creation of a Boy Scout badge that normalized practices for young male collectors. Club collectors balanced the advantages of sharing their hobby with wide audiences with emphasizing that true collectors belonged to a community of practice.

Public Stamp Exhibitions

Noncollectors of all ages might learn about stamps from collectors sharing their specialized knowledge at public exhibitions. Americans of all income levels were becoming accustomed to public exhibition as a form of amusement and a way to learn about faraway places from midways at world's fairs, oddities at dime museums in entertainment districts, and art and natural history at new museums opening in cities across the United States. Advertisements for large stamp exhibitions were placed in the entertainment sections of newspapers, so that in New York one found the International Stamp Exhibition among listings for musical performances at Carnegie Hall, for motion pictures starring Adolph Menjou and Harold Lloyd, for operas by Gilbert and Sullivan, and for a play by Theodore Dreiser. Museums, in particular, offered a model for viewing and revering objects within an ordered context—and in the case of stamps, the album often served as a display case in public spaces.[30] Public exhibits provided a physical venue for philatelists to show off collections and investments to a broader audience beyond fellow philatelists, Boy Scouts, or school-related clubs.

Thousands of visitors attended the New York International Stamp Exhibition in 1913, the first large American philatelic exhibition. British philatelic writer Fred J. Melville contributed a guest column to the *New York Times* during the exhibition, praising the quality of exhibits. He joked that they justified his long trip to the United States to view the show, and enjoyed seeing that Americans were beginning to appreciate the "cult" of the stamp as much as British and European collectors. Melville's article offered some reassurance to American club collectors looking for approval from their more experienced brothers in philately—the Europeans—for this exhibition.[31] Interestingly, one *New York Times* reporter covering the exhibition noticed a "democratic character" to the exhibitors, which he attributed to the popularity of stamp collecting, because a "humble artisan" or a monarch could collect stamps.[32] Anyone could collect, and many did. The collectors exhibiting, however, invested time and money in their leisure activity. Public exhibitions such as this one exposed noncollectors to the possibilities of the stamp market. Collecting, as "democratic," fit appropriately with American ideals, according to the reporter, even if philately originated in Europe and stamps themselves arose from needs of the British Empire.

Articles discussing the exhibition also emphasized that stamp collecting was not only about classifying stamps, by focusing on the monetary values of the stamps exhibited. Noncollectors learned that while postage was assigned a specific monetary value to mail a letter, collectors created their own alternate market for valuing stamps. Often articles in the mainstream press did not elaborate on how philatelists determined the value of a stamp or an entire collection. Visitors to an exhibition only saw that rare collections amassed by people like George Worthington were worth tens of thousands of dollars. One article described the rarities of Worthington's stamps, including a Cape of Good Hope stamp with a woodblock error.[33] To noncollectors, the world of stamp collecting was a bit mysterious because it valued errors in printing that elevated a stamp that originally cost two cents to a value of ten thousand dollars. Without knowing the whys of the stamp market, some noncollectors saw this enterprise as similar to a lottery—one rare stamp in a collection might bring in jackpot. At a time when no legal lotteries operated in the United States, a person might dream of stumbling upon a valuable old stamp in a trunk and selling it for thousands of dollars. In that scenario, luck trumped philatelic expertise, making the discovery of riches in stamps quite unluckily, yet possible for all.

Clubs also sponsored smaller, local exhibitions to reinvigorate dormant collectors' interest and attract new ones. The Stamp Collectors' Club of Hartford hosted a World War I–themed exhibition not only to display rare varieties from their members' collections, but also to increase collecting activities in Hartford. Sponsoring an exhibition from the US postal service, the Boston Philatelic Society gave these very reasons for pulling together this public event—to interest "our non-collecting citizens," to bring back onetime collectors, and to offer unaffiliated "worthy collectors" an opportunity to associate with the club members to encourage them to join.[34] Local press gave collecting clubs mainstream media coverage of their events and helped to spread the word about stamp collecting.

Organizers staged stamp exhibits in or near cultural centers in big cities to associate stamp collecting with other high-brow activities. Cultural hierarchies divided public events into high and low categories to distinguish behavioral norms and restricted audiences.[35] Philatelists clearly desired to associate their activities with institutions of learning and culture. The Art Institute of Chicago hosted an exhibition celebrating the twenty-fifth anniversary of the American Philatelic Society in 1911, and the Wadsworth Atheneum in Hartford, Connecticut, sponsored an exhibit on war issues in 1921. The 1913 New York International Stamp Exhibition was held at the Engineering Societies Building in Manhattan, located within one block of the New York Public Library and near the shopping district on Fifth Avenue. The exhibition opened near a busy cultural and commercial district in the city, and was located in the same building as a scientific association.[36] Locating a stamp exhibition in such spaces helped to legitimize the hobby and physically connected collectors with institutions commonly associated with learning. Philatelists not only desired to connect their practices with places of learning, but tried to attract people who valued cultural institutions.

One effort can be seen from the organizers of the 1926 International Stamp Exhibition, who targeted parents in advertisements. Ads urged parents to "give your boy a chance to learn" about "mysterious peoples" and "unusual customs" by taking him to the exhibition.

Encouraging a boy—only boys were mentioned and illustrated in this ad—to collect stamps increased his knowledge of geography and history. Looking together at a stamp album, a father points to stamps and talks to his son while the mother looks on in the background.[37]

In this traditional family unit, the father figure, wearing white-collar attire, discusses them with his son. Here knowledge is transferred from stamp to adult to the child. By giving a boy a chance to learn, philatelists argued, "the postage stamp" became the "common bond," getting him "in touch with the rest of the world," including countries "most of us never heard of." Missing from the image are reference books and maps that might help a young collector to contextualize imagery on a stamp alone. Boys and their fathers learned together, and, as the ad instructed the reader, stamps taught geography, history, and zoology, implying that some of this knowledge was inherent in the stamp, without needing outside literature.

In this ad, the learning process appears to be masculine. Interestingly, the ad makes no mention of stamp values or the possibility of earning money. When framed as an educational pursuit, the economics of collecting was often omitted from the discussion. The ad's imagery depicts a stereotypical middle-class household scene in the 1920s that combines with the copy to indicate that this indoor and nonathletic activity was indeed masculine. Employing a tone of exoticism by referring to "mysterious peoples" and "unusual customs" represented in stamps, the ad makes clearer the subtleties of collecting's connection to masculinity and empire.

Presenting collecting activities in this way reinforced the notion that while real government agencies produced stamps, the places represented on stamps are almost imaginary. If stamp collecting "implies a wide knowledge of the world," the type of knowledge may not be that wide but instead rather narrow. International stamps functioned as a type of souvenir from a country most collectors never visited, forcing both the collector and other spectators to view the stamp in uncritical ways. Stamp exhibitions perpetuated this idea, which was not an unfamiliar concept to most Americans, who regularly read cultural objects from a tourist perspective. Collectors knew that stamps carried different messages, and the noncollecting public increasingly learned to see stamps as meaning-filled pieces of paper.

Teaching Philately as Self-Improvement

For adults, adopting a hobby such as stamp collecting was often seen as an exercise in self-improvement. The self-improvement movement arose in the antebellum era but extended into the late nineteenth and early twentieth centuries with efforts to bring culture to those who might not have access to it through university life. Lyceums, women's clubs, and chautauquas organized lecturers around the country to discuss art, literature, and history. Visiting a museum exposed visitors to great works of art, while belonging to the Book of the Month Club in the mid-1920s offered participants a chance to read great literature at home.[38]

During the Great Depression, some unemployed adults learned to collect stamps in free classes offered by emergency relief programs. During a time when most Americans had less money to spend on nonessential items, stamp collecting continued to grow as a hobby, prompting one observer to note that philatelic advertisement pages thrived in stamp papers. To his surprise, people continued to spend money on things they could not eat.[39] To help manage the numbers of unemployed, some municipalities and civic groups offered adult education classes in arts and hobbies in the spirit of self-improvement. In New York City, the Emergency Relief Bureau organized and sponsored free classes for residents and in turn employed artists, musicians, and other unemployed people to teach a variety of classes at city recreation centers, parks, and playgrounds beginning in 1932. While classes were open to all residents, they were "designed especially for the unemployed," and over 19,000 adult students enrolled within the first six months. Classes in hobbies such as stamp collecting, photography, and home mechanics were available in these free institutes held across the city. Due to the city's success, other municipalities in the state emulated those public education programs.[40] Local authorities tapped into the network of established hobbyists to instruct fellow citizens who had unexpected free time on their hands. Stamp collecting was branded as a worthy way to spend time. Often contradictory to the term "leisure," many hobbies practiced during nonwork hours actually emulated work, which some scholars called "serious leisure." Because of the ethic involved in serious leisure activities, some recreation advocates suggested that hobbies actually made people better workers.[41]

Adult education programs formally taught philately and other pursuits to keep unemployed workers primed and ready for their next job. If this was true for adults, then teaching philately to children might be preparing them to enter the work world as an adult. During this time teachers enrolled in philately classes at the University of Minnesota, Temple University, and Harvard's School of Education and Social Service, and college students organized philatelic clubs. Universities hired APS members as their instructors, further extending the reach of philatelic clubs and their influence on the diffusion of philatelic knowledge to adults.[42]

During the Depression, stamp collecting was also promoted by the conservative Leisure League of America (LLA). The organization published literature, sponsored hobby shows, and embarked on a public relations blitz to encourage citizens to adopt a hobby. After its founding in 1934, president and founder James S. Stanley went on a campaign to promote 700 different recreational activities published in *The Care and Feeding of Hobby Horses* for the purpose of saving "the nation from boredom." Stanley complained that too many Americans were willing to sit and watch others play rather than doing it for themselves. Philately and other select hobbies earned a monograph. Some newspaper editors found this hobby movement a bit comical and joked that the LLA was "wasting time busily."[43]

A rise in mass cultural offerings—movies, sporting events, amusement parks—troubled Stanley because he saw participants in those activities as being passive: watching rather than playing. Stanley acted as a political conservative, worrying about communal bonds formed in public cultural venues. He declared during the first Hobby Round-Up on May 1, 1935, that "May Day is play day" and not a time for "radical demonstrations."[44] Stanley's statement shifted the focus from offering leisure-time activities merely to "cure boredom" to speaking out against radicalism in the name of hobbies. The Hobby Round-Up was Stanley's way of taking back May Day from the Communists. He pushed hobbies as a way of mollifying workers inclined toward increased union activity and New Deal policies that supported workers' rights. Factory workers and union members did bond through mass culture participation in cities like Chicago in 1930s, which worked to unite previously divided workers in pursuit of common economic and production goals.[45] Stanley praised hobbies as individualist pursuits.

Meant for general audiences, monographs published and distributed by LLA taught the basics of different hobbies, including stamp collecting. The stamp-collecting book offered a guide for novices, introducing them to collecting practices, philatelic clubs and papers, and a brief history of the postal system. Once again, stamp collecting was described as "purely educational" and had a "beneficial effect upon character." According to the author, stamp collectors "must have an orderly mind" because they must be "neat, accurate, conscientious, observant, and honest." He then admitted that it was difficult to ascertain whether these skills were developed or accentuated by stamp collecting, but that they were positive characteristics for all people, nonetheless.[46] A publication such as this summarized many widely shared feelings about the worthiness of stamp collecting as a practice and why it should be taught to children and adults alike.

By the 1930s, purchasing stamps was easy and Americans understood that stamps functioned in many ways outside of their official role as postage. Americans found stamps in cigarette packages and philatelic information published in newspaper columns, or learned about philately at the YMCA or at a local university. Stamp collecting continued to grow in popularity as a hobby because club philatelists, educators, parents, missionaries, and merchant capitalists contributed to a public dialogue in the mainstream media that framed stamp collecting as educational. By constructing stamps as educational, these groups taught others how to look for what they wanted them to see in stamps and the order placed on them through philatelic practices. Teachers wanted students to memorize geographic locations and world leaders; recreation leaders wanted students to stay out of trouble; cities wanted to keep the minds of unemployed adults active and ready for their next job; missionaries showed young people a path for doing God's work; and merchant capitalists demonstrated that stamps were consumer collectibles. Club philatelists participated in this mass pedagogical movement to bring stamp collecting to all Americans through a type of voluntarism that spread the word about their favorite hobby.

Collectors and noncollectors learned to see the world as an ordered place that could be controlled in the pages of a stamp album, and these processes emulated, in a small way, an imperialist impulse to gather and control territories for one's own gain. This process also opened the door to viewing the United States as different and exceptional when compared to other countries. Americans learned to read stamps as culturally encoded texts bearing images and phrases constructed by a government agency, whether aware or not. The USPOD understood this power as it tracked the growing interest in stamp collecting, and began printing commemorative stamps in the 1890s.

Federal Participation in Philately

After Omaha's triumph is properly won,
Other towns, not forgetting our own,
Will be fully entitled to do as she's done;
In this thing she must not stand alone.
And if some day the crush
Of the jubilee rush
Uncle Sam and his factory swamps,
Then old Sammy will moan,
"Ah, had I only known
I'd have sat on those Omaha stamps."
—Unknown, 1898

Why would philatelists debate whether the US Post Office Department should issue its second special commemorative stamp series promoting Omaha's Trans-Mississippi Exposition held in 1898? Five years earlier, the Department printed the first commemorative stamp series celebrating the World's Columbian Exposition in Chicago. The "Columbians," as they became known, were extremely popular and many Americans collected them. Viewing the Columbians as a successful way to promote and celebrate a world's fair, the organizers of the Trans-Mississippi convinced postal officials to support the 1898 exposition by printing another series of commemoratives. An unknown philatelic poet, quoted at the beginning of this chapter, represented the feelings of many philatelists who predicted that the USPOD would be crushed by the "jubilee rush" once postal officials conceded to printing the Trans-Mississippis. Every town might want a stamp celebrating a significant event in its history. As some philatelists predicted, that rush came twenty years later when commemorative requests bombarded the USPOD and the Department capitalized of the collectability of limited-issue stamps.

Until the Columbians, the USPOD was relatively indifferent to collectors and printed stamps solely designed for sending materials through the mail (known as "definitives"). Seeing the Department's increased interest in collectors' activities concerned some philatelists who believed that the USPOD and other stamp-issuing agencies might flood the stamp market—culturally regulated by philatelists who developed methods for valuing stamps beyond government-issued values. Acknowledging these public debates, the USPOD proceeded with its commemorative stamp program that promoted American world's fairs by presenting scenes from the American past. The last decade of the nineteenth century marked a turning point in the relationship among the USPOD, philatelists, and noncollectors as the post office and other government entities began influencing a leisure-time activity that the agency previously ignored. Simultaneously, the USPOD began circulating historical narratives on stamps, making stamps important artifacts that imprinted specific interpretations of the American past on cultural memory.

The Post Office in American Life

No federal agency was more closely tied to the daily lives of the American public than the USPOD. As one of the first government agencies, the USPOD connected states and territories, where only tenuous relationships existed, and helped to build a national culture by making information, communications, and consumer goods accessible through a federally subsidized mail system. When new towns incorporated following the Revolutionary War, post offices were established immediately and often acted as community gathering places. Even as the post office remained central to smaller towns, occasionally the actions and policies of the federal agency conflicted with local customs. Beginning in the early nineteenth century, Sabbatarians began a crusade to keep post offices closed on Sundays, a practice that wouldn't officially end until the 1910s. In the 1830s, when unsolicited abolitionist literature from New York was sent to South Carolinians, local officials challenged the federal authority of the USPOD to deliver materials that promoted overturning South Carolina's laws and local policies. Then Postmaster General Amos Kendall allowed local postal authorities in southern states to censor mails and to decide what was appropriate for their citizens.[1] As the main agency that facilitated communications and commerce across long distances, it was mired in cultural and political debates among various interest groups and politicians, with outcomes that carried significant repercussions.

Assessing the appropriateness of mail content and debating the breadth of authority held by the USPOD continued into the late nineteenth and early twentieth centuries. Forced to comply with an 1873 law that barred the circulation of obscene literature and materials, the postmaster general created an unpaid position for a special agent charged with authority to seize offensive literature and to arrest publishers, recipients, and circulators of such materials. Paid by a private organization, Anthony Comstock filled the role of special agent to the USPOD until he died in 1915. As a self-appointed cultural warrior, Comstock had been working for the New York Society for the Suppression of Vice—a YMCA-affiliated committee—prior to his federal appointment, bringing violators of state law to trial. The federal legislation, later known as the Comstock Act, broadly defined obscene materials to include not solely pornographic publications, but also reproductions of paintings containing nude figures, playing cards, contraception pamphlets, women's health-related literature, and packages of contraceptives. During his tenure, Comstock confiscated and destroyed millions of print materials and goods and prosecuted thousands of violators.[2] Comstock zealously enforced a federal law of questionable constitutionality, while serving in a quasi-governmental role.

As Comstock scrutinized the subjects of mailable matter, postmasters general sought ways to deliver consumer goods to remote areas of the country. Services introduced by the USPOD in the late nineteenth and early twentieth centuries, such as rural free delivery (RFD) and parcel post, generated their own conflicts. Local businesses in small towns protested the influence of large merchants on postal policy, while residents appreciated access to affordable goods available in mail-order catalogs. RFD and parcel post afforded many rural residents home mail delivery and gave large retailers the ability to send goods inexpensively to remote areas.[3] The centrality of the post office to American daily life is evident in the ways it was pulled in many directions by legislators and citizen action. As the federal communications department, the post office connected residents with one another and with services, goods, and literature offered by organizations and businesses that relied on a stable delivery system. The post office provided a public service and excelled in moving mail. It also sat in the middle of conflicting interests as it transmitted information produced by many entities. Even postal policies were not strictly under the Department's control.

Postal policy decisions varied with each presidential administration and with each Congress. From the 1820s through the 1960s, the postmaster general was a cabinet-level political appointment. The Department's budget, postal rates, and other postal-related activities were determined by a congressional committee. This meant, among other things, that policy interpretation varied by administration and that the postal service retained no control over postal rates. Rates, for second-class periodicals in particular, were contested in committee as periodicals expanded from newspapers, religious tracts, and abolitionist literature before the Civil War to include consumer catalogs, specialist literature, and magazines filled with advertising after the Civil War. Local businesses questioned whether the Department should subsidize nationwide publications paid for by advertising, and Progressive politicians sought, unsuccessfully, to reel in postal budget deficits by raising rates on second-class postage. As US geographical boundaries grew, transportation costs increased, yet a first-class letter traveling five miles cost the same to mail as the same letter traveling 2,000 miles. The Department was forced to absorb these costs, as well as others—including many transportation-related contracting frauds that eventually led to major civil service reform.[4] Congress kept postage at reasonable rates on behalf of constituents, but that prevented the Department from making decisions about budgets that were fiscally necessary.

Knowing of the budgetary realities, postmasters general tried new ways to generate revenue. One attempt was printing and selling commemorative stamps. Under the leadership of merchant-turned-bureaucrat John Wanamaker, the USPOD first recognized philatelists as consumers and tapped into an established network of stamp collectors eager to buy stamps for their albums rather than exchanging them for postage delivery. At this time, consumption was becoming more closely associated with responsibilities of citizenship as constructed by newly formed advertising agencies. Wanamaker wanted citizens to purchase the first set of American commemorative stamps that celebrated the 1893 World's Columbian Exposition in Chicago and America's past.[5] By linking stamp consumption to patriotism, Wanamaker hoped to attract future collectors/consumers through this set of stamps while also increasing public support for the Department. It was not the only federal entity involved with philately. Beginning in the late nineteenth century, the USPOD and the Smithsonian Institution established philatelic collections and mounted exhibitions that promoted the study of philately. Making collections of stamps available for the public not only encouraged collecting, but also demonstrated that the government approved of stamp collecting and provided the means for building collections.

The USPOD unequivocally demonstrated its support of philately when it established the Philatelic Agency in 1921, specifically to handle requests from collectors. This type of enthusiasm went unmatched, for example, by the Treasury Department, which occasionally produced commemorative coins and never offered the same support for coin collectors. The Philatelic Agency became the government's commemorative stamp store, officially acknowledging collectors as consumers. Regular postage stamps bought at a local post office would be used to send a letter or package for services rendered, while collectors wrote or visited the Philatelic Agency to buy limited-issue commemorative stamps for saving. As the USPOD solidified its role as a producer of collectibles, it created an infrastructure to support the consumption of stamps. Leading by example, the USPOD encouraged Americans to buy and save stamps it crafted to celebrate a triumphalist vision of the American past and present. These stamps reached millions of people in the United States and around the world as the federal government interpreted and represented American history by promoting contemporary events. The turn of the century marks a transition for the USPOD, from an organization indifferent to collecting to one that actively participated in collecting culture.

Wanamaker and the Columbians

Until the World's Columbian Exposition in Chicago (1892–93), nineteenth-century philatelists and societies functioned in a world almost completely removed from the producer of American stamps, the USPOD. Prior to the 1890s, the USPOD maintained limited contact with stamp collectors and produced a limited number of stamps. From 1847 to 1894, it contracted with five private firms that designed and printed all American stamps. The images on this early postage were most often the heads of Benjamin Franklin and George Washington, with occasional appearances by Alexander Hamilton, Thomas Jefferson, Abraham Lincoln, or other prominent white American politicians or military officers. Printing companies experimented with different aspects of the production process, introducing pregummed paper, making it easier to affix a stamp to a letter, and perforations between each stamp, making it easier to separate one from a sheet. Portraits of figures from the American past were the staple design genre of definitive stamp imagery. American stamps, unlike British ones, never represented a living head of state. Meanwhile, postmaster generals were busy with balancing the duties of the Department with business interests of the press and big business and with morality crusades. Official records of the USPOD reveal little contact with collectors.[6] Conversely, philatelic journals did not discuss the USPOD much in their pages. Philatelic societies and journals functioned independently from the federal government. Publishing news releases regarding new issues of stamps was the only role the USPOD played in the philatelic press until the Columbian Exposition.

One factor that muddied the relationship between collectors and producers was professional intermediaries who facilitated a philatelic economy outside of the government producing these stamps. Stamp dealers emerged in banking and business districts of major northern American cities during and after the Civil War, particularly because Union stamps could be used as currency. Stamps could be an investment and liquidated if necessary, as happened during the war. Recognizing the commercial potential for selling and valuing stamps, the number of dealers grew and expanded into the southern cities of New Orleans and Atlanta. Private entities could trade in stamps that changed in value, but postal authorities could never sell stamps for anything greater than their face value. Postmasters could, however, sell stamps and stamped envelopes at a discount to certain "designated agents," who then had to agree to sell them at face value.[7] While this study will not address the particulars of the stamp market, it is important to note that this private network formed outside of the government's purview and flourished before postal agencies understood the breadth of stamp collecting's popularity.

Retailer John Wanamaker, however, recognized these networks and forever changed the relationship between collectors and the USPOD during his tenure as postmaster general (1889–93), because he saw collectors as consumers of stamps. His administration is remembered most for implementing rural free delivery and postal savings plans, but Wanamaker also increased the visibility of the USPOD in the philatelic world. Known more as the creator of the modern department store than a Washington bureaucrat, Wanamaker brought his business acumen and understanding of customer relations to the Department. Additionally, Wanamaker was heavily influenced by the spectacle of the era's world fairs, making it possible for him to see great potential in promoting the USPOD through a carefully designed exhibit at the Columbian Exposition that he envisioned would become part of a future postal museum.[8]

From the early planning stages of the Columbian Exposition, Wanamaker envisioned heightening the postal service's visibility by involving philatelic organizations to assist in staging an exhibit and by issuing the first series of commemorative postage stamps. Immediately after securing funding from Congress, the USPOD solicited the assistance of philatelists, who eagerly cooperated soon after the announcement of the Exposition. Cooperating philatelists wished to display a complete set of all American stamps ever printed, and were shocked to learn that the USPOD did not keep samples from each printing. Seeing great potential to highlight philately at the Columbian Exposition, the American Philatelic Association encouraged wide participation among its members, emphasizing the great "impetus this exhibition will give stamp collecting!"[9]

Wanamaker was aware of the stamp-collecting "mania" and wanted the USPOD to capitalize on philatelists' desire to acquire new stamps and attract new collectors amazed by a beautifully designed set of Columbians. Estimating that millions of collectors, from the "school boy and girl to the monarch and the millionaire," kept stamps in collections "never [to] be drawn upon to pay postage," Wanamaker saw great potential for profit. He designed the Columbians as limited issues, combined with a larger size and elaborate designs, many based on historical paintings to attract international dealers and collectors. Not just for collecting, Columbians held real postal value as prepaid postage and did not replace the contemporary issue of stamps from that year. "Though not designed primarily for that object," Wanamaker emphasized the profit-making potential of these commemoratives, which was "of highest importance to the public service." He estimated that these stamps would bring in revenues to the federal government of $2.5 million.[10] He also saw that this practice was "in the line of a custom connected with national jubilees." To justify the upfront expenditure on extra stamps, Wanamaker noted that the Treasury Department issued a souvenir coin of Columbus for this occasion—another way that government engaged with collectors of a federal commodity. In 1890 and 1891, USPOD deficits exceeded $5 million annually, so Wanamaker's estimation of Columbian sales would reduce those budget deficiencies.[11]

A. D. Hazen, third assistant postmaster general under Wanamaker, reiterated the importance of this special issue to encourage collecting and to generate revenues for the USPOD. Referring to a past success when the Department issued commemorative envelopes for the Centennial Exhibition in 1876, he also saw revenue potential for the Columbians lying in dormant collections "without ever being presented in payment for postage," proving "a clear gain to the Department." Encouraging stamp collecting through the commemoratives not only cultivated "artistic tastes and the study of history and geography," but led to a "more accurate knowledge of their postal system."[12] Hazen incorporated language already used by philatelists in promoting their hobby to outsiders, claiming stamps held an inherently educational value. Messages embedded in the stamp's imagery were as important as selling those stamps. Wanamaker's business acumen and zeal for increasing American's access to goods logically led him, and the

Department, to seek out new customers by experimenting with new products. He wanted the general public to voluntarily walk into local post offices to purchase stamps, attracted by the design and stories told on stamps even when patrons were not mailing a letter.

Drawing heavily from historical paintings and sculptures, the Columbians demonstrated in their imagery that Columbus—even if the Exposition did not directly have much to do with him—symbolized utopian ideals of progress put forth in the construction of the White City and the Midway that celebrated empire and anthropologically based racial hierarchies.[13] The stamp series offered an extensive visual narrative tracing Columbus's life, beginning with his journeys to the Americas and his relationship with the Spanish Crown, told over sixteen stamps.

Printed across the top of each stamps were the years 1492–1892, with the words "United States of America" appearing immediately below. Americans were used to their stamps carrying the identifier "United States Postage," but adding the anniversary years to the stamp connected Columbus with the founding of the United States. In the series, while the United States of America may have been emphasized in print, only two of the sixteen stamps actually represented scenes in the Americas. Nine treated Columbus's life in Spain and his relationship to the Spanish Crown, while three represented the journey across the Atlantic. Queen Isabella appeared in seven of the sixteen stamps, leading Americans to believe that Isabella's influence on Columbus journeys could not be overstated. Additionally, Isabella and an unnamed American Indian became the first women represented on American stamps.[14] That the USPOD's stamp choices reflected themes of empire and conquest should come as no surprise, given that US foreign policy was already embarking on what would become a sustained imperial endeavor.

For the first time, the USPOD released a large limited-issue commemorative series drawing considerable attention in the philatelic and popular press. Immediately after the Columbians' release, philatelic journalist Joseph F. Courtney commented that the stamps were "the most magnificent pieces of workmanship" and very artistic. J. P. Glass wrote that collectors were "indebted for the handsomest, most interesting and most talked about series of stamps ever issued." Philatelist and editor Harry Kantner delighted in the Columbian stamps, noting that they were "the cause of our progress" in lifting philately to "a higher point of popularity than it ever yet has attained."[15] This heightened popularity was also due to increased press coverage highlighting the practice of stamp collecting. The *New York Times* featured an article on philately claiming that the new stamps gave "extra temporary impetus to the regular trade in stamps which has grown to proportions entirely amazing to persons not informed of its extent and diffusion." This journalist also recognized a profit-making potential of the Columbians, which proved "a lucky speculation on the part of the Government." They brought "clean profit" because the stamps would "be locked up in albums and never put upon letters for the Government to carry." E. S. Martin wrote in his *Harper's Weekly* column that the success of the Columbian stamps "called attention to the very lively status of the stamp-collecting mania"—so lively that in many homes collected stamps were as prevalent as soap.[16] Most collectors would not have purchased the entire series, but their presence—in post offices and in the press—heightened awareness of philately as a leisure-time activity and no doubt encouraged more people to purchase a Columbian even if they had no intention of starting their own collections.

Americans—collectors and noncollectors—were most likely to buy and see one- and two-cent issues from the series, because those denominations paid for postcards and first-class mail, respectively. Though the series was large in quantity and contained a variety of issues, 72 percent of those printed were two-centers. The first two stamps treat Columbus's initial journey and landing. Based on a painting by William H. Powell, the one-cent represents Columbus looking out to sea and sighting land from a circular vignette in the center for the stamp.[17] The circle around Columbus may represent a round world—something he is most often credited with declaring—and offers the viewer a peak at Columbus as if we were looking at him through a ship's spyglass telescope.

On the exterior of the vignette sit three Native Americans, almost docile, already in a defeated position looking away from the viewer, wrapping their arms around their bodies as if in an effort to protect themselves and their families. The images of Columbus and others traveling on board ship with him are heavily robed and clothed, contrasting greatly with the Native people. The woman and child are lightly covered, with a single cloth draped over the mother's legs. The man wears a smaller cloth covering his lower body and a headdress that triggers images of a Plains Indian rather than of a Taino or other Carib-

Fig. 7. Columbus in Sight of Land, one cent, 1892–93 (Courtesy Smithsonian National Postal Museum Collection)

bean native. These images visually foreshadowed and justified the conquest that followed Columbus's arrival. This stamp's representation of Native peoples was not dissimilar to how American Indians and other nonwhites were represented on the Midway Plaisance, as savages and ethnologically inferior to those with Anglo-Saxon blood roaming the fairgrounds.[18] Here, the stamp stages Columbus as the civilizer arriving in a savage land.

The two-cent stamp, the most widely disseminated of all in the series, also was based on a historical painting that maintained Columbus as a founding father. John Vanderlyn painted the *Landing of Columbus,* which hangs in the Capitol Rotunda. It represents Columbus's party landing, but unlike Powell's imagery, this one did not include any Native peoples.[19] Their presence is erased as if they did not exist

Fig. 8. Landing of Columbus, two cent, 1892–93 (Courtesy Smithsonian National Postal Museum Collection)

or were not important enough to be depicted in this painting-turned-stamp. Columbus touches the ground with his sword while he raises a Spanish flag and looks to the sky, claiming the lands in the name of Spain and perhaps invoking the will of God. Interestingly, the flags on the stamp appear intentionally blurry as if to obfuscate that they represented the Inquisition and the Catholic monarchs of Ferdinand and Isabella. The two-cent celebrates Columbus's "discovery" of seemingly unpopulated lands in the Americas, and does not attempt to connect how Columbus actually related to the founding of the United States as a nation—a connection that is implied with "1492–1892, United States of America" title printed across all of the stamps in the series. Instead, Columbus is a Christian civilizer.

Drawing upon the themes of triumphant human progress at the Exposition, the Columbians offered a post–Civil War story of American unity by representing Columbus's journeys as America's origins. Columbus did not land in territories that would become identified as the South or the North—Jamestown versus Plymouth. Unknown to most Americans at the time, Columbus landed in Caribbean islands that would become US territory following the 1898 war with Spain. Columbus's imperialistic endeavors in the 1490s matched with the United States' own actions in the 1890s. The stories, as retold in the stamps, obscured more complicated questions about conquest and slavery that followed Columbus's landing and served to celebrate the conquest. As the struggles over who participated in and attended the Exposition demonstrated, the Exposition and the stamps commemorating the fair were meant for racially white audiences.[20] Some of those citizens felt uneasy about their futures and took comfort in the utopian vision of the White City, while the stamps offered others a positive outlook on the American past during a time of economic crisis, Populist political debates, labor unrest, rapidly expanding industry, Jim Crow laws, and rapid immigration. For newly arrived immigrants, Columbus's story as represented in stamps provided them with a visual national narrative of their adopted country.

While collectors and noncollectors alike praised the stamps, others heavily criticized the Columbians for the size of the series and size of the stamps. Senator Wolcott (R-CO) called for a joint congressional resolution to discontinue the Columbian stamps, exclaiming that he did not want a "cruel and unusual stamp" unloaded on collectors.

Wolcott criticized Wanamaker for acting in a mercantilistic manner by trying to profit from philatelists.[21] Correct about Wanamaker's retailing instinct, Wolcott's assumptions were slightly flawed because Wanamaker would not profit personally—only the government reaped any monetary benefits. If fiscally successful, the USPOD could better manage its finances and require less in appropriations from Congress.

One major critique related to the stamps was the high monetary denominations. The one-dollar issue, for instance, which represented Queen Isabella selling her jewels to finance Columbus's journeys, was never meant to pay for actual postage, as the highest domestic rate in 1893 equaled ninety cents. This was also true for the high denominations (the one-, two-, three-, and four-dollar issues). A *Chicago Tribune* story critiqued "Uncle Sam" for playing "a confidence game on confiding nephews and nieces" with the Columbians. Large denominations, such as the four-dollar and five-dollar, would never be used for sending mail, but would be "hidden between red leather covers in stamp albums." If a collector wanted to purchase the entire series, it cost $16.34, which in today's dollars is roughly $300.[22] While higher denominations might mail a heavy package overseas, these stamps essentially were designed specifically for collectors to buy and save. Dealers placed them on envelopes to create commemorative covers purchased by collectors, even though the dollar amounts far outpriced the cost of mailing a letter.[23] Critics saw stamp collectors as vulnerable individuals falling prey to John Wanamaker and the USPOD, which wanted to milk savings from stamp collectors by issuing this special postage. These critiques may have been colored by concern over new department store-style consumerism that tempted customers into buying products they did not need.

Less concerned with being taken advantage of by the post office, some philatelists simply did not like the appearance and size of the stamps. One collector joked that he used Columbians for "sticking plaster" inside his house because the stamps were so large. A journalist noted that an "office boy," upon seeing the stamps, exclaimed, "What wrong have I committed that I should suffer this unjust punishment[?]"—licking larger-than-normal stamps proved "doubly tiresome and detestful." This tongue-in-cheek article was not as biting as other critiques of the commemorative issues, but the author admitted that one month after their release he was already tired of them.[24] Wanamaker's stamp series definitely generated discussion about the stamps themselves, and he attempted to address the concerns of his critics.

Efforts to stop circulation of the commemoratives were unsuccessful, but Wanamaker's successor, W. S. Bissel, curtailed the total number of pieces printed. Bissel found that the previous administration optimistically placed an order for three billion Columbian stamps to be sold over one year. He renegotiated the remaining contract down to two billion stamps and saved the Department nearly $100,000 in manufacturing costs. The cost for printing an equal number of smaller-sized ordinary stamps was about half that for printing the Columbians. According to Department figures, the rate of purchase for the commemoratives fell by mid-1893, and Bissel felt the collectors' purchasing power was not as great as Wanamaker predicted. At the time, sales of stamped matter provided 95 percent of the USPOD total revenues. For fiscal year 1893, total postal revenues jumped by nearly $5 million compared with 1892, but declined again by almost $2 million the following year. Increased expenses for printing the Columbians and the manufacture of a variety of new postal cards, in addition to escalating transportation costs, never allowed the Columbian sales to translate into postal profits.[25]

Despite not earning a profit for the Department, Wanamaker started a trend. The government continued to print limited-issue stamps celebrating other expositions. The Columbians were notable not only as the first series of commemoratives, but also as a turning point for the Department, which now actively encouraged stamp collecting as a hobby. Philatelists speculated about their positive influence on the hobby, while others pointed directly to the Columbian issues as the reason they started collecting.[26]

The next set of commemoratives, another world's fair series in 1898, however, attracted strong opposition from American and international philatelic organizations.

Trans-Mississippi Controversy

Following the Columbian issues, the USPOD began engaging philatelists in unprecedented ways, and some philatelists, particularly dealers, felt uncomfortable with the new role that the US and other governments played in the stamp market by printing limited-issue commemoratives. This discomfort exploded into a philatelic controversy at the end of the nineteenth century. The Columbians were among an early group of commemoratives printed by various nations to celebrate "jubilees," or significant anniversaries and events, in Japan, Portugal, Greece, San Marino, and Hungary. This small flurry of limited-issues angered some philatelists worldwide who deemed them unnecessary and believed that these nations printed the stamps solely to collect revenue from gullible collectors. To protest and dissuade collectors from purchasing such stamps, philatelists in London formed the Society for the Suppression of Speculative Stamps (SSSS). Worried about how a flood of commemoratives would affect stamp prices, the SSSS participated in letter-writing campaigns using the philatelic press to encourage collectors around the world to ignore the stamps.[27]

Two years later outrage and protest came from philatelists who tried to stop the USPOD from printing a stamp commemorating the Trans-Mississippi and International Exposition in Omaha (1898). Released to promote the fair, the series comprised nine stamps celebrating the conquest of western lands and peoples through imagery of agriculture, such as on the two-cent, and through technological developments, as found on the two-dollar. Each stamp carried identifying images of wheat stalks across the top and partially peeled ears of corn in each bottom corner, both major cash crops farmed in Nebraska and in territories across the Midwest. (See figs. 9, 10, and 11.) To safely migrate to new farming lands, federal troops were depicted as protectors of American pioneers from Indian attacks on the eight-cent stamp. America's imperialistic foreign policy and military aggression were portrayed as a natural outgrowth of westward expansion that was celebrated at the Exposition.[28]

Spurring much discussion in the philatelic press, *Mekeel's* likened the Trans-Mississippi controversy (for the stamp papers) to what "the Maine incident has been to the wider field of American journalism." Philatelic editors voiced opinions, and collectors responded; meanwhile the press printed articles composed by the newly formed Stamp Dealers' Protective Association (SDPA), SSSS, and Scott Stamp and Coin Company, which encouraged all philatelists to write in protest to the postmaster general. They claimed that the proposed commemoratives provided free advertising for the Exposition and therefore were not a legitimate use of the postal service. The Columbians, they

Fig. 9. Farming in the West, two cent, 1898 (Courtesy Smithsonian National Postal Museum Collection)

Fig. 10. Troops Guarding Train, eight cent, 1898 (Courtesy Smithsonian National Postal Museum Collection)

Fig. 11. Mississippi River Bridge, two dollar, 1898 (Courtesy Smithsonian National Postal Museum Collection)

claimed, "should not be considered a precedent for future issues," and lamented that philatelists would endure "a sad blow to (their) hobby if the government of the United States should lend itself to so reprehensible a scheme." Celebrating the founding of the United States was an occasion "of such surpassing importance" that the Columbian Exposition was not just about commemorating the fair, but also represented an important anniversary for the nation. According to some protestors, commemorating American settlement of the land west of the Mississippi was only of "passing interest." Of course, the overall theme of the Exposition and the stamps celebrated the federal government's role in "settling the west" just as the US military was occupying Cuba and the Philippines. To prevent philatelists from properly saving such unnecessary stamps, Scott Stamp and Coin, one of the largest publishers of international stamp albums, refused to print spaces in albums for collectors to save "speculative" commemorative stamps from 1897 to 1899.[29]

While the SDPA claimed that all collectors viewed the Trans-Mississippi issues as speculative and unnecessary, collectors themselves were conflicted. One individual wrote to the *Philatelic West* claiming joy in collecting commemorative stamps as soon as they were issued. Editors of the *Virginian Philatelist* endorsed the Omaha Exposition stamps and revealed that they had received only one negative response from a subscriber. These conflicts reflect some growing pains appearing in the philatelic world as it expanded. Philatelic clubs like the American Philatelic Association tried to grow their membership and attract new collectors to the hobby even as members rejected new commemoratives that drew more attention to philately. As the popularity of philately increased, hundreds of philatelic journals circulated around the world, a trend that disturbed some collectors and philatelic journalists.[30] The once-small intimate community of collectors had grown, and those collectors felt conflicted by philately's growth and the interest shown by USPOD.

Another reason some collectors hesitated to accept what they viewed as an excessive number of commemorative stamps related to an incident resulting in a stamp market flooded with reprints from Nicaragua, Salvador, Honduras, and Ecuador. This flood resulted from a deal made by Charles Seebeck, an officer of the Hamilton Bank Note Company, who offered to print stamps for no charge to the aforementioned countries. These stamps, however, actually expired, which was an uncommon practice. A U.S. two-cent stamp issued in 1898, for example, may be affixed to a letter today and combined with other stamps to mail a first-class letter. A Seebeck print, however, was invalid a few years after issued. After the expiration date, Seebeck received permission to reprint that same stamp using the original engraving plates, and he sold those issues to collectors, speculating that the sales covered his costs. Seebeck's plan resulted in thousands of Latin American stamps entering the stamp market between 1890 and 1898. After Seebeck's death in 1899, a speculator bought the remaining unused reprints—all ninety million of them—and sold, traded, and gave them away. Many of those reprints landed in starter stamp packets geared to generating interest in young collectors.[31] Concerns over the Seebeck issues certainly colored philatelists' opinions about new commemorative stamps.

Dealers in particular charged all governments with trying to fleece collectors by printing stamps with "fancy designs" that they saw as unnecessary for regular postage. The SSSS and SDPA did not discriminate in their criticism of stamp-issuing nations, as others did, because they seemed to be motivated mostly by economic factors and a desire to keep the stamp market controlled by dealers. Oddly, many dealers lacked enthusiasm for commemoratives that drew more people into the hobby of collecting and even argued that jubilees turned people away. One philatelic editorial illuminated this hypocrisy by criticizing dealers for giving away stamps in chewing gum and cigarette packages one minute while protesting commemorative issues that might more easily attract more collectors another. It was said that limited issues of US commemorative stamps, such as for the Pan-American Exposition and Louisiana Purchase, drew enough attention to stamp collecting and would not "fail to be of material value in advancing the collecting hobby, and one which could hardly be termed speculative."[32] In theory, the injection of stamps into the market that brought new collectors would have given dealers a larger pool of people from which to do business—in person or via the post. Instead, they resisted an expansion and fought the producers of stamps by attempting to maintain their stronghold on the stamp market.

As philatelists argued among themselves over the appropriateness of the USPOD's Trans-Mississippi commemoratives, a discussion emerged about the political and cultural status of the United States in their rhetoric. The timing of this particular protest is quite striking. This series specifically commemorated an Exposition that celebrated European migration to and conquest of territories across the middle section of the continent, home to many Native Americans. Concurrently, the United States and its military reached beyond the continental borders to invade and occupy sovereign nations and former European colonies in the Caribbean and Pacific. In defending the USPOD's production of American commemoratives, stamp columnists and editors stated that the United States' large population required postal services "greater than any other nation on earth" and was "privileged to some philatelic things without censure." But "petty states of Asia and Africa," or "some little bankrupt country," should be rebuked for issuing nonessential postage for the purpose of bringing in revenues.[33] The Seebeck issues were, no doubt, in the minds of some philatelists who held that the United States was unique and should be able to produce postage stamps for whatever purpose postal officials saw as necessary.

This exceptionalist argument did not merely apply to international philatelic matters, but was another extension of the constructed racial and economic privilege imagined by architects of American foreign policy.[34] Stamps commemorating American world's fairs celebrated empire and conquest and promoted scientifically based racial hierarchies leaving "petty states of Asia and Africa" at the bottom, while white America and western Europe rested at the top. Prevailing attitudes toward other nations' racial composition affected how stamp collectors viewed a state's ability, or right, to print commemoratives.

We hear in this rhetoric that collectors believed they influenced the production of stamps and decisions made by governments about their postage, but not everyone agreed. *Mekeel's* editors thought it was absurd of the SSSS and the SDPA to suppose that postal officials would pay attention to philatelists' protests over stamp production, or that the USPOD would print stamps specifically for collectors. *Mekeel's* editors believed the USPOD "almost invariably snubbed collectors wherever possible and [had] given us plainly to understand that it looked upon us with suspicion."[35] True or not, the editors of a major philatelic paper believed the USPOD was oblivious to their pursuit.

These protests highlighted growing pains felt by philatelists as the USPOD, and international postal agencies, acknowledged collectors and printed stamps for them. Prior to the Columbians, the USPOD was not concerned with attracting collectors, but soon after began to influence the stamp market gently by throwing additional stamps in the global collection every few years. Following the Columbian experiment, the Trans-Mississippis cemented the precedent. Interestingly, sixty-four years after the introduction of the postage stamp in the United States, the Department still defended using a postage-based system to collect revenues. Citizens continued to suggest alternatives, but postal officials noted in the Department's annual report of 1911 that the USPOD would expand rather than contract or replace the current stamp system.[36]

And expand it did. From 1892 to 1919 the USPOD printed forty-seven different sets of commemorative stamps, almost exclusively to celebrate world's fairs or regional expositions, including the Trans-Mississippi Exposition (1898), Pan-American Exposition (1901), Louisiana Purchase Centennial (1904), Jamestown Tercentenary (1907), the Alaska-Yukon-Pacific Exposition (1909), Hudson-Fulton Celebration (1909), and Panama Pacific Exposition (1915). After projected revenues from the Columbians fell short of Wanamaker's $2.5 million estimate, postal officials commissioned more conservative numbers for all other commemoratives and shortened the period of availability for future series from a year to a few months. Though not attracting nearly as much publicity, these stamps were collected and considered successful endeavors.[37] Governments noticed collectors and dealers of stamps and began targeting them for sales. Despite resistance by philatelists to being viewed as consumers, ultimately they could not prevent governments from printing scores of commemorative stamps.

Uncle Sam's Collections

As the USPOD developed a philatelic relationship with collectors and citizens, the federal government established a postal museum and national collections that encouraged philately and spawned interest in postal matters. In 1894, the USPOD opened a small museum in Washington, DC, that highlighted the accomplishments of the postal service. Major museums were opening in American cities by the 1890s, and in Washington the Smithsonian Institution operated the National

Museum on the National Mall. The Smithsonian had already established a philatelic collection in 1886, but did not hold a large postal-related collection until the postal service officially transferred all of its holdings to the Smithsonian in 1913.[38] Through collecting and exhibiting stamps, stamped matter, and other postal-related articles, the federal government demonstrated to its citizens that these objects possessed national significance.

John Wanamaker played a leading role, once again, in heightening the profile of the postal service to the citizens it served. Wanamaker was not the first postmaster general to suggest a museum, but he provided the means and support for creating one. Philatelists overwhelmingly supported Wanamaker's suggestion in 1890 to establish a museum. One philatelic journalist wrote that other stamp-producing nations had opened museums and hoped "that our own country may soon take a leading place among them." Rather than asking philatelists for assistance, Wanamaker instead looked to local and international postal officials for their help in collecting articles that represented "the progress of our postal system from its inception" and would "illustrate the work of the United States postal service, as well as that of foreign countries." Stamps would be among many other items on display, including postmarking instruments, mail bags, illustrations of post offices and postal transportation, ship models of mail steamers, and various objects from other postal services.[39] Not only would this museum be a place of great interest for Americans, but for philatelists from around the world who might visit Washington, DC.

At this time, some philatelists prodded the Smithsonian to collect and display stamps in the National Museum alongside "Indian relics, curios," coins, and other specimens. The National Philatelic Collection, as it would later be named, began modestly in 1886 with the donation of a few Confederate stamps. Organized with other Civil War artifacts, the stamps did not stand out among the other objects displayed in the museum. Spencer Baird, a former Smithsonian secretary, willed his stamp collection to the Institution in 1888, but it was not available for public viewing. Collector Frank Moore felt that philatelists and stamps were "completely left out in the cold by the respected managers of this great institution." To build a national stamp collection, Moore suggested in 1893 that all collectors send "good stamps" to the museum.[40] Even with these donations, stamp presence at the Smithsonian remained small until the two national collections merged in 1913.

Staged in a renovated storage room in the main USPOD building in Washington, the Department's exhibitions reused display pieces built for American world's fairs and expositions. At the museum opening, Postmaster General Bissell bragged that the first exhibits offered a strong base upon which to build a great national postal museum "for the benefit and interest of this and future generations." Meant for general audiences, this museum highlighted developments in all aspects of postal operations, including transportation and communications, and included a catalog of all stamps printed in the United States (1847–1893). Philatelists were pleased that the Department had begun collecting stamps from other countries—even "Uncle Sam cannot resist the pleasures of philately.[41]" Some philatelists were not satisfied with the state of the stamp collection and thought postal officials should have kept a complete set of US stamps. They also wanted the USPOD to hire a philatelist to curate the stamp collection.

The Department's collections addressed postal history and operations broadly, and did not hire a philatelist as its curator. Chief clerk Frank Thomas organized the opening exhibit, and then Stanley Ira Slack, another postal official, managed the Department's collection. Not a philatelist himself, Slack looked to the expertise of dealers for advice on mounting stamps and in some instances secured stamps for displays at world's fair postal exhibits and at the museum. Philatelists saw great value in a government saving its postage history but criticized the Department for not employing a practicing philatelist or even a "stamp man of medium experience" to manage the holdings in a systematic, "philatelic way." Despite collectors' concerns, this postal museum became a popular tourist destination in Washington, attracting between 75,000 and 100,000 visitors annually.[42]

Given the high visibility and robust visitation numbers in the 1910s, it is difficult to understand why Postmaster General Frank Hitchcock shut the USPOD's museum and transferred its holdings to the Smithsonian. Crowding in the main post office building, however, forced Hitchcock to evict the museum, since the USPOD needed the office space. Hitchcock wanted the objects to remain accessible to the public, while also moving visitors out of the main Department offices. Recognizing that the Department was not equipped to properly care for its objects, including the large stamp collection, Hitchcock forfeited the collection in favor of an institution that could. After two years, the collections transferred to the Smithsonian.[43] As noncollectors, postal officials did not quite understand the specific philatelic practices of caring for and displaying stamps. Hitchcock, like Wanamaker, believed that the government played a significant role in saving its philatelic and postal history even as it transferred the duties of preserving stamps as artifacts to the National Museum. A federal entity continued to collect stamps and postal-related objects under the auspices of the Smithsonian and not the USPOD—at least for the following two decades.

Club philatelists also believed that the government had a duty to recognize philatelic practices through proper care and exhibition of stamps. To the delight of philatelists, the Smithsonian hired well-known collector Joseph Leavy in 1913 as the first federal "philatelist" to care for the newly transferred collections. Philatelic papers covered the news of Leavy's hiring and praised him for his skills in mounting and organizing stamps in a "tabulated and orderly form." For the first time, according to one philatelic writer, "We now have a stamp exhibit that may be considered a credit to us all." Leavy cataloged the collection to identify missing pieces in the Smithsonian's holdings and encouraged fellow philatelists to donate stamps. Leavy also mounted stamp exhibitions in the National Museum housed in mahogany cabinets and mounted under glass frames. Following a museum visit, a writer for *Mekeel's* boasted that not even the British Museum had as "modern and up-to-date an abode" to house its philatelic collection. Even with renewed attention to stamps at the Smithsonian, members of the American Philatelic Society were extremely concerned, and a little confused, that the National Philatelic Collection might be abandoned and that the new philatelist might be fired. In response to a frantic resolution passed by the APS at its 1916 annual meeting, the assistant secretary of the Smithsonian assured APS members that the philatelic collection was "as permanent as the life of the nation and has never been regarded in any other light." In his statement, the physical permanence of that collection equated to the strength and permanence of the United States, together with all objects held by in the History Division of the National Museum that, in theory, collectively illustrated the history of the nation.[44]

This transfer from the Department that produced stamps to the federal entity charged with preservation and diffusion of knowledge signified a shift in how philatelists and citizens would view stamps. Stamps were not merely physical representations of prepaid postage, but were historically significant artifacts and worth saving. Philatelists had believed this from the earliest days of collecting. John Wanamaker and other postal officials valued public exhibition space for stamps and postal-related objects in federal buildings for fostering positive public relations. With the Smithsonian in charge, expertise was required for the long-term preservation, exhibition, and interpretation of these historical objects.

Keeping a philatelist on staff was important when Leavy left his position in 1921. Applicants needed philatelic experience, and "work as an amateur collector" would not be considered. In the job announcement, the government drew formal distinctions between casual and professional collectors, something philatelists had done for years. Just as Leavy's personal and professional life revolved around stamps, so would his successor's. The Smithsonian hired Catherine L. Manning, who became known as "Uncle Sam's First Lady of Philately." She had begun collecting when she was a girl and then worked for stamp dealers, including the well-known dealer J. M. Bartels. Manning's selection demonstrated that, while most philatelic clubs banned female membership, many women collected and studied stamps. By the 1930s, the philately section of the History Division became well established at the Smithsonian.[45] As federal institutions made space in their collections for stamps and postal history, the Department watched the popularity of collecting rise, and it needed a better way to handle requests from collectors.

The Philatelic Agency: Seeing Collectors as Consumers

The rising popularity of stamp collecting internationally, combined with increased numbers of stamp issues by the 1920s, motivated the USPOD to create a separate office to handle stamp requests from domestic and international collectors. Prior to the establishment of the Philatelic Agency, anyone could purchase ordinary stamps and limited-issue commemoratives stamps at local post offices. In 1900, the Department operated over 76,000 post offices, a total that dropped to 52,000 by 1920. Some collectors and dealers wrote to the USPOD directly to acquire limited-issue or rare stamps.[46] By providing the infrastructure through a new office, the Department could easily expand its commemorative stamp program and track those sales. Proposed first in 1917 by a congressman collector, the Philatelic Agency in Washington opened in 1921.

Postal officials and legislators understood that the revenue collected from sales for philatelic purposes could provide steady income for the USPOD, with the added benefit of promoting collecting. According to the postmaster general's annual report, the Philately Agency (PA) gave formal recognition to "the growing importance of stamp collecting" and provided a better way to handle the needs of collectors and dealers. That there was a means to buy directly and easily from Washington, where stamps were printed, delighted collectors and the philatelic press. Convinced that that the PA's establishment was a direct result of their requests, editors of *Mekeel's Weekly* declared that Postmaster General Will Hays was truly "humanizing the department."[47] This was a giant leap forward for collectors in the eyes of *Mekeel's*, which, twenty years earlier, had believed that the USPOD looked upon all collectors with suspicion.

To encourage use of the PA, the philatelic press helped by instructing readers on the new agency's policies and procedures. Stamp requests had to include cash or a money order (another postal product) to pay for stamps, and enough return postage for them to be mailed back to the collector. Unlike individuals or dealers, the agency would not trade in stamps, accept payment in stamps, or issue stamps "on approval"—meaning that buyers had to accept the stamps mailed to them and did not have the option to return the stamps upon seeing them. Additionally, no discrimination would be permitted to "any class of collector or dealer," perhaps to distinguish government service as distinct from an exclusive philatelic society or dealer. Most philatelists wanted this new system to succeed and were delighted to learn that the person in charge of the new agency, Third Assistant Postmaster General W. Irving Glover, was married to a woman who collected stamps.[48]

The United States was not alone in focusing attention and resources on philatelists. By the mid-1930s, over one hundred postal agencies worldwide served the needs of collectors. Colonial governments such as France and Portugal offered collectors the opportunity to purchase stamps from any of their territories in one centralized office. Philatelic publications provided contact information for these agencies, making it easier for casual collectors to broaden their holdings without traveling abroad or negotiating with a dealer.[49] Collectors could create global collections by contacting a postal agency directly. This practice of sending away for postage was well established in the club philatelic culture, where publications facilitated exchanges among fellow members, and dealers advertised in those pages. Those exchanges occurred among private citizens and did not involve government officials.

The PA sold all stamps at face value, a practice highlighted in the public and philatelic press when describing the activities of this new office. Knowing that old and rare issues sometimes remained in smaller post offices across the United States, the Philatelic Agency asked local postmasters to return that postage so that the stamps could be available for collectors through one main distribution center.[50] Acting as official dealers, the postal service would only sell stamps at the printed value regardless of any alternative value assessed in the stamp market. In the spirit of the civil service system in the government, the agency would not favor some collectors over others nor dealers over casual collectors. Everyone had an equal opportunity to buy stamps, new and old, from the original producer. Regular issues of stamps and some commemoratives would still be available through local post offices, but with all commemoratives available through the agency, local postmasters and their clerks focused on selling postage for the purpose of mail delivery and fulfilling other needs of their customers.

Not all philatelists, however, were pleased with the opening of the PA. Editors of *American Philatelist* disagreed with the benefits associated with national governments operating philatelic bureaus to handle collectors' requests. They believed that the challenge of pursuing an elusive stamp was eliminated. For instance, writing to the French postal agency gave one access to all of the stamps of its colonial territories, making the practice of collecting stamps too easy.[51] With enough money to cover the printed value of a stamp, plus the air mail postage and envelope to send the request, any collector could fill an album with contemporary stamps from around the world. Some philatelists struggled with the growing popularity of their pursuit as they clung to a romanticized and elitist notion that limited collecting to those few with means to travel abroad or shop regularly with dealers. The PA was doing its part to democratize stamp collecting for those who enjoyed stamps. As some had objected to the USPOD's insistence on issuing commemorative stamps series for world's fairs in the 1890s, others still did not appreciate the growing involvement of the USPOD in their hobby in the 1920s.

During its early years, the PA struggled with efficiency as it juggled a high volume of stamp requests. Some collectors demanded prompt service and were impatient when their requests were not filled quickly. Collectors were reminded that all orders were numbered upon receipt and then filled in order. They were asked to understand that some patrons requested large numbers of stamps and philatelic information that required considerable labor from the staff clerks. Clerks were overwhelmed with work, and officials reorganized and expanded staffing to handle the demand for stamps in 1924.[52]

This work did not go unnoticed, as Congressman Ernest R. Ackerman, a devoted and award-winning philatelist, became one of the PA's most ardent supporters and defenders. He remarked that governments could do no better than to assist those who wanted to collect stamps. According to Ackerman, philately had "no deleterious effects" and was democratic in practice because it was pursued by people of all ages, classes, and gender. Ackerman optimistically opined that stamps sales might be so high as to finance ventures far outside of the purview of regular postal activities.[53] The idea that stamp sales could produce enough revenue, to finance not only the stamp program but additional federal programs, came from Ackerman's zealous enthusiasm for philately.

Department officials seemed pleased that, within the first seven months of operation, the agency took in more than $20,000 in stamp sales. Those revenues continued to increase substantially. By the following year the annual receipts had increased to over $105,000. Sales continued to climb nearly every year, so that by the mid-1930s, receipts were counted in millions rather than thousands of dollars, which is astounding considering the most remarkable growth occurred in 1935 amid the Great Depression.[54] Revenues from all stamped matter consistently brought in a majority of the USPOD's revenue, receipts that continued to rise along with overall Department expenses. The PA's success, however, was less about stamp sales than about fostering good relationships with collectors and promoting stamp collecting. For instance, in fiscal year 1924, revenues from all stamped matter totaled over $483 million, representing 88 percent of the total departmental income, while the PA collected $129,646 in sales.[55] Increased popularity of collecting US stamps kept the PA busy filling orders, even if the agency did not erase departmental deficits. By establishing the agency, the USPOD gave itself a central office to handle the forthcoming expansion of the commemorative stamp program in the early 1920s.

Centralizing stamp sales for the purpose of serving collectors is another turning point in the relationship between the USPOD and stamp collectors, and is in keeping with how the federal government began supporting consumer capitalism following World War I. While it took a retailer to point the Department in this direction, the USPOD would take thirty-seven more years before officially sanctioning and encouraging collecting in such a direct way through the PA. Following World War I, the government expanded and decisively promoted a consumer-based economy by supporting business industry, not only through Herbert Hoover's Department of Commerce, but also with subsidies coming at the hands of the postal service.[56]

Capitalizing on the success of the PA, the USPOD opened a stamp exhibition room across the hall from the agency in 1935. Having transferred a majority of its collection to the Smithsonian more than twenty years earlier, the USPOD did not completely abandon its desire to maintain a Department postal museum. Again asking for assistance from local postmasters and requesting foreign stamps to be donated by international governments, the USPOD went about crafting its own museum. Although not meant to compete with the philatelic collection at the Smithsonian, the opening of this postal museum seemed a bit odd, if not duplicative of efforts at the National Museum. Within its own space, the USPOD highlighted collections of US and foreign stamps and exhibited other philatelic matter (including postcards, covers, commemorative envelopes) and stamp production machinery. According to Postmaster General Farley, this exhibit room served as an "important research center for collectors."[57]

By establishing a museum outside the doors of the PA, the USPOD made visiting the PA more than just a trip to buy stamps, offering an opportunity to learn more about stamps and stamp production. Certainly not a museum store as we understand the development and trend in the late twentieth century, the PA nonetheless appeared to play a similar role as the retail outlet that supported the museum. The genesis of this particular exhibit hall reflected the agency's success.

Many collectors and visitors planned a trip to the agency while visiting Washington and visited the USPOD museum as well. Both entities worked together in promoting philately and provided the means for easily purchasing American stamps. That the Department opened this exhibit hall in the mid-1930s is not surprising since the PA was pulling in record dollar amounts and the Department was producing large varieties of commemorative stamps. Stamp collecting was extremely popular, and having President Franklin D. Roosevelt as a philatelic role model did not hurt, either.

A retailer pointed the Department in the direction of serving collectors as consumers—consumers of products and of imagery from the American past—from which the USPOD would not return. Even when met with strong opposition from collectors, the federal government did not back down from its desire to issues commemoratives. Without nineteenth-century philatelists and the growing community of collectors, the USPOD would not have begun printing commemoratives celebrating American world's fairs in the 1890s. Those stamps promoted current events and circulated images celebrating American exceptionalism that contributed to a larger national narrative. By issuing commemoratives, the government encouraged collectors and noncollectors to buy stamps for albums, not just as postage. With the PA firmly established by the early 1920s, the Department had created an infrastructure to better handle increased production of commemoratives and to court a growing body of collectors. By the 1920s and 1930s, noncollecting citizens and collectors understood that the narratives on stamps carried legitimacy unmatched by other historical narratives, simply because a federal entity produced them.

Shaping National Identity with Commemoratives in the 1920s and 1930s

My stamps tell wondrous stories
In their own mysterious way;
Weaving a quaint fascination
That holds me in its sway.
They illustrate man's achievements,
And his victory over things;
His many modes of travel,
On water, rails and wings.
They show our nation's heroes,
Men who helped to free
Our great and might country,
Dearest land of liberty.
—Thomas G. Killride, "My Stamps," 1936

When Thomas Killride looked at the stamps he collected, he read "wondrous stories." He felt patriotic about American achievements and proud of heroes who helped to "free Our great and mighty country." Stories leaping out from American commemorative stamps, like the ones Killride alluded to, were shaped by decisions made by the postmaster general and his assistants and influenced by elected officials and the American public. Starting in 1892, the USPOD printed commemorative series advertising the US world's fairs with imagery that revered American achievements in technology and American and European conquest of lands and peoples. History as depicted on ordinary postage represented a top-down approach by honoring American political and military figures, showing the faces of former presidents and military leaders. Commemorative stamps offered a government-approved version of American history that both collectors and noncollectors noticed.

By the 1920s, Americans petitioned the government and asked the USPOD to print stamps that commemorated a local anniversary or honored their favorite hero. By doing so, petitioners sought the legitimacy of the USPOD to broaden the American national narrative distributed and presented on commemorative, limited-issue stamps. Individuals and special interest groups framed their petitions by arguing that their event or hero exemplified American values, innovation, and leadership or played a foundational role in winning independence. Most petitioners did not collect stamps as a hobby, but because most Americans had been primed to see and read stamps as something significant beyond their practical use as postage, they saw that stamps held power as unique federal documents to tell stories with images that circulated widely throughout the United States and the world.

American commemoratives served as a powerful tool for disseminating federally sanctioned episodes of American history. This strategy proved successful for the USPOD as it became more interested in fostering philately as a consumer practice and hobby. After finding that commemorative world's fair stamps would sell in the late nineteenth and early twentieth centuries, the Department looked beyond national expositions and began designing stamps that recognized regional commemorations and individuals and significantly increased the number of commemoratives printed in the early twentieth century. From 1892 to 1919, the USPOD printed forty-seven different commemorative stamps, almost exclusively celebrating world's fairs or regional expositions. Limited-issue production tripled between 1920 and 1940, when the USPOD printed and released 150 different commemoratives. After creating the Philatelic Agency in 1921, the Department was better equipped to handle the distribution of additional issues and respond to requests from collectors.

While the United States led the way in the production of limited-issue stamps, it was not the only country producing commemoratives. Latin American nations celebrated centennials of independence between 1910 and 1924 with stamps. Sixty-two countries comprising the British Empire celebrated the twenty-fifth anniversary of George V's reign by printing a stamp to commemorate this event, offering quite a catalog for the collector. Although originating the postal revolution, Great Britain did not issue its first commemorative until 1924, so this "Jubilee" set pleased collectors of British and British colonial stamps. When other nations began printed commemoratives, the USPOD was already printing a greater variety of limited issues. Global production increased greatly, so that all postal agencies printed more commemoratives during 1930–34 than had been printed in the previous decade (1920–29), or any time prior.[1]

Federal statutes restricted the USPOD from printing the portrait of any living person on stamps, which privileged stamps—definitive and commemorative—that represented snapshots from the past.[2] As citizens and politicians petitioned the postal service, the USPOD did not accept all commemorative stamp requests. Officials carefully chose subjects for commemorative printing, and this authority elevated any story or individual into a broader official American narrative that told consumers that this person or event was nationally significant and worthy of representing the United States. These carefully chosen and constructed stamps were then collected and saved by philatelists, some of whom saw American stamps not only as "wondrous stories" but as "stepping stones of history" that traced, from beginning to end, the "Alpha and Omega" of America's story.[3] This perception was perpetuated by philatelists, teachers, and the USPOD, which justified the educational value of collecting stamps. Viewing the corpus of commemoratives in this way indicated that many collectors—and most likely many noncollectors—believed that scenes printed on stamps told accurate stories from the past and that individuals were chosen because of their undisputed significance in American history. These stories became memorialized as collectors saved stamps. Those stamps were transformed into miniature memorials to the subjects represented within.

Postmaster General James Farley, appointed by "First Philatelist" Franklin Delano Roosevelt during his presidency in the 1930s, recognized that these commemorative stamps acted as "permanent memorials." Much like structural memorials built in public spaces, one vision of the past dominates the stamp's imagery, which screens out other perspectives. Stamps were small in size, but their availability made them more accessible than sites of national memory such as museums, archives, and monuments. These sites become nation-building tools that erase a personal, experiential memory of the past.[4] For this reason, it is important to examine limited-issue commemoratives and their impact as if they are miniature memorials.

As the USPOD worked to present a united vision of the past, stamp scenes showed a decisively white, male, and Protestant vision of early America that obscured more diverse and complicated realities of slavery, violence, and oppression. Conversations revolving around these stamps demonstrate how the USPOD became a powerful institution that legitimized and distributed historical narratives, and one that allowed ordinary citizens to engage with its government. Americans always maintained a close relationship with the postal service, and when successfully petitioning for a stamp on behalf of their cause, some citizens actually influenced postal decisions and public memory.

Interwar Colonial Revivals

During the interwar period (1919–1940), some Americans celebrated a nostalgic, homogenous fiction of the American colonial past. Public celebrations of historic anniversaries were filled with patriotic sentiment, weaving together local, vernacular, events, and people into official national narratives, as was the case with commemorative stamps printed in this era.[5] Commemorative committees, business leaders, and politicians actively pursued federal postage stamps celebrating regional anniversaries held at Plymouth Rock, Mayport, Minneapolis, Lexington and Concord, and Valley Forge, and states flaunted their foundings. Others fought for stamps honoring military men who transformed into cultural heroes, such as Casimir Pulaski and Thaddeus Kosciuszko. Knowing of the postal service's power to sell an idealized and patriotic vision of the American past, some sought commemoratives as part of grander strategies fighting for social and political equality, while others perpetuated a romanticized, whitewashed view of colonial America. The battle for recognition on a federal stamp also reflected contemporary struggles over the construction of race and definitions of citizenship in the United States. Residents and citizens with southern and eastern European ancestry, for instance, strove to be accepted as racially white, and that worked to further the chasm between whites and blacks, who still struggled as second-class citizens for political power and lacked visual representation on postage as actors in American history.[6]

In the early twentieth century, the increased popularity of collecting stamps occurred alongside the swell of interest in local and family history fostered by historical societies that promoted genealogical research and historic site preservation. State-funded and privately funded societies, from libraries and archives to patriotic-hereditary groups, encouraged Americans to research the history of their families and save family heirlooms. Hereditary group members took pride in tracing their roots back to pioneering families who established communities in Pennsylvania, for example, before the American Revolution. These practices helped to build regional and state pride that connected small towns and counties to broader national narratives. Encouraging family history research also created dividing lines among old and new immigrant groups, as many older immigrants grasped onto their colonial lineage while ignoring the challenges faced by late nineteenth- and early twentieth-century groups with similar European origins.[7]

Memorials and monuments reflect more about the time when they are built than about the past events and people represented. Celebrations and pageants, such as the national Pilgrim Tercentenary, used commemorative moments to define Americanness in postwar America in the eyes of the event's organizers. Regional preservation groups, such as the Association for the Preservation of Virginia Antiquities (APVA), erected memorials and preserved sites during this time tied to Virginia's founding families that recast British settlements at Jamestown and Williamsburg as harmonious and homogeneous. For elite Virginian members of the APVA, post–Civil War political and cultural upheaval left them with a present they did not like. Preservation and reconstruction efforts let them—and other groups working in different states—return temporarily to time when white elites commanded power and deference from blacks and poor whites.

Americanization efforts in the early twentieth century attacked customs and practices of new and first-generation immigrants thought to be racially and socially inferior. Historic preservation and colonial revival movements grew in popularity because those preserving and reproducing iconography from the colonial period believed this style was uniquely American. Preserved homes and historic sites were constructed to be places that taught new immigrants about America's past, while "patriotic Americans" were urged to buy and display colonial-era reproductions in their homes.[8]

Colonial-themed stamps from the 1920s and 1930s coincided with growing interest in viewing, owning, and displaying physical evidence, or material culture, from colonial and early Republic eras. Wealthy businessmen and heiresses of industrial fortunes donated money to finance wings in museums and historic preservation. The American Wing at the Metropolitan Museum of Art opened in 1924 to exhibit early American decorative arts and furnishings of "our ancestors"—where "our ancestors" meant a few selected to represent the many. Philadelphia's Sesquicentennial Exposition boasted "High Street," an attraction that featured rebuilt "colonial" structures of Philadelphia in 1776. Inspired by Henry Mercer's collections of tools, Henry Ford began voraciously collecting a host of buildings and objects in 1919—anything from agricultural machinery to household and kitchen implements—that he would eventually display in Greenfield Village, Michigan. Uninterested in financing an established historic site like John D. Rockefeller, Ford created his own emulation of an "Early American Village" that opened to the public in 1931. Physical restorations and quests for "authenticity" at Colonial Williamsburg in the late 1920s and early 1930s encouraged some Americans to purchase antiques and replicas to decorate their homes.[9] Calling upon the designs of the late colonial and early Republic periods during a time of American postwar conservatism in foreign policy, some Americans focused on building the image of United States as an exceptional place with a unique history.

This chapter will reveal how different groups reached backward to use images and individuals from the past to address cultural and political unease with 1920s and 1930s America through the medium of commemorative stamps.

Pilgrims and Origins

A new era in commemorative stamps began in 1920 with the Pilgrim Tercentenary, as the variety of commemorative subjects expanded beyond promotions of world's fairs to include significant anniversaries, military victories, and heroic individuals. The Pilgrim Tercentennial celebrated the landing of religious separatists on Cape Cod and their eventual settlement in the town of Plymouth, Massachusetts. From December 1920 through the summer of 1921, towns in many states organized pageants and parades to commemorate this anniversary. The stamp series created for this event was not the first to represent America's founding mythologies (see the Columbians, 1892–93, and the Jamestown Tercentennial Exposition, 1907); the series was significant because it sparked interest from many citizens to ask the USPOD to highlight their community's history and connections to America's origins on stamps.[10] As a reflection of contemporary politics, elected officials and patriotic-hereditary groups invoked the legacy of Plymouth Pilgrims both to assert the primacy of Plymouth as America's birthplace and to speak to local and national anxiety over immigration in the 1920s.

Organized after World War I during a time when many US citizens were in favor of severe restrictions on immigration, the Pilgrim Tercentennial events highlighted perceived differences among good and bad immigrant groups. Poems and speeches glorified the legacy of the Massachusetts Pilgrims as nation builders and model immigrants, in contrast with a widely held belief that immigrants in the twentieth century tore apart an imagined American fabric. Plymouth was proclaimed to be the "corner stone of the Nation," by Mayflower descendant Senator Henry Cabot Lodge, who detailed how the Pilgrims' success against adversity allowed America to grow into a great nation.[11] Vice President Thomas Marshall also touted the achievements of the "pilgrim fathers" who "prepared the way" for "the birth of a new and mighty world." He used the opportunity to argue for immigration restrictions, advocating that contemporary immigrants needed to follow the example set by the Pilgrims and commit to staying in United States rather than merely coming to work and returning home. According to Marshall, the Pilgrims came to America "to worship God and to make homes, determined never to return to Europe."[12]

The stamp designs commemorating the celebration promoted the Pilgrims' cultural legacy as America's first founders. Interestingly, none of the three postage stamps printed in the series contained the identifying words "U.S. Postage," which all other stamps prior and since carried. This cemented the story of the Pilgrims' landing at Plymouth as quintessentially American, as it needed no marking as US postage. Even the US Mint's commemorative anniversary coin imprinted the words "United States of America" on the front of the half-dollar coin.[13] Philatelists noticed this omission, concerned—and interested—that it might be an error in the printing, but the USPOD did not recall the stamps because the design was intentional. Editors of *American Philatelist* were disappointed with the series, claiming that the two- and five-cent issues were far too crowded with figures and decoration to be enjoyed.[14]

Mayflowers, fittingly, flanked each stamp's scene, and like the Columbians, the Pilgrim Tercentenary series formed a short narrative. The story began on the one-cent stamp with the *Mayflower* sailing west across the ocean on its journey with no land in sight—origin or destination (fig. 12). Similar to the Columbians, the landing occurs in the two-cent stamp—the most commonly used stamp to mail a letter and the standard rate of first-class postage until 1932.[15] This stamp's engraving makes the landing look harsh, unexpected, and jolting for the party at Plymouth Rock (see fig. 13). Men, women, and children huddle together, illustrating that family units migrated to the New England coast. Although this image suggests that struggles lie ahead for the settlers, the rock is what grounded the travelers, and is the object that grounded those celebrating the anniversary in the past. Plymouth was the ceremonial ground in 1920 and provided the physical connection to the past events.

Fig. 12. Pilgrim Tercentenary, one cent, 1920 (Courtesy Smithsonian National Postal Museum Collection)

Fig. 13. Pilgrim Tercentenary, two cent, 1920 (Courtesy Smithsonian National Postal Museum Collection)

The journey's symbolic end revealed itself in the five-cent (see fig. 14), where the Mayflower Compact was signed, indicating permanence, and showed the first document of self-governance in what would become the United States. Copies of the Compact were printed and distributed for the Tercentenary. Divine right blessed this settlement as the central figure points toward the light illuminating the signing. Drawn from a painting by Edwin White, the signing image illustrates families migrating together, even though only men signed the document.[16] The scene emphasizes that there was a community, comprising family units, who crafted the Mayflower Compact and pledged to work together. At the time of the anniversary, New England preservationists and genealogists argued that the Plymouth Pilgrims were the true first Americans because family units arrived together to form a permanent settlement through signing the Compact, unlike the commercially mind individuals who sailed to Jamestown. By representing this scene, the Tercentennial committee reiterated their argument and wanted all Americans to consider Plymouth as the birthplace of the America.

Virginians and New Englanders regularly argued over the true origins of the American story and which settlements contributed more to the development and character of the United States. Post–Civil War regional tensions can be read in written evidence found in newspapers and journals such the *William and Mary Quarterly*. In 1909, shortly after the tercentenary celebration of Jamestown's founding, Virginia historians refuted declarations published by members of the New England

Fig. 14. Pilgrim Tercentenary, five cent, 1920 (Courtesy Smithsonian National Postal Museum Collection)

Historic Genealogical Society that there were "radical differences of character and influence" between Mayflower descendants and Jamestown settlers, because Plymouth "subordinated the commercial spirit (of Jamestown) to that of securing ecclesiastical and political freedom for themselves"—seen in the five-cent stamp. The *William and Mary Quarterly* responded that those charges were "so gross, so unprovoked, so untrue," and the statement of such freedoms and strength of character in the north were exaggerated.[17]

Rivalries die hard, and Virginians did not let the Pilgrim Tercentenary pass without reminding Americans of their claim to the origins and contributions to American politics and governance. One address given at the College of William and Mary noted that Virginia's contributions to the forming of the United States were far greater than any other state, but that Massachusetts came in second place. During the national celebration of the New England Pilgrims, this effort reminded Americans that the "first" settlement was at Jamestown.[18] No one at this time recognized other colonial settlements in the western United States or acknowledged that the original residents of "America" were Native peoples who were displaced, attacked, manipulated, and feared by European colonizers.

Virginians and New Englanders weren't the only ones wrestling over founding stories publicly, through representation on stamps, as descendants from other European "pilgrims" argued successfully for their stories to be told on commemoratives.

New Netherland Pilgrims

In 1924, the Huguenot-Walloon New Netherland Commission organized a series of events in New York to celebrate the first permanent settlement of Huguenots (French Protestants) on American soil, as well as the founding of New Netherland. They wanted to harness the circulation power of postage to share the story of their ancestors by requesting a Huguenot-Walloon commemorative stamp series. Framing the founding of New Netherland as the "Huguenot-Walloon" anniversary was contested at the time. The Dutch, including Henry Hudson, fur trappers, and merchants from the West and East India Companies were commonly seen as the founders of New York. The commission included the settlement of Walloon families, who were French-speaking Protestants from Belgium who had settled in Holland, in its narrative, while obscuring the role of the Dutch government and its business endeavors in the settlement story. Anniversary literature framed the founding of what became New York as motivated by religion rather than mercantilism by identifying the Huguenots and Walloons as pilgrims who were persecuted for their religious beliefs like those who landed near Plymouth. Formed by the Federal Council of the Churches of Christ in America, the commission worked to make the Walloons' history visible to all Americans, because their "advent marks a new epoch in the history of both Church and State." Obtaining a set of commemorative stamps, and a coin, performed some of the work to acknowledge the little-known Walloon arrival as a significant episode in the American past.[19]

The commission understood the challenges it faced educating Americans about their history. After the release of this commemorative stamp series, a few collectors wrote to the postmaster general puzzled by the subject of the series and questioned the significance of those events. One collector begged for a short bibliography about the Huguenots or Walloons, because "all of the histories I have at hand seem to be a bit deficient in matters relating to the events these stamps commemorate." Collectors and citizens occasionally questioned the criteria that qualified an event or subject as nationally significant and worthy of printing on a commemorative. According to the post office, this anniversary was "of more than ordinary interest particularly in those sections of the country where these colonists originally settled."[20]

Fig. 15. Huguenot-Walloon Tercentenary, one cent, 1924 (Courtesy Smithsonian National Postal Museum Collection)

Fig. 16. Huguenot-Walloon Tercentenary, two cent, 1924 (Courtesy Smithsonian National Postal Museum Collection)

The silver half-dollar coin minted by the commission included the phrase "Founding of New Netherland" below the announcement of the "Huguenot-Walloon Tercentenary, 1624–1924," alerting those purchasing the commemorative coin of the significance of the celebration. The stamp series, however, was not well described in print, baffling collectors and citizens confronted with the Huguenot-Walloon issues. Deciphering these stamps proved challenging for all, because the designs lacked readily identifiable images. On the one-cent issue, the *Nieu Nederland* sails in 1624 east toward America, and families land in the two-cent stamp with no visual aide indicating where the ship sailed from, where it landed, or who the Huguenot-Walloons were.

The third stamp in the series is even more cryptic, picturing an

Fig. 17. Huguenot-Walloon Tercentenary, five cent, 1924 (Courtesy Smithsonian National Postal Museum Collection)

unnamed monument facing a rising sun in what appears to be a tropical climate. Palm trees and plants surrounding the structure contrast with the rocky, sparsely planted landscape pictured in the two-cent settlement stamp. The five-cent issue actually represents a stone monument erected by Jean Ribault, who explored the area near Mayport, Florida, in the 1560s to establish a refuge colony for French Huguenots. Before returning to France to pick up passengers for the sail back to Florida, Ribault erected a stone column festooned with the French king's coat of arms to claim Florida in the name of France. As part of the Huguenot-Walloon anniversary in 1924, the Florida chapters of the Daughters of the American Revolution financed the construction of a similarly shaped monument to honor Ribault and the "first landing of Protestants on American soil."[21] Interestingly, the memorial to the Walloons erected in Manhattan's Battery Park during the 1924 tercentennial does not mention their religion or status as persecuted religious refugees.

The Huguenot-Walloon Tercentenary committee specifically wanted the memorial commemorating Jean Ribault's settlement to appear on a stamp representing the first Protestant settlement in America. Seeking to redefine the chronology and attribution of religious tolerance in colonial America, committee members claimed that the Huguenots and Walloons brought with them a strong commitment to religious tolerance that "neither Pilgrim nor Puritan possessed." Reacting to the Pilgrim Tercentenary three years prior, descendants of Huguenots and Walloons desired the stamps and the celebration to counteract the "forgetfulness" of the "names and race of its founders" due to lost records.[22] With the endorsement of the federal government, this stamp series elevated the narrative framed by the anniversary committee to make a claim on New York's colonial history, and positioned the Walloons among America's earliest religious pilgrims.

Norwegian Pilgrims

The Norse-American Centenary stamp series provides another example of how the government endorsed a narrative of ethnic pride proposed by a regional commemorative committee. Much like the Huguenot-Walloon stamps, this series promoted a regional celebration of another group of pilgrims whose event committee desired the stamps to be one piece of a large festival honoring first waves of immigrants. The Norse-American Centennial Committee secured a congressional joint resolution that commended Norwegian immigrants for contributing to the "moral and material welfare of our Nation." They were credited with settling the "great Midwest," rather than pouring into cities, crowding them, like contemporary immigrants were doing in St. Louis, Chicago, and other Midwestern cities.[23] Imagery and narratives presented by the Centennial Committee sought to connect the story of Norwegians in America to a heroic past that could be traced to Vikings such as Leif Erikson, whose arrival in the New World predated Columbus and the Plymouth Pilgrims. The Pilgrim Tercentennial influenced how the Norse-American Centennial Committee shaped its message and why the committee rooted the message in celebrating pioneer fathers and their (debated) status as religious pilgrims. Like many other immigrant communities, the Centennial Committee balanced celebrating their distinct Norwegian heritage and culture with claiming their piece of the American past by earning a place on federal stamps.[24]

Following the convention of earlier stamp series, this set emphasized the immigration and a journey across the Atlantic as way to assert status as original immigrants, distinguishing their stories of migration from that of new immigrants arriving in the early twentieth century. On the two-cent, *Restaurationen*, "the Mayflower of the Norsemen," carries the first Norwegian immigrants to the United States, sailing west across the stamp without land in sight on July 4, 1825.[25]

Fig. 18. Norse-American Centennial, two cent, 1925 (Courtesy Smithsonian National Postal Museum Collection)

The second stamp does not represent the landing, but the five-cent issue features an engraving of a Viking ship built for the Columbian Exposition. That ship sailed from Norway to Chicago to remind fairgoers and stamp consumers in the 1920s that Norwegian explorers visited America long before Columbus, the English-Dutch Pilgrims, the Huguenots, or the Walloons. This particular image, interestingly, pointed the ship's bow toward the east, or toward the homeland. On the stamp, the Viking ship sails from a banner or shield of Norway toward one of the United States, and the Norse-American Viking ship is flying colors similar to an American flag.

These stamps were in high demand from collectors because of the design and intensity of the ink colors, and they sold out. The USPOD

Fig. 19. Norse-American Centennial, five cent, 1925 (Courtesy Smithsonian National Postal Museum Collection)

received letters requesting the issues be reprinted. Postal officials regretted that they had to treat all commemoratives consistently and could not reprint this series alone because they would hear protests from other groups claiming the Norwegians received preferential treatment.[26] In this case, the USPOD understood that the subject matter represented on the stamp held great meaning for petitioners—past and future—and citizens. Postal officials were careful to balance the sensitivities of commemorative scenes chosen with interests of some collectors who focused more on the particulars of stamps' designs and artful quality of the production.

Descendants of these early European settlers wanted to demonstrate that their immigrant ancestors were good immigrant-citizens and worked to transform the United States into a great and prosperous nation. Difficult to read in the stamps' images, these feelings were expressed by the Norse-American Centennial Committee, which wanted to celebrate ethnic pride, but designed the celebrations to focus on messages of good citizenship and patriotism. Even the planning committee and other Norwegian Americans involved with the centennial felt conflicted over the messages of the celebration. Many Norwegians opposed American involvement in World War I and faced nativistic attacks, not as severe as German Americans, but strong enough to identify their group as outsiders. By 1925, Norwegian communities in the northern Midwest still debated how to balance Americanization and ethnically constructed heritage activities.[27] Through public commemoration, Norwegian Americans of the Midwest declared that they were nation builders like the Pilgrims at Plymouth Rock. And with an episode of their past represented on commemorative stamps, the reach of their story stretched far beyond Minnesota.

Regional anniversary committees took advantage of the opportunities available from the USPOD's commemorative stamp program to legitimize their interpretation of the past and to ensure that the founding stories of their ancestors were included in the broader story of America's origins. Stamps represented European settlements and transatlantic journeys with images of ships and family groups of white Protestant settlers. Appeals to congressmen for stamps, and even for coins, emphasized the positive contributions each group and their descendants made to the character and strength of the United States.

The timing of these stamps and the language used to justify recognition also spoke directly to the contemporary fights over immigration. Legislation in 1921 and 1924 established eugenically minded quotas developed by Congress to shape the racial biology of future American citizens. The Quota Act of 1921 limited the numbers of immigrants to 3 percent of that nationality's presence in the 1910 US census, which drastically reduced the number of southern and eastern Europeans entering the United States. The Johnson-Reed Act of 1924 further limited quotas and completely eliminated immigration from all regions in Asia.[28]

Support of these restrictive laws was equally strong across political parties in Congress, with only a few congressmen speaking out in opposition. Some spoke loudly in favor of restrictions, including Ellison DuRant Smith. He believed that selective criteria and limited quotas would help the United States to thrive. "Without offense, but with regard to the salvation of our own, let us shut the door and assimilate what we have, and let us breed pure American citizens and develop our own American resources."[29] At a time when defining who was an American and who wasn't changed, regional anniversary celebrations commemorated on stamps reinforced the idea that the United States was founded by white western European Protestants. Stamps contributed to the ongoing ways that the US government defined Americanness and constructed official founding stories. Starting in 1925, sesquicentennial celebrations of Revolutionary War battles moved discussions of colonial founding origins into dialogues about who fought to create the United States as an independent nation.

Humble Heroes of the Revolution

Commemorations of persevering Pilgrims figuratively gave birth to Revolutionary War heroes who fought for freedom against British oppressors as represented in stamps. Starting in 1925, a flurry of activity surrounded the 150th anniversary of the American Revolution, including many regional and local celebrations held across the country. Following the lead of the Pilgrim anniversaries, local committees petitioned their legislators seeking commemorative stamps and coins to recognize regionally significant battles and heroes. The House Committee on Coinage, Weights, and Measures grew tired of such requests for commemorative coins. Responding to a request for a silver half dollar celebrating the Battle of Bennington and the independence of Vermont in 1925, the chair noted the committee did not favor "legislation of this class, because of the great number of bills introduced to commemorate events of local and not national interest."[30] Anniversaries of local interest, however, continued to win commemorative stamps.

The national sesquicentennial celebration in Philadelphia in 1926 encouraged a colonial revival, not only of design and style, but in storytelling through stamps. Surprisingly, while the Pilgrim anniversaries yielded small stamp series each, the "Sesqui" exposition itself did not. No narrative was told across three issues, leaving the Liberty Bell—the iconic symbol of the fair—to stand in as the only symbol of independence. Beginning in 1925, the USPOD told the story of the Revolution over fourteen stamps, or stamp series, related to these anniversaries.[31]

Images from the Revolutionary War issues often represented portraits of victorious generals and elite soldiers or engravings of battle scenes. This was the case for the Lexington and Concord stamp series printed in 1925, which ushered in the anniversary celebrations. The Department released the stamps on April 4 to long lines of interested collectors and citizens waiting to purchase these stamps in Massachusetts. In April ceremonies commemorating the skirmish were celebrated in and around Boston, where salutes were fired and Paul Revere's ride into Boston was reenacted on April 19 and 20, during Patriot's Day festivities.[32]

Unlike other series, the Lexington and Concord commemoratives did not proceed chronologically by denomination. The one-cent represented Washington assuming command of the Continental Army in Cambridge months after the initial skirmish. It was followed by a two-cent depicting the actual confrontation, and the five-cent completed the series memorializing the minuteman soldier.[33] The image of Washington taking command of the Continental Army in Cambridge was a conglomerate of nineteenth-century prints that represented Washington on horseback, while the stamps shows Washington standing among his soldiers. This interpretation implies that Washington was a man equal to his soldiers, standing as a fellow citizen, even as he is set apart because he was not equal in rank or status. Ready for war, the collected armies are dressed uniformly, while one company marches in the right of the scene and another, larger company stands at attention

Fig. 20. Washington at Cambridge, one cent, 1925 (Courtesy Smithsonian National Postal Museum Collection)

Fig. 21. Birth of Liberty, two cent, 1925 (Courtesy Smithsonian National Postal Museum Collection)

in the background. The viewer is led to believe that the Continental Army organized soon after the first confrontation and was prepared for combat.

Based on a painting by Henry Sandham, the two-cent issue borrowed its victorious vision of the battle (fig. 21). The stamp mislabels the painting as "The Birth of Liberty," while it is titled *The Dawn of Liberty*. Sandham painted the Minutemen as a disadvantaged band of soldiers on foot who engaged the British, who charged on horseback.[34]

The Minutemen appear larger in size but smaller in number in the foreground, standing victoriously with their arms in the air, shaking fists at the enemy, who appear smaller in size and larger in number and to be retreating in the background. This painting contrasts drastically with the vision etched by contemporary artist Amos Doolittle in May 1775. Doolittle represented the small band of Minutemen in disarray after the first shot was fired as they scattered across the Lexington green in retreat. From other sources available, including other engravings by Doolittle, this representation seems to more accurately describe the events at Lexington.[35]

While the British eventually retreated to Boston after a stand-off in Concord, the colonists did not defeat the British. The two sides exchanged fire and lost lives in this brief skirmish. Accuracy, however, was irrelevant to local history enthusiasts and residents who believed in the town's centrality to the Revolution's narrative, as its birthplace. The Lexington Historical Society purchased Sandham's painting in 1886 to hang in the town hall, and this scene was an integral part of local history.[36] Embedded in the residents' memory was that their fictive ancestors were a victorious band of volunteer soldiers who held off the well-trained British and forced a retreat. This image of local importance circulated across the country and the world and confirmed what most schoolchildren learned as part of the War for Independence narrative.

Prior to the 150th anniversary, poems written by Ralph Waldo Emerson and Henry Wadsworth Longfellow cemented this mythical interpretation of Lexington and Concord in American memory during the nineteenth and early twentieth centuries. An engraving of Daniel Chester French's *The Minute Man* statue, dedicated in 1875, appeared on the five-cent stamp, which also included the first stanza of Emerson's 1837 poem "The Concord Hymn." Emerson composed the poem for one commemoration ceremony, and later it was engraved at the base of French's statue commemorating the battle's centennial. Most stamps include few words other than "U.S. Postage," relying on the imagery to illustrate the stamp's theme. By reprinting the first stanza of Emerson's poem, readers of the stamp, most of whom would never see the statue in person, understood the symbol. Emerson's words would have been very familiar to many Americans because "A Concord Hymn" often appeared in textbooks and school readers. The government endorsed this vision celebrating humble, inexperienced, and "embattled farmers" who "fired the shot heard around the world."[37]

French's monument was similar in design to that of the common-soldier Civil War memorials erected in municipalities across the country in the late nineteenth century. Civil War memorials crafted as standing soldiers holding a rifle, not embattled, remembered those who fought and died in the 1860s and transformed into places for honoring all

Fig. 22. The Minute Man, five cent, 1925 (Courtesy Smithsonian National Postal Museum Collection)

veterans. In the case of the *Minute Man,* though the physical statue stood in Massachusetts, once on a stamp its representation became a national symbol of the earliest citizen soldiers who fought for independence. It was the stories of these men "who helped free our great and mighty country" represented on postage that collectors like Thomas Killride spoke of in his poem "My Stamps."[38] Civil War monuments acted in ways to unify the country by focusing on the individuals who fought rather than the reasons for fighting. During the Revolutionary War, northern and southern colonies fought together, even if it was for a loosely knit union. In 1925, the Massachusetts Minuteman acted as a unifying figure for celebrating white male citizenship throughout the United States.

Consumers of the Minuteman commemorative saw in the stamp design that this figure was to be remembered as a heroic freedom fighter. All commemorative stamps become miniature memorials once saved by collectors, but this particular stamp was designed to look like a memorial. The stamp represents the original sculpture and then frames it as if French's piece was part of a large neoclassical memorial. Unlike the statue that stands in a field in Concord, the Minuteman on the stamp is flanked by two Doric order columns and two tablets bearing verses from Emerson's hymn as if the verses are commandments, giving the statue the appearance of standing in an architectural niche. A niche highlights the figure inside it, and very often the figure is one to be worshipped or revered. Reverence of the Minuteman is reinforced with lighter shading behind the statue's head on the stamp that draws the eye in to focus on an archetypal American hero.

Like physical memorials, commemoratives do not allow space for questioning of the subject's interpretation. The Battle of White Plains and Vermont Sesquicentennial issues in 1926 and 1927 continued the theme of citizen soldiers as battle heroes. Unnamed, without military uniforms, men fought and represented the Green Mountain Boys in Vermont, for example, to defend their territory against British forces. In these stamps, and in the spirit of the commemorations, the white citizen-farmer-soldier stood as the archetypal American hero.

Washington as Common Man

In contrast to the Lexington and Concord series, which elevated the white citizen-farmer-soldier to the status of national hero, the 1928 Valley Forge anniversary stamp represented a mythical story about General George Washington that made him seem humble, like a common man. In the 1920s, Washington lived prominently in popular and political cultural as his name and face were used to market dishes, sell movies, and justify immigration restrictions. Prior to the Sesqui, mail-order catalogs sold colonial-themed, mass-produced knickknacks containing George's image. One familiar scene was Washington kneeling in prayer at Valley Forge. A nineteenth-century print of this vignette, based on a painting by Henry Brueckner, circulated widely after the Civil War and again following World War I. A bas-relief of a similar image was installed at the YMCA West Side Branch in New York in 1904, and replicas were created and installed in churches, schools, and historical societies. Many viewed this print as visual evidence of Washington's true piety, even though the image was completely contrived. Imagery that illustrated how a military leader turned to God for help in hard times was powerful. The scene was based on a tale first recanted by Parson Mason Weems in 1804. Weems perpetuated a cult of Washington through many stories he published about Washington, including the myth about chopping down the cherry tree.[39]

Supporters of the anniversary encampment at Valley Forge wanted to incorporate this familiar image on a stamp and began petitioning the USPOD in the mid-1920s. Malcolm H. Ganser asked in a letter to the editor of the *New York Times* for other readers to write to a very reluctant postmaster general to sway him into printing a stamp commemorating this event. Requests were honored and the image of Washington kneeling in prayer would represent the anniversary at the encampment even as Rupert Hughes and other historians began questioning the accuracy of that scene. One newspaper columnist opined there was "no good reason to doubt," and another stressed that neither the stamp engraver nor historians were at Valley Forge with Washington, so why would he doubt Washington's actions?[40] The myths of Washington were difficult to challenge in public.

Hughes was a biographer of Washington and was extremely critical of those wishing to mythologize Washington. Hughes and others criticized the stamp because they recognized that the government held immense power by endorsing images that stamp consumers might assume to convey historical fact. Interestingly, while Hughes was concerned about representations of the general and president, others were thankful that remembrances of the Revolution were not solely militaristic. Other anniversary stamps, including Lexington-Concord (1925), the Battle of White Plains (1926), and the Burgoyne Campaign (1927) depicted battle scenes and images of soldiers, cannon, rifles, and powder horns. Postal officials approved of Washington kneeling as a way to please those seeking representations of the "spiritual" side of war.[41]

The stamp engraving is a voyeuristic view of Washington kneeling in prayer in the woods surrounding the Valley Forge encampment as if from the perspective of Isaac Potts, who was shown hiding behind a large tree. According to Weems's tale, Potts was delighted when he came upon Washington praying in the woods. Potts decided at that moment that he could support the Revolution because Washington demonstrated that one could be a Christian and a soldier without moral conflict.[42] This image provided a comforting message for some. Washington kneeling at Valley Forge also spoke powerfully to those who believed that the United Sates was not only a Christian nation, but one that benefited from the grace of God during hard times.

Four printed words solidified the notion that the entire nation believed in God: "In God We Trust." These four words distinguished this stamp from any others printed at the time. This phrase appeared on contemporary US coins, but never on stamps. It would not be until another Red Scare in the 1950s when a stamp, this time a definitive, carried the motto.[43] On the Valley Forge stamp, however, the phrase

Fig. 23. Valley Forge issue, two cent, 1928 (Courtesy Smithsonian National Postal Museum Collection)

acts as a label interpreting the scene, telling consumers that this is why we trust in God, because Washington trusted in God and the United States reaped the blessings of independence. Any debates over Washington's religious beliefs or his aversion to prayer were settled in the minds of some Americans because the USPOD printed and circulated this interpretation of Washington's private life.

This stamp held great meaning for some, particularly the Daughters of the American Revolution (DAR). They included the Valley Forge stamp together with a collection of papers and objects in a copper box—together with a Bible, a copy of the US Constitution, various DAR publications, including immigrant handbooks, and signed cards by President and Mrs. Calvin Coolidge—buried in the cornerstone of Constitution Hall in November 1928.[44] That this stamp was included in this time capsule further illustrates how powerful, and sometimes transitive, stamp messages could be. The representation of Washington as a pious man held value for the DAR because the organization believed it was upholding ideals held by descendants of Revolutionary War heroes. Washington's actions and values were therefore theirs because their ancestors served under Washington. One could argue that a stamp was chosen to represent these connections to Washington because of its small size, making it fit neatly inside a capsule. If true, the DAR easily could have purchased a definitive two-cent stamp used every day by millions of Americans to send first-class letters with Washington's portrait. It had been a mainstay of US definitives since the mid-nineteenth century.[45] Instead, the DAR chose the Weems-inspired image of Washington in prayer.

We can see from the Revolutionary War sesquicentennial commemoratives that the USPOD glorified individuals and selective battles to instruct Americans, immigrants, and international collectors as to what and who was important to remember. Other stamps reflected similar patterns in design and message. Common white men were the heroes, and leaders were not elites but rather depicted as strong men who walked among their soldiers, and sometimes prayed. Seeing these stamps representing Revolutionary War men motivated other heritage and hereditary-based groups to pursue commemoratives for their humble heroes.

Revolutionary Heroes from Poland

Polish Americans and immigrants fought to honor two Polish Revolutionary War heroes on stamps as part of a larger strategy to portray Polish Americans as good Americans with ancestral ties to the birth of the United States as a nation. In the 1920s, Congress overwhelmingly approved immigration restrictions that imposed strict quotas on individuals arriving from eastern and southern Europe. Restrictions came in reaction to both political concerns over post–World War I radicalism and eugenically influenced charges of racial inferiority based on biology. Poles, for example, were described as a distinct "race" of people.[46] Few legislators spoke out to oppose the quotas. Representative Robert H. Clancy, however, defended immigrants, including the Polish, for their positive contributions to the United States: "Polish-Americans are as industrious and as frugal and as loyal to our institutions as any class of people who have come to the shores of this country in the past 300 years." Clancy also mentioned the contributions of Polish citizens during the Revolution to highlight a "high place" they had earned in American history.[47] Polish American groups broadcast the achievements of Revolutionary War heroes to anchor their people to the origins of the United States and to distinguish themselves from other eastern Europeans by showcasing their long history of being loyal Americans.

Efforts began in the early twentieth century to recognize the contributions of Count Casimir Pulaski and General Thaddeus Kosciuszko with statues and postage memorials. In 1910, monuments honoring both men were dedicated in Washington, Pulaski's financed by Congress and Kosciuszko's donated to "the people" by the Polish American Alliance.[48] Pulaski was a Polish nobleman who volunteered to fight for the colonies and is known as the Father of the American Cavalry. He fought and died at the Battle of Savannah in 1779, and the city honored him as a local hero. To further extend Pulaski's reputation as a national hero, the local chapter of the Daughters of the American Revolution spearheaded a stamp campaign in 1929, cosponsoring an event commemorating the 150th anniversary of the death of Count Pulaski. Supporting the DAR's efforts to secure a stamp was Georgia congressman Charles Edwards, who petitioned the postmaster general to support a Pulaski commemorative and commented that "the Daughters of the American Revolution would not sponsor anything that is not real meritorious and entirely worthy." According to Edwards, the DAR properly vetted the stamp's subject matter and it passed the patriotic test, demonstrating Pulaski was an early model Polish immigrant. Honoring Pulaski as a war hero was not in question when President Herbert Hoover declared October 11, 1929, as "Pulaski Day," yet no stamp came.[49] Hoover and Congress acknowledged Pulaski as a national hero, but earning a commemorative stamp proved more difficult.

Surprisingly, the following year, strong rebukes came from a Polish newspaper that may have influenced the government's decision to print a Pulaski commemorative. The paper accused US postal authorities of using a "double standard" when choosing whom to honor on stamps with the headline, "Polish Proposition Refused—Germans Favored." According to this paper's editor, the USPOD honored a German Revolutionary War hero, Baron Frederic Wilhelm von Steuben, on a stamp, and refused to reciprocate for a Polish Pulaski. French newspaper editors even decried the choice of the von Steuben stamp. They did not seek a Pulaski stamp, but rather sought recognition for French military officers who fought for independence, including Lafayette and Rochambeau. Missing from the correspondence file were panicky or angry letters from government officials strongly urging the postmaster general to order a Pulaski stamp quickly. A few months later, however, nearly fifteen months after the Savannah anniversary celebration, a Pulaski issue was announced.[50] This episode demonstrates that the world noticed when a government printed new stamps, placing postal officials in a challenging role. Their decisions held enormous political weight and carried cultural meaning far beyond those petitioning for stamp subjects.

This can be seen in the ways that noncollecting Americans noticed new stamps and questioned the reasoning behind postal choices. Present in the archive's files for the Pulaski stamp was an angry letter from a citizen who asked why the USPOD honored Pulaski with a stamp and did not chose an American soldier instead. She spoke of her fears of first-generation immigrants held by many fellow citizens. Mrs. M. A. Van Wagner criticized Polish immigrants for coming to the United States only to "get employment here and take our American dollars back to Poland," while others remained unemployed (presumably she meant native-borns) in the early years of the Depression. For Van Wagner, the Pulaski stamp signified another way that America had been "forgnised," as was the case with the "gangs" of foreigners who were responsible for importing "poison" liquor during Prohibition.[51] Her letter stands alone in the Pulaski file as one of protest, but her emotional reaction to this stamp reflects real sentiments felt by some Americans in the interwar period not only toward eastern European immigrants, but also the power stamps possessed in representing, or perhaps misrepresenting in this case, an official narrative of her country. Stamps may have been small, but their images were powerful.

Many Americans supported the immigration restrictions in Johnson-Reed, so viewing an eastern European, Pulaski, on a stamp may have angered them. It seemed hypocritical of the government to limit immigration of specific groups of people because they were not considered fit for citizenship, and then a few years later honor an individual representing one of those groups on a federal stamp. This occasion was not the first time the US government recognized the achievements of Pulaski, but the accessibility of a commemorative stamp meant that more people—across the United States and around the world—saw firsthand that the federal government celebrated a Polish hero as an American one.

Concurrent to the Pulaski stamp campaign, petitions arrived at the USPOD seeking a stamp to honor another Polish Revolutionary War hero, Thaddeus Kosciuszko. At the time of his death in 1817, Poles and Americans mourned his legacy as a war hero and his commitment to fighting for liberty worldwide. His legacy continued on in the form of monuments and celebrations dedicated in his honor.[52] Among those commemorative efforts was one to immortalize his legacy on a postage stamp that would reach across the United States and abroad to his homeland of Poland. The Kosciuszko Foundation first petitioned the postmaster general in 1926, by way of New York senator Royal S. Copeland, to commemorate the 150th anniversary of the general's "coming" to the colonies.[53]

After those attempts failed, queries were reshaped and the Foundation asked for a stamp that would instead honor the 150th anniversary of his "naturalization as an American citizen." From 1931 to 1933, hundreds of endorsement letters arrived in the office of the postmaster general supporting this stamp, accumulating a greater volume than supported Pulaski's stamp just a few years earlier. Seven years after the first requests, Postmaster Farley fittingly chose to announce the Kosciuszko issue on Polish Day at the Century of Progress World's Fair in Chicago (1933). Farley claimed that he was "happy to convey (his) highest regard for the American citizens of Polish extraction" and declared that Kosciuszko's name would be "forever perpetuated in the hearts of American people."[54]

Citizenship was a key element in pitching this stamp, which also was reflected in the announcements printed in newspapers. Kosciuszko's "admission to American citizenship" and the "privilege of becoming a citizen" were celebrated alongside his military service. Much like Farley, who paid homage to Polish citizens, other reactions to the issue emphasized that the general's legacy on a stamp "honors not only the man himself, but his countrymen who have come by the hundreds of thousands to the country he helped to establish as a land of liberty for all men."[55] Whether Kosciuszko actually became an American citizen was not questioned at the time, but the stamp offered a strong symbolic gesture and honor for all people with Polish heritage as bestowed upon them by the government. Like the pre-Revolutionary Pilgrims, the Polish were nation builders, too.

Choosing to honor Kosciuszko's "naturalization" proved to be a curious claim made by the Foundation. There appears to be no documentary evidence to support the claim that he became an American citizen, even though he was held in high regard and called a friend by George Washington, Thomas Jefferson, and other notable figures.

After the war, Kosciuszko, like other soldiers, haggled with the new Congress to be paid back wages for his service in the Continental Army. He earned membership in the Society of the Cincinnati, which was limited to military officers who served during the Revolution. Kosciuszko returned to his native Poland, where he led resistance and fought, unsuccessfully, against Russian occupation and oppression. He published the "Act of Insurrection," similar to the Declaration of Independence, and also freed the serfs in Poland in 1794. After some initial victories, Kosciuszko's resistance was crushed by the Russian forces, and he was taken prisoner and held in Russia. A few years later he returned to the United States, committed to freeing his homeland.[56]

Kosciuszko hoped to lobby support for Polish independence from American and French governments, but found himself politically opposed to John Adams's anti-France policies. In light of the Alien and Sedition Acts of 1798, Thomas Jefferson urged Kosciuszko to leave the country to avoid imprisonment. If Kosciuszko had been naturalized, he would not have needed to flee the country. According to congressional records in 1976, Representative John H. Dent tried to rectify that by submitting a resolution to confer citizenship upon Kosciuszko, perhaps in the spirit of the bicentennial celebrations. Kosciuszko's actual status was less important than the way that Polish-American cultural groups constructed his historical identity as an American citizen.[57] These groups believed there was a lot at stake by representing Kosciuszko as a citizen as well as a military hero. Polish immigrants and Polish Americans were conflicted, much like immigrants and citizens of Norwegian descent discussed earlier, about how best to balance their cultural and political identities as Poles and as Americans.

Unlike the Norse-American stamps that depicted ships and represented migration, the Pulaski and Kosciuszko stamps depicted each man in very different ways. Pulaski visually is associated with Poland with his portrait flanked by the modern flags of Poland and the United States. Generally, other commemoratives did not print the US flag. Pulaski's portrait appears in the center, where he casts his glance to his left, to the side where the Polish flag appears from behind his portrait. In contrast, the Kosciuszko design did not feature either flag. Perhaps because the stamp commemorated the 150th anniversary of his "naturalization" as an American citizen, flags were not necessary for indicating his nation of origin; Kosciusko was American, Pulaski was Polish.[58]

Fig. 24. General Pulaski, two cent, 1931 (Courtesy Smithsonian National Postal Museum Collection)

The final design represented Kosciuszko standing as a military officer, distinguishing his stamp from other Revolutionary War citizen-soldier stamps, and instead identified him as a leader.

The stamp engraving reproduces the full-bodied statue of him that sits in Lafayette Park across from the White House in Washington. Kosciuszko appears larger than life as he looks down upon the stamp reader from his pedestal. Like many other Revolutionary War officers represented on stamps, he is standing, not on horseback, with sword drawn, and appears ready to lead a battle. Pulaski, who was a royal count, looks out from his portrait wearing a dress military uniform. Oddly, he is not on horseback, although he is credited as founding the American cavalry. No identifying language tells a stamp consumer that Pulaski died at the Battle of Savannah. And unless one read the newspaper announcements discussing the stamp, or as a collector purchased the first-day cover, the average American probably did not understand that the dates printed on the Kosciuszko, 1783–1933, celebrated his fictional naturalization.[59]

Obtaining these commemoratives was a great achievement for the fraternal and Polish heritage organizations that fought for these stamps to demonstrate ethnic pride and claim a piece of American heritage, and as another means for establishing their status as racially white. Even as cultural and legal definitions of whiteness were changing in the United States in the 1920s and 1930s, their members experienced discrimination and understood that Poles and other eastern

Fig. 25. Kosciuszko, five cent, 1933 (Courtesy Smithsonian National Postal Museum Collection)

European immigrants were defined as racially different from old stock immigrants hailing from western Europe. Celebrating Kosciuszko's naturalization tells us that it was important for the Polish National Alliance, Polish Roman Catholic Union, and other organizations to broadcast their hereditary claims to Revolutionary lineage and American citizenship. The first naturalization law in 1790 dictated that only a "free white person" was eligible for citizenship. Kosciuszko qualified as white and fit for citizenship, contradicting the justifications behind immigration restrictions of people from Poland found in the Quota Act and Johnson-Reed. In the early twentieth century, Polish Americans were inching their way out of an in-between status, racially, and used the accomplishments of two Polish military men who volunteered (and died, in Pulaski's case) for the American cause during Revolutionary War as their connection to the origins of the republic.[60]

Polish American groups received help from the USPOD in proving their people to be fit and loyal American citizens, since their ancestors fought to establish the United States as an independent nation. The legal and cultural murkiness of racial classification in the early twentieth century made it more imperative for first- and second-generation immigrants to be able to stake their claim to whiteness. For Polish immigrants, earning two stamps helped.

Commemorative stamp subjects from the 1920s and early 1930s tell stories about America's origins and the nation's founders. All of these subjects are male and of European descent. We can see through the petitioning process that ordinary citizens became invested in the subjects of commemorative stamps. Civic, cultural, and political groups saw power that the USPOD held in influencing public understanding of the American past through printing and circulating historical narratives on stamps. Campaigning for and against commemoratives would continue into the 1930s, by unrepresented groups, as the number of stamps printed increased during Franklin D. Roosevelt's presidency.

Representing Unity and Equality in New Deal Stamps

> I am but a postage stamp
> Bit of paper, and bright colored ink,
> I certainly cause lots of attention
> And make many people think.
> —"A Postage Stamp" by A. W. Pfeiffer

The last chapter discussed how the interwar years in the United States brought tremendous interest in local and regional history, and commemoration of colonial and Revolution-related events. These activities continued into the 1930s with a big booster: the federal government. Letter-writing campaigns to the USPOD continued into the 1930s, as civic and political groups saw there was power in circulating messages on stamps. Beginning in 1933, commemorative selections retreat from featuring regional and local anniversaries, and instead focus on state anniversaries, broad national themes, and contemporary federal programs. Much of this shift comes after the election of President, and philatelist, Franklin Delano Roosevelt. He used the commemorative stamp program to build popular support for his federal initiatives. He understood that the visual language of stamps, printed by the USPOD, carried great power and could reach large numbers of Americans. Stamp collecting already appealed to many different people in first half of twentieth century, and as a philatelist, FDR saw collecting grow as a hobby from the nineteenth into the twentieth century. During FDR's first term, the USPOD printed more special commemoratives than in previous administrations.[1]

During Franklin D. Roosevelt's presidency, federal participation in and supervision of historical interpretation, practices, and preservation grew tremendously through a number of Depression-era programs. Prior to his election, federal public history work was very decentralized. There was no national archive or federal history museum system, and the Smithsonian's National Museum divided its exhibition space among collections representing many fields in the arts and sciences. Congress hesitated to take over locally controlled sites when asked, while other sites maintained a strong legacy of female management through heritage societies who fought to keep interpretative control over sites they cared for.[2] Interest in promoting local and regional traditions continued as more Americans researched their family histories with help from genealogical bureaus that assisted researchers and encouraged individuals from non-elite families to discover their ancestral roots. These strong localized components complemented federal history initiatives during the New Deal. Folklife and the arts received attention as essential components of American culture, while the Federal Writers' Project, various federal art projects, and the Historical American Building Survey employed hundreds of artists, historians, and writers and elevated their work in communities across the country as nationally significant. Through these programs, the federal government demonstrated a serious commitment to preserving history from the ground up and as a patron of the arts in ways not been in the past.[3]

The Treasury Department's Section of Fine Arts (the Section) commissioned art and murals for local post offices and other public buildings. Unlike New Deal programs that offered employment aid, this federal program selected artists through a competition and then encouraged artists to seek input from local communities. Artists then composed mural scenes reflecting regional practices, significant events, and individuals, and occasionally aspects of postal operations. Citizens, local press, postmasters, and the Section engaged in dialogue and debate over the subjects and artistic styles represented in murals.[4] Given the centrality of post offices to American life in the early twentieth century, murals in post office buildings were widely seen—enjoyed or disliked—across the country. Citizens saw federal investment in historical narratives circulated on stamps, on post office walls, and in national parks and historic sites.

The expansion of the National Park Service (NPS) into historic preservation and interpretation is seen as a watershed moment for federal involvement in spreading historical knowledge and in constructing professional public history practices. In 1933, FDR officially consolidated all federally managed battlefields and historic sites under the management of the NPS under the direction of Harold Albright. Prior to 1933, the Park Service focused on the conservation of natural resources and interpretation of geological history in national parks, rather than on interpreting human history. Albright established a museum program that opened the door for historical interpretation to coexist in national parks alongside beautiful scenery and physical science research. Professional historians, like Verne Chatelain, were hired to create interpretative strategies for sites, and to develop criteria for selecting new parks. Guiding the selection of new sites was the idea that all parks would be connected across a narrative arc representing "important phases" in American history. This approach privileged event-based sites over person-driven sites—battlefields over birthplaces. Some states, like Minnesota, had already developed a robust program for integrating a state-driven narrative across multiple sites for the NPS to borrow. Early Park Service historians shaped a national narrative about the American past by connecting sites across different states. With many locally run sites petitioning for inclusion in the new park system, NPS developed practices for negotiating with local boosters about the conditions for acceptance. These practices would hold for decades to come and firmly established "history as a function of government service."[5]

The USPOD had been involved in history work since the late nineteenth century with its commemorative program, but that work never included historians. NPS officials were much more systematic in their approach to selecting sites for federal protection and interpretation. They developed criteria based on persistent themes they devised for major time periods to construct a progressive narrative of the American past.[6] In contrast, the USPOD never turned to or employed historians for guidance in making commemorative selections. Instead, the office of the third assistant postmaster general in consultation with the postmaster general—political appointees—balanced the requests, and pressure, from citizens and their congressional representatives when selecting figures and historical scenes for stamps that carried national significance. By the time the NPS sought suggestions for new historic parks, civic boosters and history enthusiasts already knew they could petition their government to ask that their favorite historic site, event anniversary, or hero represent the United States through publication on a postage stamp. The NPS may have benefited from the USPOD's established process.

During the 1930s, individuals and political groups demanded commemoratives that more fully represented the American past, including African American achievements and women's suffrage, as the USPOD continued its role as an arbiter of cultural symbols. For the first time, a president who was an avid collector directly influenced stamp selection and production, and used his office to create stamps that supported federal and quasi-federal pursuits. Stamp collecting surged in popularity during the Depression years, and more individuals saw, saved, and valued commemoratives as miniature memorials. When stamps were saved in an album, collectors reviewed and reflected on a stamp's imagery and often researched the scenes and individuals represented. Subjects chosen to represent the United States on a commemorative stamp lived on beyond the time period of their issue.

First Philatelist, FDR

Beginning with the 1932 presidential campaign and continuing through his presidency, FDR's stamp-collecting activities were highlighted in the mainstream and philatelic press. During the 1932 campaign, the *Wall Street Journal* discussed the presidential candidates' hobbies, telling readers they were choosing between an avid fisherman in Herbert Hoover and a voracious stamp collector in Roosevelt. George W. Linn, publisher of *Linn's Weekly Stamp News*, openly endorsed FDR by printing, on the front page of his widely read philatelic paper, "Boost a Philatelic brother," proclaiming, "A million stamp collectors want a stamp collector for President." Not to be left out of the philatelic community, President Hoover spoke at the convention of the Society of Philatelic Americans to declare that his entire family had collected stamps for many years even if he wasn't actively collecting at the time.

Discussing leisure-time pursuits in the 1930s gave voters a means of identifying with these elite male candidates.[7] Discussions like this in the media continued to boost popular awareness and interest in stamp collecting.

Mekeel's Weekly and other philatelic papers were thrilled when American voters elected the first active philatelist as president. Stories about Roosevelt's collecting habits generally repeated that he began collecting stamps when he was eight years old, a practice he learned from his mother. His interest was piqued when he traveled abroad as a youngster and again later in life when he served as assistant secretary of the navy. To the disappointment of philatelists, FDR would not display his albums publicly or appear at philatelic club meetings. Any meetings he arranged with fellow philatelists took place in private. While he was a very public advocate of stamp collecting, FDR guarded his collection.[8] Yet Roosevelt's collecting activities were covered in the mainstream and the philatelic press. *New York Times* readers learned that he stayed up sorting his stamps to relax while waiting for the Seventy-Third Congress to vote on bills proposed during his famous first one hundred days. White House staffers reportedly gathered stamps from letters sent to the president, other executive offices, and the State Department, and brought them to FDR's private quarters for him to sort through in the evenings. Philatelists honored Roosevelt for his advocacy role in increasing exposure to stamp collecting when one of the oldest philatelic clubs awarded him the Hanford Cup.[9]

Shy about displaying his own collection, Roosevelt boldly used his power as president to influence stamp production. He submitted ideas for stamps that promoted current government and quasi-public programs that supported economic recovery and national unity. Often, he sketched the design he wished to be printed, or suggested an artwork to use as the model for engraving the stamp. Some have suggested that his stamp subjects were designed in light, soothing colors to reflect a sense of optimism during the Great Depression.[10]

Avid philatelists grew skeptical of FDR's efforts to encourage collecting after learning that the president and his postmaster general, James A. Farley received their own sets of first-day issue souvenir stamps that would not be available for other collectors to purchase. Farley purchased and autographed these ungummed and unperforated sheets soon after the printing. Some sheets were also signed by FDR, and Farley gave them to family members and friends. In 1935, a congressional inquiry asked the USPOD to respond to complaints by philatelic societies about this practice. These special sheets and the scandal were known as "Farley's Follies," and demonstrated special privilege and access offered to the executive offices. While no congressional action was ever taken, Postmaster General James A. Farley announced soon after the inquiry that any souvenir sheets printed by the Department would be made available for collectors to purchase through the Philatelic Agency.[11] As demonstrated in previous administrations, philatelists closely watched activities of the USPOD to see how it influenced their hobby. Collectively, their voices were strong.

Promoting Federal Programs with Commemoratives

Roosevelt used all of the mechanisms available to him to generate support for his New Deal relief programs, including the accessibility of commemorative stamps and the reach of the USPOD. The third assistant postmaster general in charge of the stamp division, Clinton B. Eilenberger, communicated regularly with philatelic societies, discussing new stamps and encouraging them to stay involved in collecting. At the Mississippi Philatelic Convention in 1934, Eilenberger stroked the egos of those attending, proclaiming that "stamp collectors and those interested in this happy avocation are above the average in intelligence and cultural attainments." That declaration was then printed in the *Washington Post* for all to read. Knowing that club philatelists disliked the commemorative series from the 1920s and early 1930s that celebrated regional events, he assured the crowd that under the new administration, the Department would only issue stamps that represent "the best in our history and tradition" of "national importance."[12]

Speaking to the Society of American Philatelists that same year, Eilenberger assured collectors that the Roosevelt administration would only honor subjects of "national importance" on limited-issue stamps. The criteria also included FDR's newest relief program. Designed and issued soon after the establishment of the National Recovery Administration (NRA) in 1933, the National Emergency Relief stamp worked to influence participation in and support of FDR's earliest New Deal initiatives. FDR established the NRA with an executive order to promote industrial planning in establishing codes to regulate labor, prices, and production. To make the NRA stamp fit logically with the spirit of the existing commemorative stamp program, Eilenberger created a narrative of American progress that wove together the stories behind two other commemorative stamps issued by Hoover's administration in 1933. Beginning with the "Proclamation of Peace" stamp that celebrated the ceasefire ending the Revolutionary War, Eilenberger spoke how this memorial acted as a tribute to the "fortitude" and achievement of those who fought for independence "against almost unbelievable odds."[13]

Similarly, in the Century of Progress stamp that promoted the 1933 World's Fair in Chicago, Eilenberger saw the "fulfillment of sacrifices and struggles of the early pioneers," such as the sons of Washington's soldiers from Newburgh who migrated west and south "in search of better homes and greater opportunities for their children." Their "success" was aided with developments of science and technology, but it really was due to "self-reliance" and the "American spirit."[14] The NRA stamp, representing a voluntary collective effort to manage labor, wages, and pricing in a time of economic depression, was crafted as the logical next step in the progressive and triumphalist vision of American history that prized individualism and encouraged individuals to work together for a greater good. As support for the NRA's voluntary codes and wage equality waned in 1934, Eilenberger gave a political speech to philatelists using the language of stamp imagery to seek support for the New Deal program.

Fig. 26. National Recovery Act issue, 1933 (Courtesy Smithsonian National Postal Museum Collection)

After a strong start, support for the NRA waned in 1934 as the initiative struggled to work with private industry, even when those businesses received exemptions from other federal regulations. According to Eilenberger, if everyone cooperated with the administration's recovery efforts—industry magnates and trade manufacturers, farmers and factory workers—then the stamp would represent the beginning of the end of economic hardship. According to Department, the stamp depicted "a farmer, a business man, an industrial worker, and a woman employee united in a common effort to banish unemployment and distress from the land." If the same "courage and perseverance" read in the historical scenes represented on stamps was shown by the American people in the 1930s, then, Eilenberger declared, "The National Recovery Stamp will indeed be a memorial of victory."[15]

The stamp's first design incorporated the NRA's blue eagle, but people won out over the symbol. The faces united "in common determination" on this stamp were racially white, representing different ethnic backgrounds of American workers. The absence of an African American in the crowd accurately reflects that most black workers did not benefit from the NRA programs. Many lost their jobs because white employers refused to grant African Americans the same pay and benefits as their white workers, or employers ignored the industry codes to retain their discriminatory pay practices.[16] On the other hand, a white woman stands as an independent person walking equally next to the industrial worker, farmer, and businessman. Three of the four are looking ahead in the same direction with a "common determination." This image also represents nameless citizens who are not soldiers or fighting in the name of independence. Instead, they are going to work together with a shared purpose, on equal ground.

In the stamp, the businessman stands slightly apart from the others as he looks directly out of the stamp to its viewers. Collectors noticed this difference and wrote to the postmaster general and to President Roosevelt asking why the individual representing "Business or Capital is out of step" with the others, when the stamp should represent the nation moving forward together. Department responses to collectors noted that the image came from an NRA poster indicating that in fact the businessman is "a pivotal figure of the group, rather than being out of step."[17] An alternative stamp design actually drew FDR into the illustration among the workers. As a living person, he could not appear

Fig. 27. Rejected design for the National Recovery Administration stamp (Courtesy Smithsonian National Postal Museum Collection)

on a stamp, but we then can see that the businessman in the printed stamp who is pivotal in the recovery efforts is Roosevelt. The rejected design also represents academia, with a male graduate dressed in cap and gown, and a woman looks over the shoulders of the farmer and Roosevelt, relegated to the background of the image and not standing equally among the men. The final NRA stamp represented citizens as active in their own recovery.

By the mid-1930s, the Department connected directly with philatelists in ways that it had not in the many years prior, while it also dramatically expanded the commemorative stamp program to attract new collectors. The president and USPOD together worked to foster positive relationships between collectors and the Department to support the hobby, and to bolster optimism about the future of the United States by showcasing specific initiatives, including Admiral Byrd's trip to Antarctica.

Supporting Exploration, from the Poles to the Parks

Another stamp printed in 1933 came as a suggestion from President Roosevelt. The Philatelic Agency sold a stamp, designed primarily for philatelic purposes, that supported an expedition to Antarctica led by Admiral Richard E. Byrd. Admiral Byrd served as a naval (reservist) officer and scientist who explored regions near the North and South Poles during his career. As he prepared for his second voyage to Antarctica in 1933, Byrd visited his friend FDR, who asked if Byrd could send him a stamped envelope canceled at the Little America outpost. Roosevelt thought other collectors also might want a unique souvenir envelope canceled at the Little America post office by the expedition crew. FDR asked Farley to print a limited-issue stamp. Farley developed a plan allowing collectors to send a self-addressed stamped envelope with a postal mail order of fifty-three cents to the expedition's headquarters in Norfolk, Virginia, or to the PA.[18] Covers were gathered and sent down to the "most southerly" post office. Byrd secured private financing for his polar journeys, but the expeditions were expensive. While FDR did not divert federal dollars toward Byrd's second Antarctic exploration (1933–34), FDR facilitated a path allowing the proceeds from the limited-issue commemorative stamp to go toward the expedition expenses.

FDR also participated in the expedition stamp's design and production. Designers at the Bureau of Engraving and Printing prepared four drafts that were rejected in favor of a vertical design FDR sketched himself. He then encouraged collectors and interested citizens to support the expedition by buying the stamps. Byrd's expedition team carried letters with the limited-issue three-cent stamp to the Little America camp, where each piece of mail was canceled with a seal from Antarctica by a newly appointed postmaster for the outpost. Because of the distance carried, a fifty-cent transportation fee was imposed. This fee helped finance the expedition's transportation expenses. Postal workers Leroy Clark and Charles Anderson were overwhelmed by the volume of mail and canceled more than 150,000 envelopes in Little America.[19]

Prior to Byrd's expedition, another pioneer relied on philatelic funding for her travels. Amelia Earhart also carried mail with her on her first transatlantic flight in May 1932, but her flight was not autho-

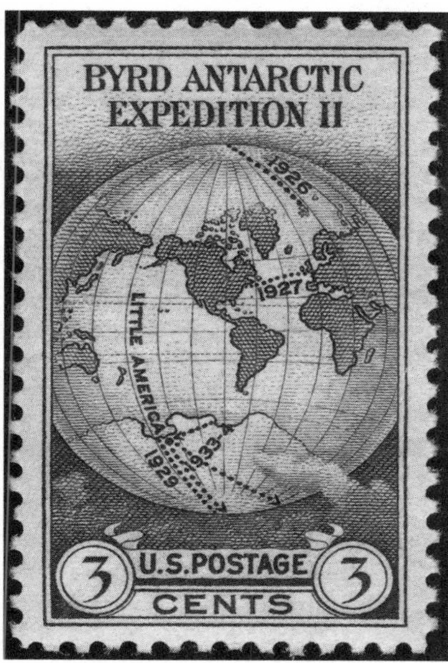

Fig. 28. Byrd Antarctic issue, 1933 (Courtesy Smithsonian National Postal Museum)

rized by the USPOD. Instead, philatelists paid her to postmark each of fifty letters in Newfoundland and after landing in Ireland, and she numbered and autographed each cover. News spread through philatelic circles, and Earhart carried mail with her on additional flights. She also saved and exhibited examples of her stamped envelopes, or covers, at philatelic exhibitions. On her final, fatal, flight she carried approximately $25,000 in souvenir envelopes.[20] Sales of the Earhart covers and the Byrd stamp contributed to the expenses of both Earhart's and Byrd's expeditions. Earhart appealed directly to philatelists for her support; Byrd appealed to his friend the president and was officially supported by the federal government.

The Department received many negative responses from philatelists who did not approve of federal promotion of the Byrd expedition through sales from a commemorative issue. Unlike other limited-issue commemoratives, these stamps were only available through the Philatelic Agency and not at local post offices. The souvenir covers were also sold at Gimbels Department Store, as were Earhart's for her final flight in 1937.[21] This move led to confusion as to whether the Antarctic stamps could be used to mail a letter in the United States. Additionally, the three-cent stamp was dyed blue rather than the usual purple tint for stamps printed in that denomination at that time. Philatelic community reactions against this type of current-event limited issue never escalated to a protest like the one over the Trans-Mississippi issues in 1898. While some philatelists complained, no one began a massive letter-writing campaign. In fact, many Americans thought this was a worthy cause because the Philatelic Agency sold over six million Little America stamps. Admiral Byrd wrote to FDR expressing his gratitude, saying that the stamp "helped us immeasurably in a number of ways." The stamp and cancellation from a remote post office offered a new way to publicize the Antarctic expedition, and Byrd welcomed the increased exposure.[22]

FDR continued to capitalize on the Department's ability to promote federal programs in the 1930s by encouraging the printing of a series to highlight the growing network of national parks. Declaring 1934 as the National Parks Year, Secretary of the Interior Harold Ickes worked closely with Postmaster General Farley to create a ten-stamp series featuring picturesque scenery from ten parks. Issued in rapid succession primarily during summer months, the series was designed to encourage domestic tourism.[23] A collector could buy all ten and assemble them as souvenirs from a cross-country road trip to visit those natural wonders.

The National Parks Year also coincided with the expansion of the National Park Service to include battlefields and historic sites. None of the new sites appeared in this series, but the stamps reinvigorated interest in the federally managed park system. Without naming a New Deal program, this series also subtly promoted the work of the newly created Civilian Conservation Corps. Beginning in 1933, the CCC employed hundreds of thousands of young men who built infrastructure at national parks and forests across the United States. Tourists, collectors, or relatives of CCC workers might decide to buy one or more stamps in the national park series. Similar to the Antarctic stamp, this limited-issue series did not represent a historical narrative but, rather, promoted contemporary government initiatives. Roosevelt's administration showed its acumen for marketing federal programs by piggybacking on the success of the Post Office Department's commemorative stamp program. Stamp sales increased and the receipts from the Philatelic Agency during fiscal year 1935 were the highest to date. The

Fig. 29. Little America post office overrun with covers awaiting cancellation (Courtesy Smithsonian National Postal Museum Collection)

Fig. 30. National Parks Mt. Rainier, three cent (Courtesy Smithsonian National Postal Museum collection)

USPOD interpreted this growth as "further evidence of the increasing attention that is being directed to stamp collecting."[24] Popular participation in and media attention of stamp collection was beginning to peak nationwide.

Federal efforts to unite Americans during an economic depression included stamps in their portfolio that showcased the beauty of national parks, the common determination of citizens, and the achievements of explorers enduring extreme condition for scientific research. Another Rooseveltian effort to promote feelings of nationalism came with a series of stamps honoring military heroes. The announcement of this series surfaced regional, gender, and racial tensions, while also questioning who qualified to represent national character on American commemoratives.

Susan B. Anthony and the Military Series

In the early twentieth century, the USPOD positioned itself as a producer of historical narratives representing the American past, and laid a foundation that privileged the stories of elite white men. Citizen petitioners worked to break that foundation during the 1920s and 1930s, demonstrated by the Polish American campaigns to honor Pulaski and Kosciusko, described in an earlier chapter, and by women and African Americans who simultaneously campaigned for commemoratives to make their political achievements visible to collectors and noncollectors alike.

Until the late 1930s, US commemorative stamps almost exclusively honored the achievements of white men. In the corpus of commemoratives, women and all people of color played almost no role in US history. This is not surprising given the "great men" approach to teaching history in schools and presented in historical sites, but it also reflected contemporary discriminatory laws, practices, and violence directed against people of color and women. Petitioners for stamps honoring Susan B. Anthony and Booker T. Washington were astute observers of USPOD stamp production and understood that the government almost exclusively honored white male contributions in commemoratives. The stakes were high for these stamp supporters. As a result, they positioned the achievements of Anthony and Washington in the context of other commemorative issues and hoped that federal approval was a small step in a very long battle to achieve full political equality.

Commemorating the work of suffrage activists through a postage stamp was a key piece of a broader agenda for the National Woman's Party and the Susan B. Anthony Memorial Committee. Committee chair Ethel Adamson, noticed great public honors were bestowed on men "for much smaller achievements" than Anthony's and believed that her suffrage legacy deserved public recognition. Some of the federal neglect, supporters suggested, could be repaired by issuing a stamp honoring Anthony. Groups of women met with Third Assistant Postmaster General Eilenberger in 1934 and in 1935 to persuade him to accept their petitions to print an Anthony or a suffrage stamp. He did not support the stamp and claimed that stamp collectors showed no interest either. Even during the 1930s, white men comprised the memberships in philatelic associations. Speaking to philatelists at the American Philatelic Society's annual convention in 1934, Eilenberger maintained that the USPOD wanted to "revive the memories of historic events" with the commemoratives, and dismissed rumors that his department might print a stamp honoring a woman, including actress Mae West.[25]

Before the fight over an Anthony issue, collectors of American stamps most likely held few images of identifiable women in their albums. In the Columbian commemorative series, Queen Isabella of Spain appeared on six stamps. A portrait of Pocahontas dressed in English clothing, mistakenly represented as royalty, was printed on the five-cent issue in the Jamestown Exposition series (1907). In 1902, and again in 1922, the USPOD released a series of definitive stamps and chose Martha Washington's face as the first American woman to grace the eight-cent (1902) and four-cent (1922) issues. Persons and places represented in these everyday stamps from 1922 were selected to "stand for America as it might be viewed by a newly arrived immigrant." According to Third Assistant Postmaster General Glover, the Department chose Washington over other possible well-known American women, including Anthony and Clara Barton, because she "more nearly typified the women who were closely identified with the groundwork of American national life in its first phases."[26] Washington was known as a wife and mother, not as a nurse and organizer or political activist like Barton or Anthony. Selecting Washington as the first woman represented on a stamp sold everyday freed the USPOD from any controversy, because few would argue against choosing the country's original First Lady.

Still fighting for a stamp in 1936, women campaigning for Anthony were outraged when they heard that the Department planned to print a series of stamps honoring US Army and Navy commanders, including Robert E. Lee and Stonewall Jackson. Former president Theodore Roosevelt initiated the idea for a stamp series honoring American military heroes during World War I, but it was not until his cousin Franklin pushed for it that the series was approved. In February 1936, a list of military heroes was leaked after Secretary of War George H. Dern submitted his proposal to Roosevelt and the postmaster general. Prior to any stamp printing, citizens began to react. Letters flooded the Department and the White House, mainly from Southerners who supported a stamp honoring Robert E. Lee. Other letters, such as one from New York congresswoman Caroline O'Day, remarked that Republican women of her state would not like seeing Lee representing the United States on a stamp in the series. She noted that politically it would be important for elected officials to support the initiative, because the negative reaction from southerners would be far greater if there was no stamp honoring Lee.[27]

A long fight over the army-navy issues soon ensued. Images of military leaders from the army and navy were printed in a ten-stamp series released in small sets during 1936 and 1937. Each service received a set containing one- through five-cent denominations. Proceeding somewhat chronologically, the one-cent honored Generals Washington and Greene and Captains Barry and Jones and continued through the War of 1812, Civil War, and Spanish-American War. While the series was planned in advance, the release of the Grant-Sherman-Sheridan stamps in February 1937 and the Lee-Jackson stamps in March drew the biggest public responses once the stamps were printed. Southern congressmen, collectors, and interested citizens decried Sherman as a "common murderer" and defended Lee as a wronged hero who was unintentionally demoted by the Department because the stamp showed his uniform's shoulder boards carrying two stars instead of three. Protests against the Confederate generals became battle cries for the Anthony committee and African American newspapers asking for a stamp honoring Booker T. Washington because "he has surely done

Fig. 31. Lee-Jackson, four cent, Army-Navy series, 1936 (Courtesy Smithsonian National Postal Museum Collection)

more for American Democracy than Gen. Lee or Stonew(a)ll Jackson."[28] The USPOD stood squarely amid a cultural debate over political equality and the legacy of the Civil War in the 1930s. Commemoratives representing Confederate officers acted as another attempt by the FDR administration to use stamps to promote nationalism, but these stamps were read as a clear rejection of political equality promised at the end of the Civil War. By appearing on US stamps, Lee and Jackson were not traitors, but American war heroes who looked out from postage alongside the portraits of George Washington, William Sherman, and Ulysses S. Grant.

Protectors of Susan B. Anthony's legacy were also disturbed: "Why should such men, fighting for the principle contrary to our present standard of life and liberty, be given honors in advance of an individual who gave her services freely for the cause of freedom for all of the people—men and women alike?" According to the chair of the National Woman's Party (NWP), the Department was not impressing women voters and urged Postmaster General Farley "to be fair with your women constituents and glorify some of our outstanding women with Susan B. Anthony leading them all." Understandably, members of the NWP could not reconcile the contradictions of their government that honored men who led a secessionist fight against the Union and fought for oppression and slavery, while ignoring the accomplishments of one woman who represented the struggle for female voting rights. While the NWP often ignored voices and concerns from African American women, the party leader's rhetoric indicated that they and Anthony fought for equality for all persons. Releases of the first issues

Fig. 32. Susan B. Anthony, three cent, 1936 (Courtesy Smithsonian National Postal Museum Collection)

in the army-navy series coincided with further indecision by Farley about an Anthony stamp. The Anthony Memorial Committee believed Farley kept "giving the women the run-around" by misleading them as to when the USPOD might issue an Anthony stamp: "First, we are too early, now we are too late." The timing was never right, and seemed like an impossible battle to win.[29]

Amid the military series debates, the Post Office Department announced in July 1936 that it would print a suffrage anniversary stamp using a portrait of Susan B. Anthony in August. The stamp's engraving was drawn from a bust sculpted by Adelaide Johnson that represented her as a classically inspired figure. Johnson described her sculpture as "expressing the entire life of Miss Anthony" by emphasizing her strength and spirituality. The stamp engraving depicts Anthony's left profile with her hair wrapped into a bun in the center of the stamp. A wide oval frame encases her portrait, making the vignette look like a cameo. Wearing cameo brooches became popular in the Victorian Age, recalling the classical Greek art form of carving figures in stone relief. Many female cameo figures created for brooches were dressed in flowing robes, with their curly hair pulled back from the face.[30] Anthony's clothing was not necessarily flowing and her hair was not curly, yet her image alludes to the form of a cameo that presents an idealized female figure inside representing virtue. In this style of image, Anthony is not an annoying agitator but, rather, a nonthreatening, admirable citizen. The stamp's purple ink aided in the stamp's appearing like a cameo brooch, even though all three-cent stamps were tinted violet. For example, in the army-navy series Admirals David Farragut and David Porter appeared on a violet three-cent stamp. In contrast, however, the stamps of military heroes represented their bodies mostly looking outward from the stamps. Unlike other three-cent single issues from the 1930s, the Anthony was cut to a smaller size and shape, similar to a definitive stamp. Other single-issue commemoratives, such as the Texas Centennial (March 1936), Rhode Island Tercentennial (May 1936), and Ordinance of 1787 Sesquicentennial (July 1937) were rectangular in shape and distinctive as a commemorative.[31] With its monetary value equaling postage for mailing a first-class letter, this Anthony-suffrage commemorative stamp actually appeared in size and functioned very similarly to a definitive. This was as close to a regular issue stamp as possible.

NWP members and other supporters of Antony's legacy and an equal rights amendment believed the stamp's production was a real political victory. The USPOD, however, drew substantial criticism from collectors and other citizens. Since the stamp commemorated the sixteenth anniversary of the Nineteenth Amendment, some believed honoring an ordinary anniversary should not be eligible for a commemorative, unlike a twenty-fifth, fiftieth, or centennial. Some collectors questioned Farley's rationale for printing an excessive number of commemoratives throughout this tenure, and specifically questioned his choice of Susan B. Anthony. *Washington Post* reader C.N. Wood warned of an "epidemic" brought on by the Anthony stamp that would open the door to the printing of stamps honoring Booker T. Washington, Esperanto, Babe Ruth, Al Capone, and former summer Olympian Eleanor Holm Jarrett.[32] Wood expressed his displeasure that the Department had moved beyond honoring white, native-born men as representatives of American history to include what he saw as undeserving figures. Wood marginalized the accomplishments of Anthony and Washington in particular. John Pollock, then chair of the Democratic Party, wrote to Farley indicating that some of his members might even leave the party in protest over the Anthony stamp. He warned Farley that if he did not suppress the Anthony stamp, "It will prove a political boomerang." Despite these warnings, the stamp did not damage Roosevelt's chances of winning reelection, and Farley kept his job as postmaster general.[33] As a handful of commemorative subjects slowly interjected American stories outside of that exclusive white male perspective, some citizens rejected the stamps as ahistorical as a screen for their animus. These negative reactions showed that even working for a stamp was a political battle, one these women continued to wage through the mid-twentieth century.

That debates over the military series and the Anthony stamp played out in government offices, philatelic meetings, mainstream media, and political organizations further illustrates the power Americans believed stamps held to circulate messages. Petitioners worked with sense of urgency to earn stamps for their cause, because they understood that the USPOD held power to spread historical and political ideas, and that those stamps would be saved by collectors. Importantly, stamps carried a federal endorsement of a particular narrative. Women and African Americans understood that they needed representation of their stories on stamps as they pushed for political equality. Congressional resolutions were submitted to the postmaster general that did not win approval, including one in 1935 authorizing a stamp commemorating the "romantic settlement" of Indian tribes in Oklahoma that would honor Sequoya, inventor of the Cherokee alphabet.[34] Who was missing from the commemorative corpus was as important as who was represented. The USPOD controlled a platform where citizens, collectors, and federal officials negotiated meanings of contemporary cultural and political issues.

Anthony was not the first woman engraved on a stamp, but it could be said that she was the first politically active woman chosen. Another would not be chosen until the 1940 Famous American series, when Jane Addams and Frances Willard were among thirty-five Americans honored for their achievements in the fields of literature, music, education, and technology.[35] Among those in this series was Booker T. Washington, the first African American pictured on a US stamp. The USPOD understood that issuing commemorative stamps brought great joy to petitioners, but that not all Americans, noncollectors and collectors, approved of its choices. This may be why the USPOD slipped Washington into a large series of stamps honoring men and women famous for diverse accomplishments to avoid backlash and make Washington more acceptable to white Americans.

Booker T. Washington and the Emancipation Stamps

During the struggle over the Anthony-suffrage stamp, the widely circulated African American newspaper *Chicago Defender* asked, "How About Us?" Acknowledging that women ought to be represented on stamps, the paper pressed that there "should be some stamps bearing black faces" as well. When the USPOD expanded its commemorative program in the 1920s, the *Defender* and many citizens called for stamps celebrating the heroism and achievements of Frederick Douglass, Booker T. Washington, and Crispus Attucks. Bostonians hailed Attucks as a martyr who was remembered as the first casualty of the Revolution. Why wouldn't he qualify as an American hero equal in valor to Nathan Hale, whose likeness appeared on a stamp in 1925?[36] Many African Americans were frustrated that the Department, and their government, continued to ignore the achievements of people of color.

The most ardent supporter of a Washington stamp was Major Richard Robert Wright Sr., an accomplished formerly enslaved person who fought in the Spanish-American War, served as the first president of the Georgia State Industrial College for Colored Youth (now Savannah State University), and founded the Citizens and Southern Bank and Trust Company in Philadelphia. With a seemingly sympathetic administration in office, Wright began petitioning President Roosevelt and Postmaster General Farley in 1933 and regularly wrote scores of letters through 1939. By the mid-1930s, as the number of commemoratives grew at a rapid rate, African American newspapers again called on the government to choose Washington, Attucks, or Douglass for a stamp. The *Defender* asked citizens across the country to write personal letters to Farley requesting a Washington stamp. Momentum also was building for a Frederick Douglass stamp, pushed by another commemorative committee that also waited and waited for the Department to choose their African American hero. The secretary of Dunbar High School's stamp club in Washington, DC, appealed to President Roosevelt asking for a stamp honoring "members of the Negro race" because "we are loyal citizens and always answer when our country calls, regardless of the discriminations we are forced to suffer."[37] Constantly reminded of their status as second-class citizens, some African Americans fought for a stamp as a small step along a long road to achieving full political equality. Achievements made by African Americans would gain legitimacy when representing the United States on a stamp.

In July 1939, the USPOD announced that Washington's image would appear as part of the series honoring thirty-five famous Americans. Though he was not honored separately, like Anthony, the Washington stamp was lauded as a victory by African American leaders because it finally broke the color barrier imposed on postage subjects. Throughout the late nineteenth and early twentieth centuries, Washington was the most widely recognized African American, so it comes as no surprise that he was the first black person to earn a stamp. Known internationally for founding the Tuskegee Institute in Alabama, Washington created a path for African Americans in the rural South to achieve economic equality through mastery of trades and skills first, before agitating for full political and social rights. Often described as an accommodationist, Washington was an acceptable representative of African American achievement to many white Americans who believed in racial segregation and the genetic inferiority of African Americans. His approach, thought to be very practical, was acceptable to many southern African Americans. Conveniently, Washington's philosophy was also acceptable by the federal government, which would soon ask African Americans to fight in another world war for a country that did not allow them full rights as citizens.[38]

Three months after this announcement, the Diamond Jubilee of the Emancipation Proclamation event in Philadelphia celebrated the printing of the Washington stamp. Postal officials attended this "grand" celebration, and Major Wright and Mary McLeod Bethune, a prominent civil rights leader and advisor to FDR as a member of the Federal Council on Negro Affairs, were on hand. They distributed miniature busts of Washington to white and black children who attended, representing more than five hundred public schools in the Philadelphia area.[39] These busts served as physical reminders of Booker T. Washington's self-declared legacy as one who raised himself "up from slavery" and would not agitate for social equality. Celebrating these two events together with a mixed-race audience gestured to Washington's autobiography, where he recalled that newly freed enslaved persons felt no bitterness toward their white masters upon hearing the Emancipation Proclamation read. Whites and blacks came together in another symbolic gesture during the ceremony as four girls—two black, two

Fig. 33. Booker T. Washington ten cent, Famous American series, 1940 (Courtesy Smithsonian National Postal Museum Collection)

white—marched on stage in military costumes, carrying an American flag that they then draped across the shoulders of Major Wright "in token of his victory in securing" the Washington stamp.[40] The multiracial audience and participants appeared to "cast down" their buckets in a joint celebration of Washington's work.

This was a significant symbolic moment indicating that an African American was worthy of representing the entire nation and population by appearing on a stamp. Wright's successful efforts created a space where an African American stood alongside white Americans in the catalog of US stamps, and opened the door for other black heroes to earn a place in the official narrative of the American past told through commemoratives.

Washington was selected as one of five educators in the Famous American series, which also recognized achievements of authors, poets, scientists, composers, inventors, and artists. As one in a series, Washington's stamp appeared similar to others, with only the portrait and ink color distinguishing each issue. Washington's engraving came from a familiar photograph where he looks outward from the stamp. While the Washington stamp was colored brown, it was in keeping with the colors established for other ten-cent stamps in this commemorative series. Washington's ten-cent issue was the highest-priced stamp in the group of five educators honored in the series. Major Wright and others worried that the price might hinder purchases from African Americans. Despite his concerns over the higher price, the Washington was one of the most widely sold stamps ($23 million) in the Famous Americans series.[41]

The Washington stamp was first released and sold at the Tuskegee Institute's Founder's Day celebration on April 7, 1940, which brought postal officials together with the Tuskegee community. At the celebration, Postmaster General Farley sold the first Booker T. Washington stamp together with the Tuskegee Philatelic Club. Farley spoke at the ceremony, hailing Washington's legacy as a "pioneer educator" and spokesman of his race. The *Defender* devoted tremendous amounts of copy to the events at Tuskegee by publishing photographs and large portions of the speeches. According to Farley, "Negro progress" could be traced directly to the "humanitarian work, noble ideals, and practical teachings" that Washington put into place at Tuskegee. Importantly, according to Farley, Washington taught that "merit, no matter under what skin was in the long run recognized and rewarded." His other greatest achievement was in "his interpretation of his people to the white men," read as his accommodationist approach to the fight for political equality. To compliment Washington's dedication to training young people of the South, Farley jarringly associated Washington's "refusal to accept personal gain with that of Robert E. Lee." Farley furthered the comparison by weaving into his speech a statement by Lee about his strong obligation to train young men of the South after the Civil War. According to Farley, not "one word of that declaration need be changed were the speaker Booker T. Washington." Not surprisingly, the *Defender* omitted this portion of the speech.[42]

Farley cleverly connected Washington's work with that of Robert E. Lee during this first-day ceremony for an audience of Americans not attending the Tuskegee events. One can imagine that a few gasps were heard in the audience upon their hearing a comparison. Perhaps anticipating angry letters from white southern citizens, Farley explained that Washington was another southern leader who devoted himself to bettering the lives of the region's young people. To make the Washington stamp acceptable to white southerners, Lee, the hero of the "Lost Cause" (honored a few years earlier on postage) was called upon to make Washington's achievements appear equally heroic.

Booker T. Washington stood distinguished alongside fellow famous Americans, but the stamp commemorating the seventy-fifth anniversary of the signing of the Thirteenth Amendment issued the same year looked backward. News of this stamp came as a surprise to many, as the USPOD announced the printing only one week before it was available for sale during the final days of the New York World's Fair in October 1940. Generally, the Department announced commemorative stamps at least a few months before printing to allow first-day ceremonies to be planned and to build anticipation from collectors and the petitioning communities or commissions.[43] By debuting the stamp at the world's fair, the USPOD missed an opportunity to promote the stamp earlier that year at the American Negro Exposition in Chicago, which celebrated seventy-five years of freedom. Black achievements were celebrated while federal agencies and private corporations demonstrated concern for African American welfare through agricultural, housing, and employment exhibits. The USPOD was one of the agencies that staged a small exhibit to sell the Washington stamps—and easily could have sold the Thirteenth Amendment issue. Additionally, the world's fair was rife with racial tensions. At the opening in 1939, African Americans protested a lack of representation in the fair's planning, management, and exhibits.[44]

Labeled as a "New Deal masterstroke," the stamp was released just prior to the presidential election of 1940. While all commemoratives represented someone's agenda, this one in particular appeared to be politically motivated by FDR. Major Wright was delighted because he had been working for nearly a decade, petitioning for both an African American figure and an emancipation stamp. Wright wanted a three-cent stamp specifically, because it could be used to mail a first-class letter, which happened to be the same denomination as the Anthony and other single commemoratives issued during the Farley administration. While various ceremonies celebrated this diamond jubilee of the Emancipation Proclamation, the true anniversary was of the passage of the Thirteenth Amendment to the Constitution.[45] Wright's vision for celebrating emancipation as an uplifting and powerful moment in American history was not realized in the imagery chosen for this stamp.

During the first-day release ceremony, President Roosevelt used the stamp as a vehicle to praise African Americans' achievements after slavery, even when the image chosen to represent emancipation was actually one of subservience. The stamp featured an engraving of the Freedmen's Memorial depicting Lincoln standing over a kneeling enslaved man, bowing at Lincoln's feet, struggling to break the chains

Fig. 34. Thirteenth Amendment, three cent, 1940 (Courtesy Smithsonian National Postal Museum Collection)

of bondage. Although the sculpture was financed partially by formerly enslaved people, a white commission controlled the sculpture's construction and chose a design representing emancipation as a generous act of moral leadership by Lincoln and enfranchised whites. Supposedly honoring freedom from bondage, the sculpture as composed by artist Thomas Ball did not represent a newly freed male figure on equal ground with Lincoln. The enslaved figure was still breaking away from slavery, with no symbols of hope designed into the memorial to indicate that freedmen could ascend to a position of equality promised by emancipation. Given to the city of Washington in 1876 by the "colored citizens of the United States," the memorial reasserted racial hierarchy in which descendants of enslaved people would always be inferior to white men.[46] In choosing this image to commemorate emancipation with the Freedmen's Memorial, the USPOD celebrated Lincoln, not freedom and equality, but instead a racial order in which descendants of enslaved people could never realize full equality in the United States.

Choosing to commemorate the Thirteenth, and not the Fourteenth, Amendment, which gave all adult males full rights of citizenship, seemed deliberate, to focus attention on the abolition of slavery and not on citizenship equality. Similar to the choice of Washington, the USPOD chose Lincoln to represent black freedom by printing a nonthreatening stamp that also did not challenge the authority of state laws that legalized segregation.[47] Complicating the matter was FDR's speech read at the fair. In addition to lauding achievements of African Americans who had "enriched and enlarged and ennobled American life," his language emphasized the need for American unity as he gestured toward the war in Europe. Liberty was "under brutal attack" and peaceful lives were challenged by "brute force" that would "return the human family to that state of slavery from which emancipation came through the Thirteenth Amendment." Through this celebration, he called Americans to "unite in a solemn determination to defend and maintain and transmit to those who shall follow us the rich heritage of freedom which is ours today."[48] FDR rhetorically ignored the fact that the entire "human family" was not enslaved until 1865—slavery was very specifically reserved for those of African descent. For FDR, the emancipation stamp was not a celebration of freedom for African Americans, much like the statue representing emancipation, but rather a call for unity under the false pretense that all Americans were created equal.

Prior to these stamps, the absence of African Americans symbolized their lack of political power. The publication signified a slow shift in nationalized political and cultural agitation. This shift, of course, was not without many contradictions in implementation. During FDR's administration, African Americans did not benefit equally with whites from New Deal–funded programs because of the ways federal programs were constructed and implemented at a local level. At the same time, civil rights groups began publicizing their agendas more loudly and making their fight more visible to federal officials and the general public. Labor and civil rights leader A. Philip Randolph threatened to march on Washington in 1941 to demand an end to racial discrimination in the defense industries and in the military. FDR partially conceded to some of Randolph's demands by signing Executive Act 8802 in June 1941, which ended discrimination in the defense industries and federal defense positions. Randolph canceled the march, but FDR never desegregated the military. Individuals like Randolph laid groundwork for additional legislation and executive orders to come that slowly repealed legal segregation.[49]

Both stamps printed in 1940 illustrated the contradictory ways the US government treated African Americans. As the individual achievement of Booker T. Washington—as an educator and not as a political figure—was revered in April, African Americans, as a race, were reminded in October that their freedom and equality still depended on whites. The Washington issue directly honored the achievements of one man and gestured toward millions of people defined and segregated by their race, yet the emancipation stamp reinforced racial hierarchies that prevented former slaves from achieving equality. The Thirteenth Amendment stamp, coupled with Washington's, sent a message that the federal government approved of individual but not racial group achievement. FDR demanded desegregation of private industry but did not desegregate the military. Even so, FDR deftly combined Washington's and Lincoln's images as symbols of American progress to pave the way toward asking African Americans to work hard for a greater cause, and he suggested that their skills, labor, and duty would be rewarded with full equality under the law.

Touring with Commemoratives as the National Story

Earning a commemorative held a great payoff for those advocating that their hero or historic event deserved a place in the corpus of American postage stamps. Figures such as Booker T. Washington and Susan B. Anthony became part of a mainstream visual narrative of American history. Spaces with their names appeared in empty stamp albums calling out to be filled. And the USPOD invested in promotional efforts to encourage citizens of all ages to fill those pages and to read commemorative stamps in the context of American history.

On the eve of entering the next world war, the USPOD went on a patriotic history tour of the United States, using its catalog of commemorative stamps as the guide. In addition to the collecting and exhibiting efforts begun earlier in the century, the USPOD engaged in another intentional effort to encourage stamp collecting and reading the visual historical narratives printed on stamps. It outfitted a special truck designed to tour the United States. The philatelic truck drew upon a successful tradition of circulating books and connecting communities through traveling library programs and bookmobiles in

Fig. 35. Philatelic truck at White House, May 9, 1939 (Harris & Ewing, photographer, Library of Congress, Prints and Photographs Division)

the early twentieth century. While bookmobiles served statewide or regional populations, the philatelic truck's audience was national.[50] With assistance from the Bureau of Engraving and Printing, the Philatelic Agency designed exhibit cases to fit inside of a panel truck that traveled 20,750 miles, visiting 490 towns and cities. The truck carried displays of US definitive, airmail, and commemorative stamps; postcards and envelopes; and a miniature printing press that stamped out souvenirs while demonstrating the printing processes.[51]

Intending to stimulate interests of young Americans living in rural areas, the truck was a popular attraction every place it visited. Interest in the truck began before the tour routes were solidified. Many local postmasters and stamp club members wrote to Postmaster General Farley asking that the truck stop in their town. To encourage visitation and community participation while the truck was in town, local newspapers promoted the truck's stop in their town and the mission of the USPOD's stamp program.[52] Like many traveling cultural exhibitions, the truck offered citizens who could not visit the home institutions in Washington an opportunity to view the catalog of US stamps.

While touring, the truck's staff did not sell any stamps, but instead sold a small booklet intended for young collectors. The cover art pictured two girls and a boy organizing stamps into an album, illustrating that stamp collecting could be equally interesting to girls and boys. Inside the booklet, young readers found a complete illustrated catalog of US commemorative stamps from 1893 to 1938 and two welcoming notes: one from President Roosevelt and the other from Postmaster General Farley.[53]

Addressing the "Junior Philatelists of the United States," Roosevelt wanted readers to know that he began collecting stamps as a child. Even as president, his stamp-collecting practices helped him to "keep up" his interest in history and geography. Importantly, FDR closed his note by telling readers that he believed collecting stamps made individuals better citizens.[54] A presidential endorsement carried weight and influence with parents, educators, and young collectors.

Postmaster Farley more directly extolled the role and value represented with the catalog of special issue stamps:

> The purpose of this booklet is to bring to the Youth of America the history of our great Nation as pictured on commemorative and other special issues of postage stamps, and to awaken in the citizens of tomorrow a keener sense of appreciation of the vision and faith of our forefathers who founded on these shores a new form of government, dedicated to the enduring principles of freedom and equality for all.[55]

Farley clearly articulated his vision for reading American commemorative stamps as a picture book of American history. Stamps held transformative power that he argued could unite all citizens. This vision told through stamps is progressive and triumphalist, and ridden with holes in its historical perspective. The truck delivered this message as it traveled. The exhibits were popular with all audiences, and the truck drew its largest crowds in cities, such as Pittsburgh and New York. USPOD officials believed that the effects of the traveling exhibits stimulated philately and gave the public a better understanding of US history as told through American stamps. The truck toured from May 1939 until December 1941, taking occasional breaks when postal officials granted time off for its crew. Touring stopped permanently after the Japanese attacks on Pearl Harbor on December 7, 1941. Visiting western states that December, the truck was ordered to San Diego for its last call, where it retired permanently.[56]

Since Postmaster General Wanamaker's successful attempt to sell commemorative stamps to citizens in 1892, the USPOD appealed to collectors with varying waves of enthusiasm through the US involvement in World War II. US entry into World War II changed commemorative production. The USPOD reduced the number of stamps produced and focused subjects directly on supporting the military, celebrating American technological achievements, alongside nationalistic themes. FDR and his administration used all of the resources available to them during his terms to promote federal programs and the hobby of stamp collecting. If noncollecting citizens did not know before FDR took office, they understood during his administration that the USPOD held power to endorse and promote specific interpretations of American history and played a role in the reification of national heroes.

As a philatelist, President Roosevelt deliberately employed commemorative stamps as tools for garnering popular support for New Deal programs and federal initiatives. For those campaigning for a cause, earning a stamp was considered a victory for all those involved. Commemoratives from the 1930s also represented efforts to unite Americans across regional, gender, and racial divides. Supporters of the Anthony, Washington, and emancipation stamps, particularly, enjoyed great victories when those stamps were printed and were available for wide distribution. Earning that place on an American commemorative ensured that the legacy of those individuals and events chosen would live on as miniature memorials when saved in collectors' albums and when displayed at small philatelic exhibitions and in large national collections.

Afterword

After World War II, postal officials began to rethink the selection process for printing commemoratives. By 1957, the USPOD established the Citizens' Stamp Advisory Committee (CSAC) to assume the task of selecting American commemorative stamps.[1] Citizens had influenced commemorative choices since the 1920s, but the CSAC formalized this relationship. In the process, postal officials created some space between themselves and cultural debates that arose from stamp requests from fellow citizens, collectors, and elected officials. By appointing a body of stamp enthusiasts who weighed proposals and made recommendations to the postmaster general, the Department lifted some pressure from executive-level political appointees, who no longer evaluated every commemorative stamp suggestion.

Giving Americans official procedures for suggesting stamp topics means that identifying commemorative subjects became easier for everyone because the Department articulated clear criteria. For example, CSAC criteria mandate that historic anniversaries may only be considered in multiples of fifty years. By limiting anniversaries, the CSAC reduces the number of eligible requests. The Susan B. Anthony stamp that honored the sixteenth anniversary of the Nineteenth Amendment's ratification never would have been approved under these guidelines. Additionally, the committee also only considers subjects with "national significance," specifically prohibiting local and regional anniversary commemoratives. Instead, local postmasters may request a special inked stamp to hand-cancel mail dropped at their post office with a seal acknowledging that significant anniversary of a local event.[2] Amid the Cold War, local history remained local, and the committee decided what qualified as nationally important and worthy of representing the United States on commemoratives.

Through the Cold War period, postal services remained central for personal and business-related communications, delivering mail, magazines, and packages, even as the system for moving mail aged and postal workers grew frustrated. As an agency designed to be self-supporting, the postal service always struggled to balance its budget. After years of debate about how to handle postal operations, the Postal Reorganization Act of 1970 transformed the USPOD into the USPS, or United States Postal Service, as a semipublic institution. The postmaster general no longer ranked as a member of the presidential cabinet, and the Department's centrality in government services started to wane. Even with those major institutional changes, Congress still wielded control over postal rates and mandated certain expenditures, making major systemic reform difficult for future postmasters general.[3]

Despite desires for the postal service to be self-sustaining, postal operations and activities from the earliest days always required some government funding. Lawmakers and federal officials at all ranks believed that facilitating a system of open and inexpensive communications was critical to supporting a sprawling nation. In the United States, operating an accessible, reliable, and affordable postal system was akin to maintaining a public utility. The postal revolution in the 1840s, born out of the needs of empires, gave birth to stamps, some that actually celebrated empire. With prepaid postage based on weight, rather than distance traveled, communicating across miles remained inexpensive, and the post office shaped American life as it facilitated the interconnectness of people across the country and the world. The need for accessible and inexpensive communications remains even in the digital age. As other federal agencies consider regulations that threaten that affordability, we as citizens need to be active defenders of values that the postal service promotes and maintains today. We must not forget that the federal government subsidized the communication and the circulation of ideas from the earliest days of the nation.

The post office's influence on our daily lives has diminished, and stamps do not serve the same functional role they once did, because of the ubiquity of electronic communications. Fewer letters are mailed requiring fewer stamps, and more bills are paid online than through paper remittance. Most mail delivered to our boxes contains indicia, or a stamp that prints the amount paid, and not a colorful stamp. Even with this reduction in mail volume, the USPS prints nearly twenty-five commemorative stamps each year.[4] Other than holiday-themed stamps affixed to seasonal cards, most Americans no longer see stamp imagery of new commemoratives on their mail, and they don't read about new issues in their daily newspaper. Stamps' power to naturalize historical narratives is changing in the digital era.

While Americans are not seeing stamps as regularly as they once did, interest in stamps and collecting is not dead. In many ways, the Web reinvigorated stamp collecting for philatelists and enthusiasts. Early stamp collectors joined clubs or purchased philatelic publications to find collectors with similar interests to share, buy, and trade stamps. Since the late 1990s, many collectors have traded and sold stamps on auction sites like eBay, and some create websites to share their personal collections, such as *Justine's Stamps* or to create resources for others identifying stamps, such as *1847USA*. Collectors can easily communicate with one another in online forums, email groups, and meetups. The *Crying of Lot 49* will be livestreamed. Followers of the Smithsonian National Postal Museum (NPM) on social media will see stamps and facts related to the images on each stamp in their stream. Finding, researching, organizing, and discussing stamps has never been easier.[5] Using collected stamps to create art or to decorate furniture, in ways that appeared in the pages of *Ladies' Home Journal* in the early 1900s, is also popular. Examples of stamp art can easily be found on Etsy and Pinterest, and the NPM organizes philatelic art programs.

Federal and private institutions of public memory that collect, preserve, and exhibit stamps demonstrate their worth as cultural artifacts. The NPM is a joint venture between the USPS and the Smithsonian Institution, making objects related to postal operations and philately part of our national cultural heritage. University museums are rediscovering their stamp collections and mounting exhibitions to focus on the cultural meanings and designs of stamps. In 2012, the Africana Studies Department at the University of North Carolina, Charlotte, developed *Blacks on Stamp* and in 2016 a museum studies graduate course at Brown University curated *Thousands of Little Colored Windows* at the Jay Hay Library. Visitors to these exhibits are encouraged to look closely and read stamps like documents containing symbols and meaning within each design.[6] Stamps and the process by which the USPOD selected commemorative subjects remain important and under-examined pieces of evidence that can increase our understanding of the construction of American identities in the early twentieth century. Stamps are coded with racial, gendered, and cultural understandings of the time when they were selected, and have many stories to tell. These messages are legible through imagery and design, and historical research done by historians and philatelists who work to keep these little colored bits of paper accessible to nonspecialist audiences. By collecting something originally designed to be functional, stamp collectors in the nineteenth century influenced postal authorities, who printed commemorative stamps and promoted the philatelic hobby that continues today.

In studying and writing about popular collecting practices, I encourage others to look more seriously at collectors and collecting processes to gain a greater appreciation of the history work performed. Objects collected and saved by individuals often land in museum collections to be incorporated into exhibitions and interpreted as primary sources by researchers. Yet collectors of those objects often are viewed as quirky people obsessed with the minutiae of the things they collect. They have not always been invited to share their expertise with museum staff, but this trend is changing. Some museums embrace collectors and other subject enthusiasts as valuable experts with specialized knowledge who can help interpret the material culture found in artifact rooms. Web platforms that facilitate sharing and co-creation of knowledge encourage historians and curators to invite others to share in the processes of saving and interpreting their own history, or to crowdsource descriptions of digitized objects and records posted online. If historians and museum professionals can see collectors as valued and respected members of the historical enterprise, then this type of collaboration ushered in by the Web may seem less radical.

American Commemorative Stamps Issued, 1892–1940

The following list was created from the online philately collection at the Smithsonian National Postal Museum, *Arago: People, Postage, and the Post,* http://arago.si.edu

1892–93	World's Columbian Exposition (16 stamps)
1898	Trans-Mississippi and International Exposition (9 stamps)
1901	Pan-American Exposition (6 stamps)
1904	Louisiana Purchase Exposition (5 stamps)
1907	Jamestown Exposition (3 stamps)
1908	Lincoln Centenary of Birth
1909	Alaska-Yukon-Pacific Exposition
1910	Hudson-Fulton Celebration
1915	Panama-Pacific Exposition (4 stamps)
1919	Victory Stamp
1920	Pilgrim Tercentenary (3 stamps)
1923	Harding Memorial (issued following President Harding's death)
1924	Huguenot-Walloon Tercentenary (3 stamps)
1925	Lexington Concord Sesquicentennial (3 stamps)
	Norse-American Centennial (2 stamps)
1926	Sesquicentennial Exposition (Philadelphia)
	Ericsson Memorial
1926	Battle of White Plains Sesquicentennial

1927 Vermont Sesquicentennial (Green Mountain Boy)
Burgoyne Campaign Sesquicentennial (150th anniversary of the battles of Bennington, Oriskany, Fort Stanwix, and Saratoga)

1928 Valley Forge, Sesquicentennial of Washington's Encampment
International Civil Aeronautics Conference (2 stamps)
Battle of Monmouth Sesquicentennial (Molly Pitcher overprint)
Hawaii Sesquicentennial overprint

1929 George Rogers Clark (150th anniversary of the surrender by the British of Fort Sackville at Vincennes, Indiana)
Electric Light's Golden Jubilee
Sullivan Expedition (Major General John Sullivan's military campaign against the Iroquois)
Battle of Fallen Timbers (135th anniversary of the battle near the Maumee River, Ohio)
Ohio River Canalization (1875–1928)

1930 Massachusetts Bay Colony (300th anniversary)
Carolina-Charleston (260th anniversary of the founding of Carolina Province and the 250th anniversary of the establishment of the city of Charleston, South Carolina)
Braddock's Field (175th anniversary of the Battle of Braddock's Field, Pennsylvania, 1755)
Von Steuben (200th anniversary of the birth of Baron Frederick Wilhelm von Steuben)

1931 Pulaski (Anniversary of General Casmir Pulaski's death at the Battle of Savannah, Georgia, 1779)
Red Cross (50th anniversary of founding of organization)
Yorktown (150th anniversary of the Battle of Yorktown)

1932 Washington Bicentennial (12 stamps)
Olympic Winter Games (Lake Placid, New York)
Arbor Day (60th anniversary)
Olympic Games (Los Angeles, California) (2 stamps)
Three-cent Washington
William Penn (250th anniversary of Penn's 1682 landing)
Daniel Webster (150th anniversary of his birth)

1933 Peace of 1783 (150th anniversary of George Washington's proclamation of peace ending the Revolutionary War)
Century of Progress World's Fair (2 stamps)
National Recovery Act
Byrd Antarctic Expedition
Kosciuszko (150th anniversary Kosciusko's naturalization as an American citizen)

1934 Maryland Tercentenary (anniversary of establishment of the colony of Maryland)
Mothers of America
Wisconsin Tercentenary (anniversary of explorer Jean Nicolet's "discovery" of Wisconsin)
National Parks Year (10 stamps celebrating national parks)

1935	Connecticut Tercentenary (anniversary of charter granted by Charles II)
	California Pacific International Exposition
	Boulder Dam (marked the completion of Boulder, now Hoover, Dam)
	Michigan Centenary (anniversary of statehood)
1936	Texas Centennial (anniversary of Texas Declaration of Independence)
	Rhode Island Tercentenary (anniversary of the first settlement)
	Arkansas Centennial (anniversary of Arkansas statehood)
	Oregon Territory (anniversary of the establishment)
	Susan B. Anthony (16th anniversary of the 19th Amendment)
1936–37	Army and Navy (10 stamps honoring military men)
1937	Ordinance of 1787 Sesquicentennial
	Virginia Dare (350th anniversary of the birth of Virginia Dare)
	Constitution Sesquicentennial
	Territorial (tributes to territories of Hawaii, Alaska, Puerto Rico, and the Virgin Islands) (4 stamps)
1938	Constitution Ratification
	Sweden-Finnish Tercentenary (anniversary of founding of New Sweden, Delaware)
	Northwest Territory Sesquicentennial
	Iowa Territory Centennial
1939	Golden Gate International Exposition
	New York World's Fair Issue
	Washington Inauguration (150th anniversary of Washington's inauguration)
	Baseball Centennial
	Panama Canal (25th anniversary of the opening of the canal)
	Printing Tercentenary (anniversary of printing in colonial America)
	50th anniversary of statehood (North Dakota, South Dakota, Montana, and Washington)
1940	Famous Americans (35 stamps honoring American artists, scientists, educators, authors, poets, composers, and inventors)
	80th anniversary of the Pony Express
	Pan American Union (50th anniversary of the founding of the Pan-American Union)
	50th anniversary of Idaho statehood
	50th anniversary of Wyoming statehood
	400th anniversary of the Coronado Expedition
	National Defense (coincided with the first day of registration for America's first peacetime draft)
	Thirteenth Amendment (75th anniversary)

Notes

Introduction

Epigraph: Thomas Pynchon, *The Crying of Lot 49* (New York: J.B. Lippincott, 1965), 31–32.

1. Pynchon, *The Crying of Lot 49*, 149.

2. Mary H. Lawson, "Philately," in *Arago: People, Postage and the Post* (Washington, DC: National Postal Museum, 2006), http://www.arago.si.edu/index.asp?con=1&cmd=1&mode=1&tid=2027477

3. Jack Child, *Miniature Messages: The Semiotics and Politics of Latin American Postage Stamps* (Durham: Duke University Press, 2008).

4. Russell W. Belk, *Collecting in a Consumer Society* (London: Routledge, 1995); Leah Dilworth, ed., *Acts of Possession: Collecting in America* (New Brunswick, NJ: Rutgers University Press, 2003); Susan M. Pearce, *On Collecting: An Investigation into Collecting in the European Tradition* (London: Routledge, 1995); Susan Stewart, *On Longing: Narratives of the Miniature, the Gigantic, the Souvenir, the Collection* (Baltimore: John Hopkins University Press, 1984).

5. William J. Reed, "The Sun Never Sets in Philately Land," *Philatelic West* 85, no. 2 (February 1927): n.p.

6. Belk, *Collecting in a Consumer Society*; Daniel Horowitz, *The Morality of Spending: Attitudes toward the Consumer Society in America, 1875–1940* (Baltimore: Johns Hopkins University Press, 1985).

7. William Leach, *Land of Desire: Merchants, Power, and the Rise of a New American Culture* (New York: Pantheon Books, 1993).

8. Matthias Judt, Charles McGovern, and Susan Strasser, eds., *Getting and Spending: European and American Consumer Societies in the Twentieth Century* (Washington, DC: German Historical Institute, 1998); Charles McGovern, *Sold American: Consumption and Citizenship, 1890–1945* (Chapel Hill: University of North Carolina Press, 2006); Gary Gerstle, *American Crucible: Race and Nation in the Twentieth Century* (Princeton: Princeton University Press, 2002). See also Lizabeth Cohen, *Making the New Deal:*

Industrial Workers in Chicago, 1919–1939 (Cambridge: Cambridge University Press, 1990).

9. Gerstle, *American Crucible.*

10. Stewart, *On Longing,* 132–51.

11. Marita Sturken, *Tourists of History: Memory, Kitsch, and Consumerism from Oklahoma City to Ground Zero* (Durham: Duke University Press, 2007).

12. Maurice Halbwachs, *On Collective Memory,* trans. Lewis A. Coser (Chicago: University of Chicago Press, 1992); Pierre Nora, "Between Memory and History: Les Lieux de Memoire," *Representations* 26 (Spring 1989): 7–25. Stewart's and Nora's definitions draw upon the concept of a screen memory developed by Sigmund Freud. A screen memory stands in for an original unpleasant personal memory from the past in order to protect an individual as he or she lives in the present. Sigmund Freud, *The Standard Edition of the Complete Psychological Works of Sigmund Freud,* trans. James Strachey (London: Hogarth Press, 1948).

13. John E. Bodnar, *Remaking America: Public Memory, Commemoration, and Patriotism in the Twentieth Century* (Princeton: Princeton University Press, 1992); Kirk Savage, *Standing Soldiers, Kneeling Slaves: Race, War, and Monument in Nineteenth-Century America* (Princeton: Princeton University Press, 1997); Susan A. Crane, ed., *Museums and Memory* (Palo Alto, CA: Stanford University Press, 2000); James E. Young, *The Texture of Memory: Holocaust Memorials and Meaning* (New Haven: Yale University Press, 1993); Kristin Ann Hass, *Carried to the Wall: American Memory and the Vietnam Veterans Memorial* (Berkeley: University of California Press, 1998); John R. Gillis, ed., *Commemorations: The Politics of National Identity* (Princeton: Princeton University Press, 1994); Michael Kammen, *Mystic Chords of Memory: The Transformation of Tradition in American Culture* (New York: Knopf, 1991).

14. Marita Sturken, *Tangled Memories: The Vietnam War, the AIDS Epidemic, and the Politics of Remembering* (Berkeley: University of California Press, 1997); Halbwachs, *On Collective Memory.* I favor Sturken's concept of "cultural memory" here rather than Halbwachs's "collective memory." Certainly, Americans could be categorized as one social group, and stamps contributed to the memories of that group. Stamps, however, live beyond the countries where they are printed and have lives within homes and stamp albums of individuals. The interpretation of stamps also lies "entangled" between history and memory, because they are produced by governments in an official capacity yet are used by collectors and noncollectors in different ways to suit their interests and needs.

15. Tom Stammers, "The Bric-a-Brac of the Old Regime: Collecting and Cultural History in Post-Revolutionary France," *French History* 22 (September 2008): 295–315; Paul A. Gilje, ed., *Wages of Independence: Capitalism in the Early American Republic* (Madison, WI: Madison House, 1997); Pearce, *On Collecting*; Douglas Rigby and Elizabeth Rigby, *Lock, Stock, and Barrel: The Story of Collecting* (Philadelphia: Lippincott, 1949).

16. *Guide to the American Art-Union Print Collection, 1840–1851* (New York: New-York Historical Society, 2002), http://dlib.nyu.edu/eadapp/transform?source=nyhs/artunion.xml&style=nyhs/nyhs.xsl&part=body. Rigby and Rigby, *Lock, Stock, and Barrel,* 277–78.

17. William R. Weeks, *History of the American Numismatic and Archeological Society* (New York: American Numismatic and Archeological Society, 1892); Neil Harris, "American Poster Collecting: A Fitful History," *American Art* 12, no. 1 (Spring 1998): 13–15.

18. Ellen Gruber Garvey, "Dreaming in Commerce: Advertising Trade Card

Scrapbooks," in Dilworth, *Acts of Possession*, 66–85; Susan Tucker, Katherine Ott, and Patricia Buckler, eds., *The Scrapbook in American Life* (Philadelphia: Temple University Press, 2006); and Colleen McDannell, *Material Christianity: Religion and Popular Culture in America* (New Haven: Yale University Press, 1995).

19. Originally published as a column in the *Paris Spectator*, January 4, 1812; collected and translated in Etienne de Jouy, *The Paris Spectator, Or, L'hermite de La Chaussée-d'Antin, Containing Observations Upon Parisian Manners and Customs at the Commencement of the Nineteenth Century*, trans. William Jerdan (Philadelphia: M. Carey, 1816), 96. This article was then republished in "A First Night in Racine," *Knickerbocker*, April 1844, 345; and "Collectors and Collecting," *Chicago Tribune*, November 22, 1868, O3.

20. References to "collecting mania" are easily found in the Library of Congress's database of digitized newspapers, Chronicling America: http://chroniclingamerica.loc.gov/search/pages/results/?date1=1836&sort=date&date2=1922&searchType=basic&state=&rows=20&proxtext=collecting+mania&y=0&x=0&dateFilterType=yearRange&page=3&sort=date. Searching for the term in the Google Books corpus illustrates that the term's usage peaked in the 1880s, http://books.google.com/ngrams/graph?content=mania&year_start=1800&year_end=2000&corpus=15&smoothing=3&share=

21. Elaine S. Abelson, "The Invention of Kleptomania," *Signs* 15, no. 1 (Autumn 1989): 123–43.

22. The Collecting Fiend," *New York Times*, March 20, 1877, 4; and "Stamp Collecting," *Boston Daily Globe*, July 11, 1896, 6; and "Collecting Souls," *Youth's Companion* 94, no. 29 (July 15, 1920): 422. After keyword searching through Proquest newspaper and periodical databases, the term "collecting mania" appears most often—in 40 separate articles—between the 1890s and 1900s. Between 1840 and 1940, the term appears 134 times.

Building Philatelic Communities

Epigraph: "The Prevailing Malady," *New York Times*, July 15, 1895, 7.

1. Stanley M. Bierman, *The World's Greatest Stamp Collectors* (New York: Frederick Fell Publishers, 1981); and "Good as Chest Protectors," *New York Times*, January 23, 1893. Some European collectors preferred the term "timbrology" to refer to stamp collecting. *Timbre* is the French word for stamp. Mauritz Hallgren, *All about Stamps: Their History and the Art of Collecting Them* (New York: Alfred A. Knopf, 1940), 177–85; and Mary H. Lawson, "Philately," *Arago: People, Postage and the Post* (Washington, DC: National Postal Museum, May 16, 2006), http://www.arago.si.edu/index.asp?con=1&cmd=1&mode=1&tid=2027477

2. "The Collecting Mania," *Washington Post* (originally published in *New York Tribune*), March 17, 1889, 12; E. D. Koontz, "'Collectin' Stamps," *Philatelic West and Collectors World* 77, no. 1 (September 1920): 29.

3. Gabriel P. Weisberg et al., *Collecting in the Gilded Age: Art Patronage in Pittsburgh, 1890–1910* (Pittsburgh and Hanover: Frick Art & Historical Center and University Press of New England, 1997), "Collecting Past and Present," *The Nation* 109, no. 2841 (December 13, 1919): 736–77.

4. Kristen Haring, *Ham Radio's Technical Culture* (Cambridge, MA: MIT Press, 2007).

5. An example of that tension is found in the establishment of the Book of the Month Club; see Janice A. Radway, *A Feeling for Books: The Book-of-the-Month Club, Lit-*

erary Taste, and Middle-Class Desire (Chapel Hill: University of North Carolina Press, 1997).

6. Albert R. Rogers, *Roger's American Philatelic Blue Book, Containing a List of Over Two Thousand Stamp Collectors and Dealers, Philatelic Papers and Societies, with Valuable Information Concerning Them, and Seven Hundred Advertisements of Collectors and Dealers* (New York: Albert R. Rogers, 1893). See transcriptions and totals of collectors from *Roger's Blue Book,* https://docs.google.com/spreadsheet/ccc?key=0AswRKpQyX0l4dDNCbHJ2V2RXQzV3NGN4RThKbWpwRFE&usp=sharing

7. Rogers, *Roger's American Philatelic Blue Book.* He placed ads in various stamp publications and sent notices to stamp clubs in the United States and Canada to gather the names in the publications. A handful of individuals listed a business or school address, so it is possible to see the occupations of these collectors. It is unclear whether some of those listed under colleges are students, staff, or professors. Mekeel required payment of one dollar to be listed in his directory, but all of those listed also received free space for an exchange notice where they described what type of stamp varieties they collected. Mekeel, *Mekeel's Stamp Collectors' and Dealers' Address Book,* 138.

8. Work Department, *Godey's Lady's Book* 101, no. 605 (1880): 477. Reported by London Tit-Bits but reprinted in "Costume of Postage Stamp," *Eagle County Blade,* 1905. MacClung Strickler, "To Make a Postage Stamp Collection," *Ladies' Home Journal* 18, no. 4 (1901): 6. In the fad party, stamps were hidden around the house and participants had to find as many stamps as possible until a bell sounded to end the hunt. Bertha A. Law, "A Novel Fad Party," *Ladies' Home Journal* 21, no. 12 (1904): 57.

9. "The Beginning of Philately," *American Philatelist* 33, no. 5 (1919): 161. Other stories referenced included how one woman placed an advertisement in the London *Times* in 1841 seeking canceled stamps to decorate her dressing room. And in 1842, *Punch* poked fun at female collectors who anxiously sought out the queen's head by collecting images of Victoria postage stamps.

10. Due to the subscriptions of services like ProQuest and Readex, it is not possible to share these exact results from these queries of large national and regional and major African American newspapers. Additionally since subscription packages change, the same selection of papers is not available through all institutions with memberships. Numerous regional and local papers are available in the Library of Congress's *Chronicling America* digital newspaper project.

11. Crawford Capen, "Stamp-Collecting: How and What We Learn From It," *St. Nicholas, An Illustrated Magazine for Young Folks,* January 1894; "Stamps to Stick," *Youth's Companion,* March 20, 1919; Russell J. Reed, "Junior Philatelist," *Christian Science Monitor,* August 13, 1910.

12. "The Growing Interest in Philately," *Collectors Club Philatelist* 11, no. 2 (April 19, 1932): 133; H. M. Harvey, "Philatelic Departments," *Mekeel's Weekly Stamp News* 46, no. 46 (November 14, 1932): 564; "Announcing a New Department on Stamps and Stamp Collecting," display ad, *Chicago Daily Tribune,* September 4, 1932; J. C. Salak, "Philately," *Los Angeles Times,* December 16, 1928, sec. L; "The Stamp Album," *Washington Post,* July 23, 1933; "For Stamp Collectors," display ad, *Chicago Daily Tribune,* May 2, 1934; and Frank L. Wilson, *The Philatelic Almanac: The Stamp Collector's Handbook* (New York: H. L. Lindquist, 1936), 107–9.

13. I have not been able to locate any transcripts or recordings of these stamp programs. Powers's programs were broadcast in different stations and markets. It is possible that the programs began because radio stations needed to fill airtime and daytime programming lacked competition in the early days of broadcasting. "Today's

Radio Program," *New York Times*, January 15, 1924, 21; "Today's Radio Program," *New York Times*, February 5, 1924, 17; "Today's Radio Programs," *Chicago Daily Tribune*, January 3, 1924, 6; "Radio Programs," *Washington Post*, March 25, 1924, 16; "Broadcasts Booked for Latter Half of the Week," *New York Times*, August 12, 1928, sec. XX, 16; "Chicago Radio Talks," *Mekeel's Weekly Stamp News* 46, no. 39 (September 26, 1932): 476; "Radio Philately," *Mekeel's Weekly Stamp News* 46, no. 41 (October 10, 1932): 504; and Wilson, *The Philatelic Almanac*, 110–11. For a few sources on the history of commercial radio, see Alice Goldfarb Marquis, "Written on the Wind: The Impact of Radio during the 1930s," *Journal of Contemporary History* 19, no. 3 (July 1984): 385–415; Susan Smulyan, *Selling Radio: The Commercialization of American Broadcasting, 1920–1934* (Washington, DC: Smithsonian Institution Press, 1994); Susan J. Douglas, *Inventing American Broadcasting, 1899–1922* (Baltimore: Johns Hopkins University Press, 1987).

14. Mark A. Swiencicki, "Consuming Brotherhood: Men's Culture, Style and Recreation as Consumer Culture, 1880–1930," *Journal of Social History* 31, no. 4 (Summer 1998): 773–808; Thorstein Veblen, *The Theory of the Leisure Class: An Economic Study of Institutions* (New York: Mentor, 1899); Charles McGovern, *Sold American: Consumption and Citizenship, 1890–1945* (Chapel Hill: University of North Carolina Press, 2006); Daniel Horowitz, *The Morality of Spending: Attitudes toward the Consumer Society in America, 1875–1940* (Baltimore: Johns Hopkins University Press, 1985).

15. Paul Lucier, "The Professional and the Scientist in Nineteenth-Century America," *Isis* 100, no. 4 (December 1, 2009): 699–732; Dorothy Ross, *The Origins of American Social Science* (Cambridge: Cambridge University Press, 1991).

16. Joyce Oldham Appleby, *Telling the Truth about History* (New York: Norton, 1994).

17. "Recent Sales of Postage Stamps," *Chambers's Journal of Popular Literature, Science, and Art* 6 (May 4, 1889): 287–88.

18. Arthur J. Palethorpe, *The Study of Philately* (Bury S. Edmund's, England: Nunn, Christie & Co, 1886), 6; John M. Luff, *What Philately Teaches: A Lecture Delivered before the Section on Philately of the Brooklyn Institute of Arts and Sciences*, February 24, 1899 (New York: n.p., 1915), http://www.gutenberg.org/files/15713/15713-h/15713-h.htm

19. *American Journal of Philately*, 2nd ser., 1 (1888): i; *Northwestern Philatelist: A Monthly Magazine Devoted to the Science of Philately* (Elk Point, SD: J. C. Richard, R. J. Ellis, 1899–1900).

20. Eva Earl, "A Girl's Philatelic Reminiscence," *Pennsylvania Philatelist* 5, no. 3 (February 1894): 207–8.

21. H. A. Talbot, "Communications Report," *American Philatelist and Yearbook of the American Philatelic Association* 12 (1898): 27; "Collectors of Stamps Are Now Scientists," *Pensacola Journal*, February 3, 1907, sec. 2; H. Toelke, "Section of Philately, Brooklyn Institute of Arts and Sciences—an occasional correspondent," *Weekly Philatelic Era*, 14, no. 2 (October 30, 1899): 20; and "Second Exhibition of Postage Stamps by the Section of Philately of the Brooklyn Institute of Arts and Sciences," *Weekly Philatelic Era* 14, no. 14 (December 30, 1899): 118. Even the correspondent from the Brooklyn Institute signed off his contributions to stamp papers with "Yours in Science." "Stamp Collecting Raised to Science," *Washington Post*, June 19, 1925.

22. Theo. F. Cuno, S. B. Bradt, and W. G. Whilden Jr. to The Philatelists of the United States, June 25, 1886, in *Official Circular Number 1*, American Philatelic Association (November 1886): i.

23. Robert H. Wiebe, *The Search for Order, 1877–1920* (New York: Hill and Wang, 1967).

24. American Philatelic Association, *Official Circular Number 1*, 6; S. B. Bradt, O. S. Hellwig, and R. R. Shuman, "National Organization of Philatelists," Announcement (Chicago, April 19, 1886), American Philatelic Society Archives, http://www.stamps.org/Almanac/history1.htm

25. By-laws and constitution published in American Philatelic Association, *Official Circular Number 1* (November 1886): 2–3, 4–8.

26. American Philatelic Association, *Official Circular Number 1*, 6.

27. Charles P. Karuth, *American Philatelist and Yearbook of the American Philatelic Association* 8 (1899): 32–34. Much is said about the "science of philately," yet little is defined within the stamp journals. It seems as if careful study of subject representations on stamps or the specifics about the production of stamps qualify as science.

28. Philatelia appears as the APA's seal on the first *Year Book* from the American Philatelic Association in 1886. Use of Philatelia by other clubs can be found in catalogs such as Rigastamps, Fields-Picklo Catalog of Philatelic Show Seals, Labels, and Souvenirs, May 2005, http://www.cinderellas.info/philexpo/philp-r.htm. For references to the goddess, see Cullen Brown, "Classes to Collect," *Canadian Journal of Philately* 1, no. 1 (June 1893): 15; and American Philatelic Association, *The American Philatelist Year Book* 7, no. 13 (1893): 53.

29. Joshua Charles Taylor, *America as Art* (Washington, DC: Smithsonian Institution Press, 1976), 3–34; and Bailey van Hook, "From the Lyrical to the Epic: Images of Women in American Murals at the Turn of the Century," *Winterthur Portfolio* 26, no. 1 (Spring 1991): 63–80.

30. *Weekly Philatelic Era* 9, no. 10 (1894): 91. Often collectors referred in exchanges to their membership number and organization, perhaps to indicate that they were serious collectors. For example, Anna Lambert, of St. Paul, Minnesota, identified herself a member of the Philatelic Sons of America in an exchange notice she submitted to the *Weekly Philatelic Era*. This identification as a club member may have been more important to a female collector to demonstrate that she was a philatelist and not merely a collector.

31. Gordon H. Crouch, "On Collecting," *American Philatelist* 28, no. 13 (1915): 222.

32. Roy Rosenzweig, *Eight Hours for What We Will: Workers and Leisure in an Industrial City, 1870–1920* (Cambridge: Cambridge University Press, 1985); Swiencicki, "Consuming Brotherhood; and "Stamp Collecting as a Hobby," *Weekly Philatelic Era* 16, no. 28 (1902): 227–28.

33. American Philatelic Association, *List of Members of the American Philatelic Association*, 1889 (Ottawa, IL: American Philatelic Association, 1887); Col. Lector, "Filatelic Figures," *American Philatelist* 39, no. 6 (March 1926): 362; and Edwin Christ, "The Adult Stamp Collector," PhD diss., University of Missouri, Sociology, 1957, 91. Cheryl Ganz, curator of philately at the Smithsonian Institution's National Postal Museum, threatened legal action against the Collectors Club of Chicago because it did not accept female members. It acquiesced and she became a member. Cheryl Ganz, conversation with author, May 25, 2007, Washington, DC.

34. David G. Hackett, "The Prince Hall Masons and the African American Church: The Labors of Grand Master and Bishop James Walker Hood, 1831–1918," *Church History* 69, no. 4 (December 2000): 770–802. I also found that there was a Tuskegee Philatelic Club in 1940 for the issuing of the Booker T. Washington stamp, but it's

unclear to me when the club began. "Tuskegee Philatelic Club Prepares Booklet on Art," *Chicago Defender* (National Edition), January 27, 1940.

35. "For President of the United States Senator Joseph Benson Foraker of Ohio for Vice-President of the United States," *Washington Bee*, June 29, 1907, sec. XXVII, issue 5, 4; "Capital's Negroes Fight White Negro: Black Professor Was Barred from Cyrus Field Adams's Philatelist Society. Race Leaders Are Angry Declare Adams Poses as a White Man and Will Seek His Dismissal from the Treasury," *New York Times*, June 11, 1907, 7; "Washington Letter," *Rising Son*, July 6, 1907, 8.

While African Americans were not welcomed into most philatelic clubs, it is probable that some were familiar with the practices of collecting through philatelic literature. Stamp trading and buying often occurred through the mails and one did not have to identify oneself by race or gender to participate. In philatelic literature, individuals identified as African American are almost completely absent until the 1930s, when they appear in pejorative and cartoonish ways. Examples include G. R. Rankin and Al Pois, "Philatelic Tragedies," *American Philatelist* 43, no. 5 (February 1930): 220; "A Fiji Variety," *Mekeel's Weekly Stamp News* 46, no. 45 (November 7, 1932): 555; and "A Specialist in Turkey," *Mekeel's Weekly Stamp News* 46, no. 47 (November 21, 1932): 580.

36. Bradt, Hellwig, and Shuman, "National Organization of Philatelists."

37. "The Philatelist's Dream," illustration, *American Philatelist and Yearbook of the American Philatelic Association* 20 (1906): n.p.

38. "Rah! For the American Philatelic Association," *American Philatelist* 20 (1906): 57.

39. Kristin L. Hoganson, *Fighting for American Manhood: How Gender Politics Provoked the Spanish-American and Philippine-American Wars* (New Haven: Yale University Press, 1998); and Amy Kaplan and Donald E. Pease, eds., *Cultures of United States Imperialism* (Durham: Duke University Press, 1993).

40. *American Philatelist* 22, no. 1 (1908): 72, 141; John W. Scott, "A Few Lines from the President," *American Philatelist* 31, no. 6 (1917): 86–87; and Max Casper, "All Together for the Good of the A.P.S.," *American Philatelist* 31, no. 9 (February 1, 1918): 134–36.

41. Benedict R. Anderson, *Imagined Communities: Reflections on the Origin and Spread of Nationalism*, rev. ed. (London: Verso, 2006).

42. Edward Denny Bacon, *Catalogue of the Crawford Library of Philatelic Literature at the British Library*, rev. ed. (Fishkill, NY: Printer's Stone, with the British Library, 1991). First printed as a bibliography of James Ludovic's (the Earl of Crawford), personal collection of philatelic literature, the *Crawford Catalogue* has become the best reference guide to early stamp-related publications. An ardent stamp collector in the 1860s while attending Eton, Ludovic lost interest until he encountered stamps at a Sotheby's auction in 1898 that he decided to buy; he then reopened his collection. According to his introduction, the earl sought out literature on stamp collecting and found an abundance of resources, but most were difficult to obtain. He started his own library and increased it substantially when he bought the library of J. K. Tiffany, a philatelic writer from St. Louis, Missouri, who began collecting stamp papers from their earliest days. Eventually, the Earl of Crawford donated this large collection of philatelic literature to the British Museum, where it resides today.

43. Wayne E. Fuller, "The Populists and the Post Office," *Agricultural History* 65, no. 1 (Winter 1991): 1–16; and Jane Kennedy, "Development of Postal Rates: 1845–1955," *Land Economics* 33, no. 2 (May 1957): 93–112.

44. Scott and Company produces the standard catalog for stamps. *Mekeel's Weekly*

Stamp News (Portland, ME: Severn-Wylie-Jewett Co, 1891–1996). *Mekeel's* is still an active publication, but with a different publisher. In 1901, *Philatelic West* changed its name and broadened its focus, including articles about other hobbies. *Philatelic West and Camera News* became the official publication of the following clubs: Nebraska Philatelic Society, Nebraska Camera Club, Kansas Philatelic Society, American Camera Club Exchange, Stamp Collectors Protective Association of America, Boy's Collecting Society, Michigan Camera Arts Association, Pennsylvania Camera Club Exchange, Spanish-American Philatelic Society, International Souvenir Card Exchange, and the Stamp Dealers Protective Association. For listings see *Philatelic West and Camera News* 15 (March 1901): boilerplate. While claiming to have the largest circulation, *West* opened its subscription books for others to count, but the actual numbers are absent. See "Philatelic Advertising," *Philatelic West and Camera News* 18, no. 3 (March 1902): n.p. *Philatelic West* expanded into a general hobby-collecting magazine that became *Hobbies* by the 1930s.

45. Bacon, *Catalogue of the Crawford Library of Philatelic Literature at the British Library*, 770. There is some confusion as to where Baum's paper resides. Neither the American Philatelic Society library nor the library at the National Postal Museum has it available, but it is believed to be in a special collection. Paula Petrik, "The Youngest Fourth Estate: The Novelty Toy Printing Press and Adolescence, 1870–1886," in *Small Worlds: Children and Adolescents in America, 1850–1950*, ed. Elliot West and Paula Petrik (Lawrence: University Press of Kansas, 1992), 127. Young journalists even formed their own society, the National Amateur Press Association, elected officers, and held a conference.

46. *Philatelic Journal of America* (1893): 168.

47. Harry Franklin Kantner, "The Philatelic Writer," *Pennsylvania Philatelist* 2, no. 1 (June 1892): 3; and H. Franklin Kantner, "The Philatelic Publisher's Soliloquy," *Pennsylvania Philatelist* 2, no. 1 (June 1892): 3.

48. H. Franklin Kantner, "Philatelic Journalism," *Pennsylvania Philatelist* 3, no. 3 (February 1893): 49–52"Review of Philatelic Press," *Weekly Philatelic Era* 9, no. 18 (1894): 141; and "Philately in 1895," *Philatelic West and Collectors World* 77, no. 1 (1920): 28. Kantner's use of "young men" indicates that a majority of the publications were headed by men in the late nineteenth century. Few female writers appeared in the journals I reviewed, but some, like Eva Earl, mentioned earlier in these notes, encouraged women to collect and participate in philatelic societies.

49. Lawrence W. Levine, *Highbrow/Lowbrow: The Emergence of Cultural Hierarchy in America* (Cambridge, MA: Harvard University Press, 1988).

50. Kantner, "Philatelic Journalism," 52. For a discussion of nineteenth-century cultural hierarchies see Levine, *Highbrow/Lowbrow.*

51. W. C. Eaton to *American Journal of Philately* editors, May 25, 1894, in *American Journal of Philately* 7 (June 30, 1894): 288; *Philatelic West* (Superior, NE: Brodstone & Wilkinson, 1896–98). The *American Journal of Philately* published minutes from many of these smaller societies. *Quaker City Philatelist* (Philadelphia: Quaker City Philatelic Publishing, 1886–94).

52. Warren H. Colson, "Advertisement," *American Philatelist* 36, no. 4 (1922): 161, 91; and Halgren, *All about Stamps*, 186. I reviewed many journals to discover these patterns, including *American Philatelist*, 1886–98; *American Journal of Philately*, 1888–99; *Pennsylvania Philatelist*, 1891–1900; *Philatelic West*, 1896–98; *Quaker City Philatelist*, 1891–94; *Texan Philatelist*, 1894–98; and *Weekly Philatelic Era*.

53. C. H. Mekeel, *Mekeel's Stamp Collectors' and Dealers' Address Book*, 2nd ed. (St.

Louis: C. H. Mekeel Stamp and Publishing Co., 1891), 8, 10, 24, 42; and J. de Q. Donehoo, *Mekeel's Address Book of Foreign Stamp Collectors and Dealers: Containing over 9000 Names and Addresses from 127 Countries and Colonies, Being the Most Complete Work of the Kind Ever Issued* (St. Louis: C. H. Mekeel, 1897).

54. George J. Remburg, "The Modern Maud Muller," *Philatelic West and Camera News* 15, no. 2 (1901): n.p.

55. Verna Weston Hanway, "Philatelic Complaining," *Philatelic West and Camera News* 29 (1904); "An Aside," *Philatelic West and Collectors World* 63, no. 2 (1914); and Bradford Peck, *The World a Department Store; a Story of Life under a Coöperative System* (Lewiston, ME: B. Peck, 1900), 61.

56. The first column of the Woman-Collectors' Department I found was from September 1905 in the back of the *Philatelic West* portion of the journal when it was printed together with *Camera News*. By December 1906, Alma Appleton took over the column. Verna Weston Hanway, "Woman-Collectors' Department," no title, *Philatelic West and Camera News* 31, no. 1 (September 1905): n.p., and Verna Weston Hanway, "Old Manuscripts," *Philatelic West and Camera News* 32, no. 3 (April 1906): n.p.

57. "The Outbursts of Mr. Phil A. Telic," cartoon, *A.C. Roessler's Stamp News* 97, no. 1 (1917).

58. "Stamp Collecting as a Hobby," 227–28; and Fred J. Melville, *ABC of Stamp Collecting* (London: Drane, 1903).

59. Lewis G. Quackenbush, "The Evolution of the Stamp Album, from Lallier to Mekeel," *Philatelic Journal of America* (reprinted by Earl P. L. Apfelbaum, 1894), available at http://www.apfelbauminc.com/library/evolutionalbum.html

60. For some examples of albums, see the National Postal Museum collection, http://arago.si.edu/index.asp?con=1&cmd=1&mode=1&tid=2040893&

61. Quackenbush, "The Evolution of the Stamp Album, from Lallier to Mekeel"; *The International Postage Stamp Album* (New York: Scott Stamp and Coin Co. Limited, 1894); *The International Postage Stamp Album, Nineteenth Century Edition* (New York: Scott Stamp and Coin Co. Limited, 1912).

62. Verna Weston Hanway, "Firelight Reveries," *Philatelic West and Camera News* 31, no. 2 (November 1905): n.p.

63. "1919 Scott Stamp & Coin Imperial Stamp Album," eBay item accessed August 11, 2009.

64. Susan Stewart, *On Longing: Narratives of the Miniature, the Gigantic, the Souvenir, the Collection* (Baltimore: John Hopkins University Press, 1984).

65. H. R. Habicht, "The Enjoyment of Stamp Collecting," *American Philatelist* 36, no. 4 (1922): 159–61.

66. Hanway, "Firelight Reveries."

67. This particular piece was rescued by Cheryl Ganz, curator of philately at the National Postal Museum, because it had no value at an auction. Someone planned to throw it away but thought Ms. Ganz might enjoy it because of her work.

68. "One Way of Collecting," *Philatelic West and Collectors World* 78, no. 1 (1921): n.p.; and "Work Department," *Godey's Lady's Book* 101, no. 605 (1880): 477; reported by London Tid-Bits but reprinted in "Costume of Postage Stamp," *Eagle County Blade*, 1905, 3.

69. Steven M. Gelber, *Hobbies: Leisure and the Culture of Work in America* (New York: Columbia University Press, 1999), 117–19; Herman Herst, *Nassau Street; a Quarter Century of Stamp Dealing*, vol. 1 (New York: Duell, 1960).

70. "Hobby of Business," *Philatelic West and Collectors World* 79, no. 2 (1922): n.p.

Despite admonitions that stamp papers downplay great finds, articles appeared in periodicals such as N. R. Hoover's that tell the stories of a few "almost unbelievable" lucrative stamp finds. These stories continue especially into the 1930s during the Great Depression. N. R. Hoover, "The Lure of Stamp Collecting," *Philatelic West and Collectors World,* 89, no. 1 (August–November 1930): n.p.

71. Earl, "A Girl's Philatelic Reminiscence," 207–8.

72. Clifford W. Kissinger, "The Fair Sex in Philately," *Pennsylvania Philatelist* 5, no. 2 (January 1894): 172–73.

Learning to Read Stamps

Epigraph: G. M. McCracken, "Poor Mary," *Washington Post,* August 27, 1933, sec. JP, 3.

1. William Leach, *Land of Desire: Merchants, Power, and the Rise of a New American Culture* (New York: Pantheon Books, 1993).

2. Ellen Gruber Garvey, *The Adman in the Parlor: Magazines and the Gendering of Consumer Culture, 1880s to 1910s* (New York: Oxford University Press, 1996); Steven M. Gelber, *Hobbies: Leisure and the Culture of Work in America* (New York: Columbia University Press, 1999); Lisa Jacobson, *Raising Consumers: Children and the American Mass Market in the Early Twentieth Century* (New York: Columbia University Press, 2004).

3. "Antique Stamp Dealer Trade Card Pauline Markham Bufford," eBay, accessed August 16, 2009; "Antique Stamp Dealer Trade Card Pres. Buchanan Bufford," eBay, accessed August 16, 2009.

4. Ethel Ewert Abrahams and Rachel K. Pannabecker, "'Better Choose Me': Addictions to Tobacco, Collecting, and Quilting, 1880–1920," *Uncoverings* 21 (2000): 79–105; "Postage Stamps—Loose Cards," Duke Digital Collections Item, 1880s, http://library.duke.edu/digitalcollections/eaa.D0150/

5. W. Duke Sons & Co, Duke's Postage Stamp Album (New York: W. Duke, Sons and Company, 1889), http://library.duke.edu/digitalcollections/eaa.D0003-01/pg.1/; Abrahams and Pannabecker, "'Better Choose Me'"; John Walter Scott, *The International Postage Stamp Album,* 8th ed. (New York: Scott Stamp and Coin Co. Limited, 1886).

6. Nancy Bowman, "Questionable Beauty: The Dangers and Delights of the Cigarette Industry, 1880–1930," in *Beauty and Business: Commerce, Gender, and Culture in Modern America,* ed. Philip Scranton (New York: Routledge, 2001), 52–86. This advertising tactic, combining stamps and trade cards, may have counteracted criticisms Duke faced for circulating images of "lascivious" women on other card sets. Trade card advertising generally appealed to women, but tobacco cards clearly were meant for male audiences, even if others held onto the cards within a household. It would not be until the 1920s that cigarette companies acknowledged female smokers in their advertising campaigns.

7. John M. Luff, *What Philately Teaches: A Lecture Delivered before the Section on Philately of the Brooklyn Institute of Arts and Sciences,* February 24, 1899 (New York: n.p., 1915), 4–5, http://www.gutenberg.org/files/15713/15713-h/15713-h.htm

8. Article reprinted from December 1888: J. W. Scott, "Stamps of the United States Sanitary Fairs," *American Philatelist* 32, no. 3 (December 1918): 61–63; "History in Stamps," *Chicago Daily Tribune,* October 21, 1894, 42; Crawford Capen, "Stamp-Collecting: How and What We Learn From It," *St. Nicholas, An Illustrated Magazine for Young Folks,* January 1894, 279; and Thomas Pakenham, *The Scramble for Africa: White Man's Conquest of the Dark Continent from 1876 to 1912* (New York: Avon Books, 1992).

9. Jas Lewis Howe, "Postage Stamp Collecting," *Christian Observer*, March 30, 1910, 19.

10. "A Young Collector," photograph, *Christian Science Monitor*, July 24, 1934, 6.

11. H. R. Habicht, "The Enjoyment of Stamp Collecting," *American Philatelist* 36, no. 4 (January 1922): 159–61; Anne Zulioff, "Stamps," *Washington Post*, September 2, 1934, sec. JP, 1.

12. Granville Stanley Hall is probably most notable for his recognition of a need to define the period between childhood and adulthood as distinctive developmentally; he called it "adolescence." Burk was one of Hall's students. Caroline F. Burk, "The Collecting Instinct," *Pedagogical Seminary* 7 (1900): 179–207; G. Stanley Hall and Theodate L. Smith, eds., *Aspects of Child Life and Education* (Boston: Ginn, 1907), vii.

13. Burk, "The Collecting Instinct"; Elizabeth Howe, "Can the Collecting Instinct Be Utilized in Teaching?," *Elementary School Teacher* 6, no. 9 (May 1906): 466–71; Lawrence Augustus Averill, *Psychology for Normal Schools* (Boston: Houghton Mifflin, 1921), 51–57; and William D. Johnston, "The Acquisitive Instinct in Children as an Educational Stimulus," *Science*, new series 54, no. 1409 (December 30, 1921): 662–63. Other studies of collecting habits in youth include E. Leigh Mudge, "Girls' Collections," *Pedagogical Seminary* 25 (1918): 319; and William Estabrook Chancellor, *Our Schools, Their Administration and Supervision* (Boston: D. C. Heath & Co, 1904), 189.

14. M. T. Whitley, "Children's Interest in Collecting," *Journal of Educational Psychology* 20 (1929): 249–61; Paul A. Witty and Harvey C. Lehman, "Further Studies of Children's Interest in Collecting," *Journal of Educational Psychology* 21 (1930): 112–27; Paul A. Witty and Harvey C. Lehman, "Sex Differences: Collecting Interests," *Journal of Educational Psychology* 22 (1931): 221–28; Paul A. Witty and Harvey C. Lehman, "The Collecting Interests of Town Children and Country Children," *Journal of Educational Psychology* 24 (1933): 170–84. Here we read in Witty and Lehmann's prose an unease with perceived differences between rural and urban life, and in their use of the term "American farmer" we do not hear an understanding of how rural African American children collect. Rather, their concern is based on a construction of the "frontiersman," an individualist, who is of European descent, who would not be well socialized for the modern world. Cooperation is valued in the Witty and Lehmann paradigm, and but there is no understanding of farmer cooperatives.

15. R. L. Payne, "How Shall We Keep the Young People Interested in Philately?," *Philatelic West* 7, no. 2 (August 1898): 27–28; "The Public-School Museums of Belgium," *Harper's Weekly*, August 13, 1881, 558; "A Royal Road to Learning," *Chicago Daily Tribune*, August 9, 1885, 20; and "School Stamp Exhibit Shown," *Los Angeles Times*, August 7, 1932, sec. A, 1.

16. Taught by a Stamp," *Chicago Daily Tribune*, August 26, 1894, 27.

17. Mary L. B. Branch, "The Little Stamp-Collector," poem, *St. Nicholas, An Illustrated Magazine for Young Folks* 12, no. 10 (August 1885): 732. This poem was reprinted in *Washington Post*, November 11, 1888.

18. "Lecturers Tell Teachers How to Teach Play," *Washington Post*, July 15, 1934, sec. R, 10.

19. American Institute of Child Life and After School Club of America, *Young Folk's Handbook* (American Institute of Child Life, 1913), 3–4, 73–74, available, https://archive.org/details/youngfolkshandb00lifegoog; and American Institute of Child Life and William Byron Forbush, *Guide Book to Childhood: A Hand Book for Members of the American Institute* (Philadelphia: American Institute of Child Life, 1913).

While the After School Club was established for boys and girls, the AICL's president authored studies on the "boy problem." Stamp collecting was recommended as an indoor winter activity for boys as early as 1901. See William Byron Forbush, *The Boy Problem* (Boston: Pilgrim Press, 1901).

20. Recommended reading for AICL parents included *Sacredness and the Responsibilities of Motherhood*; and *A Better Crop of Boys and Girls*; American Institute of Child Life and Forbush, *Guide Book to Childhood.*

21. A review of the "World Comrades" column appears in "Stamp Collecting as a Method," *Missionary Review of the World* 57 (August 1934): 367. Founder and editor Juliette Mather of the Women's Missionary Union of the Southern Baptist Convention created *World Comrades* in 1922 because no Southern Baptist missionary publications existed for children.

22. David Macleod, *Building Character in the American Boy: The Boy Scouts, YMCA, and Their Forerunners* (Madison: University of Wisconsin Press, 2004); untitled column, *Philatelic West and Collectors World* 75, no. 1 (October–November,1918): 31; "Education from Stamp Collecting," *Philatelic West and Collectors World* 74, no. 1 (May 1, 1918): 44; "Collectors of Dallas," *Philatelic West and Collectors World* 79, no. 2 (September 1922): n.p.; "Boys Start Stamp Club," *Philatelic West and Collectors World* 78, no. 3 (March 31, 1922): n.p.; "Lincoln Y.M.C.A., Lusty Yearling, Will Celebrate," *Chicago Daily Tribune*, October 6, 1929, 17.

23. "J.R. Stout Heads Rotary," *New York Times*, April 3, 1929, 18; Harry E. Gray, "Building Future Collectors," *American Philatelist* 46, no. 3 (December 1932): 165; "Stamp Exhibition Nearing, Boys to Display Washington Issue," *Los Angeles Times*, January 11, 1932, sec. A, 14; "City to Sponsor Stamp Exhibit," *Los Angeles Times*, April 10, 1933, sec. A, 5; "Playgrounds Foster Hobby," *Los Angeles Times*, April 14, 1933, sec. A, 16; Washington Grant, Willard O. Wylie, and Thorn Smith, *How to Deal in Stamps: A Booklet Designed for Those Who Would Like to Engage in a Lucrative and Clean Business*, vol. 5 (Portland, ME: Severn-Wylie-Jewett Co, 1931); Jacques Minkus, "Merchandising of Postage Stamps," *Journal of Retailing* 21, no. 2 (April 1945): 66–71.

24. "Lone Scouts," *New York Times*, November 6, 1926, 16; William Hoffman, "Merit Badge for Stamp Collecting Available to Boy Scouts," *American Philatelist* 44, no. 10 (July 1931): 466; and Prescott Holden Thorp, *Stamp Collecting, Merit Badge Series* (New York: Boy Scouts of America, 1931).

25. "Scouts Have Good Stamp Collections," *Washington Post*, May 20, 1934, sec. A, 9.

26. Thorp, *Stamp Collecting*; Hoffman, "Merit Badge for Stamp Collecting Available to Boy Scouts."

27. Boy Scouts of America, *Handbook for Scoutmasters: A Manual of Leadership* (Boy Scouts of America, 1932), 175–83.

28. Steven M. Gelber, "Free Market Metaphor: The Historical Dynamics of Stamp Collecting," *Comparative Studies in Society and History* 34, no. 4 (October 1992): 742–69.

29. "Scouts Have Good Stamp Collections," 9.

30. David Nasaw, *Going Out: The Rise and Fall of Public Amusements* (Cambridge, MA: Harvard University Press, 1999); Steven Conn, *Museums and American Intellectual Life, 1876–1926* (Chicago: University of Chicago Press, 1998); "These Swift Messengers," advertisement, *New York Times*, October 15, 1926, 21; and "Give Your Boy a Chance to Learn," advertisement, *New York Times*, October 16, 1926, 15.

31. "Stamp Show Drew Him Back," *New York Times*, October 30, 1913, 18; and Fred J. Melville, "Expert Praises Stamp Exhibition," *New York Times*, October 13, 1913, 18.

32. "Stamp Show Drew Him Back."

33. "Postage Stamps Worth $2,000,000 to Be Shown Here," *New York Times*, October 12, 1913, sec. SM, 9.

34. "Boston Exhibition to Contain Stamps Valued at $100,000," *Christian Science Monitor*, March 17, 1923, 4; "Rare Stamps in Morgan Memorial Exhibit," *Hartford Courant*, March 20, 1921, X6.

35. Lawrence W. Levine, *Highbrow/Lowbrow: The Emergence of Cultural Hierarchy in America* (Cambridge, MA: Harvard University Press, 1988).

36. "Solemn, Sad, Sober Stamp Men; Philatelism Is Such a Science," *Chicago Daily Tribune*, August 13, 1911, B6; and "Rare Stamps in Morgan Memorial Exhibit," X6. J. P. Morgan built and donated the Morgan Memorial building to the Athenaeum, which according to the *Christian Science Monitor* would eventually make Hartford one of the greatest art centers in the world. "Boston Exhibition to Contain Stamps Valued at $100,000," 4.

37. "Give Your Boy a Chance to Learn," 15.

38. Joseph F. Kett, *The Pursuit of Knowledge under Difficulties: From Self-Improvement to Adult* (Palo Alto, CA: Stanford University Press, 1994); Janice A. Radway, *A Feeling for Books: The Book-of-the-Month Club, Literary Taste, and Middle-Class Desire* (Chapel Hill: University of North Carolina Press, 1997). One member of the book selection board, Dorothy Canfield Fisher, suggested in her 1907 book, *What Shall We Do Now*, that children could spend their free time collecting and trading stamps or by creating paper snakes using old stamps. Dorothy Canfield Fisher, *What Shall We Do Now? Five Hundred Games and Pastimes* (New York: F. A. Stokes, 1907), 278, available, http://www.gutenberg.org/files/31186/31186-h/31186-h.htm

39. Wilds Dubose, "Stamp as a Hobby," *Los Angeles Times*, November 20, 1932, sec. F, 7.

40. Eunice Fuller Barnard, "New York Sets Out to Capture Culture," *New York Times*, September 23, 1934, sec. SM, 6; and "Jobless Teaching Jobless Who Seek Added Learning," *Christian Science Monitor*, June 17, 1933, 1.

41. Gelber, *Hobbies*; R. A. Stebbins, *Amateurs, Professionals, and Serious Leisure* (Montreal: McGill-Queens University Press, 1992); A. D. Olmstead, "Hobbies and Serious Leisure," *World Leisure and Recreation* 35, no. 1 (1993): 27–32.

42. Kett, *The Pursuit of Knowledge under Difficulties*; Radway, *A Feeling for Books*; and E. F. Sellmansberger, "Philately's Place in American Education," *American Philatelist* 50, no. 12 (September 1937): 674–75.

43. "Americans Spend 4 Billion on Play," *New York Times*, July 29, 1934, sec. N, 2; Earnest Elmo Calkins and Hugh Brotherton, *Care and Feeding of Hobby Horses* (New York: Leisure League of America, 1934), available, http://babel.hathitrust.org/cgi/pt?id=mdp.39015007025383;view=1up;seq=5; Henry Renouf, *Stamp Collecting* (New York: Leisure League of America, 1934); R. H. L., "A Very Open-Faced Letter to the President of the Leisure League," *Chicago Daily Tribune*, June 11, 1934, 14; "Designs for Loafing," *New York Times*, June 3, 1934, sec. BR, 12; and "Wasting Time Busily," *Chicago Daily Tribune* (reprint from *Detroit News*), May 2, 1934, 14.

44. "Hobby King Wars on Boredom," *Los Angeles Times*, June 11, 1934, 5; "Leisure Exhibit May 1," *New York Times*, March 10, 1935, sec. N, 10.

45. Lizabeth Cohen, *Making the New Deal, Industrial Workers in Chicago, 1919–1939* (Cambridge: Cambridge University Press, 1990).

46. Renouf, *Stamp Collecting*.

Federal Participation in Philately

Epigraph: Unknown, "Untitled Poem," *Mekeel's Weekly Stamp News* (reprinted from the *Pittsburgh Leader*) 11, no. 7 (February 17, 1898): 78.

1. Richard R. John, *Spreading the News: The American Postal System from Franklin to Morse* (Cambridge, MA: Harvard University Press, 1998); Wayne E. Fuller, *Morality and the Mail in Nineteenth Century America* (Urbana: University of Illinois Press, 2003).

2. Helen Lefkowitz Horowitz, "Victoria Woodhull, Anthony Comstock, and Conflict over Sex in the United States in the 1870s," *Journal of American History* 87, no. 2 (September 1, 2000): 403–34; Fuller, *Morality and the Mail in Nineteenth Century America*; Marshall Cushing, *Story of Our Post Office: The Greatest Government Department in All Its Phases* (Boston: A.M. Thayer, 1893), can be viewed at http://babel.hathitrust.org/cgi/pt?id=uc2.ark:/13960/t3416w09k;view=1up;seq=7

3. Wayne E. Fuller, "The South and the Rural Free Delivery of Mail," *Journal of Southern History* 25, no. 4 (November 1959): 499–521; Fuller, *Morality and the Mail in Nineteenth Century America*.

4. John, *Spreading the News*; David M. Henkin, *The Postal Age: The Emergence of Modern Communications in Nineteenth-Century America* (Chicago: University of Chicago Press, 2006); Richard B. Kielbowicz, "Postal Subsidies for the Press and the Business of Mass Culture, 1880–1920," *Business History Review* 64, no. 3, "Service Industries" (Autumn 1990): 451–88; Cameron Blevins, "Who Picked Up the Check?," *Historying*, blog, June 27, 2013, http://historying.org/2013/06/27/who-picked-up-the-check/

5. Charles McGovern, *Sold American: Consumption and Citizenship, 1890–1945* (Chapel Hill: University of North Carolina Press, 2006).

6. Alexander T. Haimann and Wade Saadi, "Philately, United States, Classic Period," *Arago: People, Postage and the Post* (National Postal Museum, May 11, 2006), http://www.arago.si.edu/index.asp?con=1&cmd=1&mode=1&tid=2027496; Peter T. Rohrbach and Lowell S. Newman, *American Issue: The U.S. Postage Stamp, 1842–1869* (Washington, DC: Smithsonian Institution Press, 1984). Overall, the USPOD records are very spotty in the late nineteenth century. Archivists from the National Archives note that federal records often are missing significant amounts of paperwork because there were no requirements to keep files indefinitely. Historians at the US Postal Service concur that few stamp-related records exist from that era. Often records were legally destroyed.

7. Henkin, *The Postal Age*; Mary H. Lawson, "Philately in the United States," *Arago: People, Postage and the Post* (National Postal Museum, May 16, 2006), http://www.arago.si.edu/index.asp?con=1&emd=1&mode=1&tid=2035125; "Act of June 8, 1872," ch. 335, 17 Stat L. 305, reproduced in William Mark McKinney, Harold Norton Eldridge, and Edward Thompson Company, Federal Statutes Annotated, vol. 8 (Northport, NY: Edward Thompson Company, 1918), 132.

8. Robert Stockwell Hatcher, "United States Postal Notes," *American Philatelist* 6, no. 11 (November 10, 1892): 185. John Wanamaker began and operated one of the first department stores in the United States, Wanamaker's, in Philadelphia. He forever transformed the retail business and was referred to as the "greatest merchant in America." As postmaster general, he spearheaded postal reform such as the rural

free delivery experiment, which some progressive reformers supported because of its capacity to unify the nation. William Leach argues that Wanamaker's goal was to increase the public's access to goods, subsidized by the government. Since he was a department store merchant, he favored other large-scale retailers, like Sears, Roebuck, and Company's mail-order business. See William Leach, *Land of Desire: Merchants, Power, and the Rise of a New American Culture* (New York: Pantheon Books, 1993), 32–35, 182–84. For Wanamaker's fascination with world's fairs, see Herbert Adams Gibbons, *John Wanamaker* (Port Washington, NY: Kennikat Press, 1971), 153–80; and *United States Post Office Department, Annual Report of the Postmaster-General of the United States for the Fiscal Year Ending June 30, 1892* (Washington, DC: Government Printing Office, 1892), 74.

9. Mekeel was interviewed in "Postage-Stamp Collectors," *New York Times*, September 7, 1890. The government's exhibit included stamped paper, models of postal coaches and mail equipment, photographs, maps, and examples from the Dead Letter Office. The USPOD also operated a working post office where Columbians could be purchased at the fair. Congress appropriated $40,000 for the postal station and an additional $23,000 for transporting the mail to and from the fairgrounds over the course of the Exposition. American Philatelic Association, *Catalogue of the American Philatelic Association's Loan Exhibit of Postage Stamps to the United States Post Office Department at the World's Columbian Exposition Chicago, 1893* (Birmingham, CT: D.H. Bacon and Company, 1893), 3; Albert R. Rogers, "American Philatelic Association's Exhibit of Postage Stamps at the World's Columbian Exposition, Chicago, 1893," *American Philatelist* 7, no 3 (March 10, 1893): 33–35; Memo, "Inventory of Articles turned over to Mr. Tyler," Albert H. Hall, "Letter to Hon. Wilson S. Bissell," in RG 28, Records of the Post Office Department, Office of the Third Assistant Postmaster General (Stamps and Stamped Envelopes) Correspondence, 1847–1907 (Washington, DC: March 2, 1894); United States Post Office Department, *Annual Report of the Postmaster-General of the United States for the Fiscal Year Ending June 30, 1892* (Washington, DC: Government Printing Office, 1892), 75–77.

10. United States Post Office Department, *Annual Report of the Postmaster-General of the United States for the Fiscal Year Ending June 30, 1892*, 75–77.

11. United States Post Office Department, *Annual Report 1892*, 77. For a comparison of budget deficits from 1890 to 1894, see United States Post Office Department, *Annual Report of the Postmaster-General of the United States for the Fiscal Year Ending June 30, 1894* (Washington, DC: Government Printing Office, 1894), 3.

12. United States Post Office Department, *Annual Report, 1894*, 910–1100.

13. Robert W. Rydell, *All the World's a Fair: Visions of Empire at American International Expositions, 1876–1916* (Chicago: University of Chicago Press, 1984), 38–71.

14. Alexander T. Haimann, "Columbian Exposition Issues," *Arago: People, Postage and the Post* (Washington, DC: National Postal Museum, May 16, 2006), http://www.arago.si.edu/index.asp?con=1&cmd=1&mode=1&tid=2027851

15. Joseph F. Courtney, "Our Columbian Issue," *Pennsylvania Philatelist* 3, no. 2 (January 1893): 33; J.P. Glass, "The Effect of the World's Fair on Philately," *Pennsylvania Philatelist* 4, no. 1 (May 1893), 9; and Harry F. Kantner, "Philately's Progress," *Pennsylvania Philatelist* 5, no. 1 (December 1893): 71.

16. "Good as Chest Protectors," *New York Times*, January 23, 1893; E. S. Martin, "This Busy World," *Harper's Weekly*, April 14, 1894.

17. Alexander T. Haimann, "2-cent Landing of Columbus," *Arago: People, Postage and the Post* (Washington, DC: National Postal Museum, May 16, 2006), http://arago.

si.edu/index.asp?con=1&cmd=1&mode=1&tid=2027853; Alexander T. Haimann, "1-cent Columbus in Sight of Land," *Arago: People, Postage and the Post* (Washington, DC: National Postal Museum, May 16, 2006), http://www.arago.si.edu/index.asp?con=1&cmd=1&tid=2027852. Powell was known for his historical paintings in the nineteenth century. Two paintings hang in the US Capitol, *Discovery of the Mississippi* and *Battle of Lake Erie.*

18. Rydell, *All the World's a Fair,* 55–65.

19. Haimann, "2-cent Landing of Columbus."

20. Rydell, *All the World's a Fair*; Alan Trachtenberg, *The Incorporation of America: Culture and Society in the Gilded Age* (New York: Hill and Wang, 1982).

21. "The New Stamps Ridiculed," *New York Times,* January 22, 1893.

22. "The New Stamps Ridiculed"; "Good as Chest Protectors"; from *Chicago Tribune,* reprinted, "The Big Columbian Stamps," *New York Times,* January 14, 1893; Haimann, "Columbian Exposition Issues."

23. Alexander T. Haimann, "1-dollar Queen Isabella Pledging Her Jewels," *Arago: People, Postage and the Post* (Washington, DC: National Postal Museum, May 16, 2006), http://www.arago.si.edu/index.asp?con=1&cmd=1&mode=1&tid=2027864; Alexander T. Haimann, "4-dollar Queen Isabella & Columbus," *Arago: People, Postage and the Post* (Washington, DC: National Postal Museum, May 16, 2006), http://www.arago.si.edu/index.asp?con=1&cmd=1&mode=1&tid=2027866

24. Col. U. M. Bus, "The Columbian Issue Criticised," *Pennsylvania Philatelist* 3, no. 3 (February 1893): 53–54.

25. United States Post Office Department, *Annual Report of the Postmaster-General of the United States for the Fiscal Year Ending June 30, 1892,* xxvi–xxx, 463–73; and United States Post Office Department, *Annual Report of the Postmaster-General of the United States for the Fiscal Year Ending June 30, 1894,* 479–90. The decline in postal revenues for fiscal year 1894 was mostly attributed to economic depression.

26. "Philately's Progress," *Pennsylvania Philatelist* 5, no. 1 (December 1893): 71; A. Pilley, "My Collecting," *Philatelic West* 1 (June 1896): 1.

27. "Revolt of Philatelists," *New York Times,* March 8, 1896, 22; "The SSSS Is Correct," *Philatelic West* 2, no. 3 (September 1896): 12; J. A. Jamesell, "Commemorative Issues," *Philatelic West* 2, no. 3 (September 1896): 11–12; "Another Scheme," *Pennsylvania Philatelist* 6, no. 6 (November 1894): 484. For the San Marino, some philatelists were angered because the republic seemed to favor those ordering large numbers of stamps by sending the stamps in commemorative envelopes (covers) that would be canceled in San Marino.

28. Rydell, *All the World's a Fair,* 105–25.

29. "The S.S.S.S. and the Omaha Stamps," *Mekeel's Weekly Stamp News* 11, no. 13 (March 31, 1898): 148; *American Journal of Philately* 9 (January 1898): opening page; "Omaha Exposition Stamps—Protest of San Francisco Collectors," *American Journal of Philately* (March 1898): 132; "Omaha Stamps at the S.S.S.S.," *American Journal of Philately* (May 1898): 209; reprinted memo from John A. Merritt, Third Assistant Postmaster General, *American Journal of Philately* (September 1898): 374–75; "Protest of the Postage Stamp Collectors," *Mekeel's Weekly Stamp News* 11, no. 7 (February 17, 1898): 78. Letters issued by the Stamp Dealers' Protective Association were also printed in the mainstream press, such as the *Chicago Daily Tribune*; "Trans-Mississippi Stamps Issued in Spite of Criticism," *Washington Post,* August 12, 1934, AM edition, 7; and "This Busy World," *Harper's Weekly* (January 22, 1898): 79.

30. H. Franklin Kantner, "Philatelic Journalism," *Pennsylvania Philatelist* 3, no. 3

(February 1893): 49–52; H. Frank Kantner, "The Philatelic Writer," *Pennsylvania Philatelist* 2, no. 1 (June 1892): 3; H. Frank Kantner, "The Philatelic Publisher's Soliloquy," *Pennsylvania Philatelist* 2, no. 1 (June 1892): 3; and H. Franklin Kantner, "Philatelic Journalism," *Pennsylvania Philatelist* 3, no. 3 (February 1893): 49–52.

31. Jack Child, *Miniature Messages: The Semiotics and Politics of Latin American Postage Stamps* (Durham: Duke University Press, 2008), 45–47.

32. "Another Protest," *Mekeel's Weekly Stamp News* 11, no. 7 (February 17, 1898): 78; Editorial," *Mekeel's Weekly Stamp News* 11, no. 7 (February 17, 1898): 78. See the chapter "Learning to Read Stamps" on the relationship between Scott Stamp and Coin and Duke Cigarette Company. L. G. Dorpat, "A Year of Philately," *Philatelic West and Camera News* 18, no. 1 (January 1902); and E. R. Aldrich, "Notes for U.S. Collectors," *Philatelic West and Camera News* 17, no. 9 (December 1901). This period of world's fair promotions after 1894 also marked the beginning of what has been categorized as the "Bureau Period" in philately because it is marks the time when the Bureau of Engraving and Printing (BEP), the agency responsible for designing the dies for all American money, took on the contract for designing and printing US stamps exclusively through 1940. For more information on the BEP's involvement in stamp production, see United States, *History of the Bureau of Engraving and Printing, 1862–1962*, reprint ed. (New York: Sanford J. Durst, 1978).

33. Missourieness, "The Proposed Omaha Exposition Stamps," *Mekeel's Weekly Stamp News* 11, no. 4 (January 27, 1898): 41–42; "Editorial," 78; "Protest of the Postage Stamp Collectors," 78; N. A. Crawford, "The Progress of Philately," *Philatelic West and Camera News* 32, no. 2 (March 1906): n.p.

34. Amy Kaplan and Donald E. Pease, eds., *Cultures of United States Imperialism* (Durham: Duke University Press, 1993); Gary Gerstle, *American Crucible: Race and Nation in the Twentieth Century* (Princeton: Princeton University Press, 2001).

35. "The S.S.S.S. and the Omaha Stamps," 148–49.

36. United States Post Office Department, *Annual Report of the Postmaster-General of the United States for the Fiscal Year Ending June 30, 1911* (Washington, DC: Government Printing Office, 1911), 272–73; "A U.S. Service for Philatelists," *Mekeel's Weekly Stamp News* 31, no. 6 (February 10, 1917): 51.

37. United States Post Office Department, *Annual Report of the Postmaster-General of the United States for the Fiscal Year Ending June 30, 1901* (Washington, DC: Government Printing Office, 1901); United States Post Office Department, *Annual Report of the Postmaster-General of the United States for the Fiscal Year Ending June 30, 1904* (Washington, DC: Government Printing Office, 1904); Kenneth A. Wood, *Post Dates: A Chronology of Intriguing Events in the Mails and Philately* (Albany, OR: Van Dahl Publications, 1985).

38. Herbert R. Collins, "Postal Museums and Collection," unpaginated (Washington, DC: National Philatelic Collection, 1986), RG 580, Box 9, National Philatelic Collection, National Museum of American History, ca. 1915–91, Smithsonian Institution Archives.

39. Postmaster General William Vilas suggested the establishment of a postal museum in 1887, two years before Wanamaker mentioned the idea. Collins, "Postal Museums and Collection"; Guy W. Green, "A Postal Museum," *Nebraska Philatelist* (March 1890): 3–4; Lawton, "A Postal Service Museum," *Southern Philatelist* 1, no. 9 (June 1890): 95–96; United States Post Office Department, *Annual Report of the Postmaster-General of the United States for the Fiscal Year Ending June 30, 1890* (Washington, DC: Government Printing Office, 1890), 43.

40. Frank Moore, "Not In It," *Golden Star* 4, no. 4 (April 1893): n.p.; Collins, "Postal Museums and Collections."

41. "Post Office Museum," *Washington Philatelist* 6, no. 2 (October 1894): 1–2; United States Post Office Department, *Annual Report of the Postmaster-General of the United States for the Fiscal Year Ending June 30, 1894*, 46–47; and "Uncle Sam Cannot Resist," *Mekeel's Weekly Stamp News* (January 31, 1895): 1.

42. "The Government's Stamp Collection," *Mekeel's Stamp Collector* 1 (July 4, 1904): n.p.; Collins, "Postal Museums and Collection"; A Collector, "Uncle Sam's Collection of Stamps," *Southern Philatelist* (November 1911): 95; "Many Interesting Exhibits in the P.O. Dept. Museum," *Atlanta Constitution*, March 27, 1910, 5. An estimated 75,000–100,000 people visited the museum in 1910.

43. Collins, "Postal Museums and Collection."

44. "The Government Collection," *Mekeel's Weekly Stamp News* (March 27, 1915); "Joseph B. Leavy, "The Govt Philatelist Who Has Achieved Great Success," *Mekeel's Weekly Stamp News* (March 27, 1915): 1; R. Rathburn to Dr. H. A. Davis, April 16, 1917, in "U.S. Government Collection," *American Philatelist* 30, no. 17 (June 1, 1917): 233–34.

45. Leavy served as editor of *American Philatelist* for one year and published articles on stamps from Holland and Belgium. According to *A.C. Roessler's*, before Leavy was hired as philatelist, he was a brewer in Brooklyn "before the anti-hootch amendment became law, but the Government does not hold that against him now." "The U.S. Stamp Section at Museum," *A. C. Roessler's Stamp News* (May 1921): n.p.; "Know Your Fellow Members," *Washington Philatelic Society Newsletter* (October 27, 1940): 27; and Catherine L. Manning, "Philately in the National Museum," *National Philatelic News* (October 15, 1930): 6.

46. The amount of those sales is challenging to determine since all revenue sent directly to the Department for philatelic purposes was included in the "miscellaneous funds" column in the annual reports, which also included money collected from dead letters, from auctioning unclaimed items at post offices, and other sources. Most of the annual reports bury this in their "miscellaneous fund" tables, such as in United States Post Office Department, *Annual Report of the Postmaster-General of the United States for the Fiscal Year Ending June 30, 1912* (Washington, DC: Government Printing Office, 1912), 267; "Publication 100—The United States Postal Service—An American History 1775–2006," 100, available, http://www.usps.com/cpim/ftp/pubs/pub100/welcome.htm

47. "A U.S. Service for Philatelists," *Mekeel's Weekly Stamp News* 31, no. 6 (February 10, 1917): 51; editorial, "Celebrate," *Mekeel's Weekly Stamp News* 35, no. 52 (December 24, 1921): 718; "Philatelic Stamp Agency," *Collectors Club Philatelist* 1, no. 1 (January 1922): 17–18; Guy U. Hardy, "Confessions of a Stamp Collector," *Mekeel's Weekly Stamp News* 36, no. 6 (February 11, 1922): 73; and United States Post Office Department, *Annual Report of the Postmaster-General of the United States for the Fiscal Year Ending June 30, 1922* (Washington, DC: Government Printing Office, 1922), 10. Hays soon left the Harding administration to become the first president of the Motion Picture Producers and Distributors Association, where he established the first set of self-regulatory guidelines for the motion picture industry in an effort to fight censorship that morphed into the Production Code in the 1930s.

48. "Philatelic Stamp Agency," 18. This is an example of what appeared in many philatelic publications. "Philatelic Agency Reports a Profit," *New York Times*, December 17, 1922, 29.

49. One example of such a publication is Frank L. Wilson, *The Philatelic Almanac: The Stamp Collector's Handbook* (New York: H. L. Lindquist, 1936).

50. "Stamp Collectors Buy Now from U.S.," *Philatelic West and Collectors World* 79, no. 2 (September 1922): n.p.; Hardy, "Confessions of a Stamp Collector," 73; "Stamp Collectors Now Making Big Purchases," *Washington Post*, May 8, 1922, 4; "Philatelic Agency Reports a Profit," 29.

51. "Editor's Column," *American Philatelist* 37, no. 5 (February 1924): 271–72.

52. Philip H. Ward Jr., "The Philatelic Stamp Agency," *Mekeel's Weekly Stamp News* 4 (October 4, 1926).

53. Ackerman's comments and a letter from the USPOD are found in *Congressional Record*, House, 68th Congress, 1st Session, LXV, part 6 (April 3, 1924), 5530–31; Ernest R. Ackerman, "In Defense of the Agency," *Mekeel's Weekly Stamp News* 38, no. 8 (May 5, 1924): 251–52. Ackerman wrote that sales could be so high as to fund commercial attachés to promote international trade.

54. The annual reports are useful for gathering numbers of stamp sales conducted through the Philatelic Agency. See United States Post Office Department, *Annual Report of the Postmaster-General of the United States* (Washington, DC: Government Printing Office), annual reports from 1922–1940 and "Philatelic Agency Reports a Profit," 29.

55. United States Post Office Department, *Annual Report of the Postmaster-General of the United States for the Fiscal Year Ending June 30, 1924* (Washington, DC: Government Printing Office, 1924), 6–9. Interestingly, sales from the Philatelic Agency are reported together with "other funds" deposited to the Treasury and not included in the totals of stamp revenues. Other stamped matter included stamped envelopes, postal cards, and newspaper wrappers.

56. Leach, *Land of Desire*, 351; Carroll Hill Wooddy, *The Growth of the Federal Government, 1915–1932, Recent Social Trends in the United States* (New York: McGraw-Hill, 1934), 261–76, 549.

57. "Postal Museum Work Is Pushed by Officials," *Washington Post*, May 26, 1935, 11; "Postal Officials Guests at Banquet of Collectors Club," *Washington Post*, June 9, 1935, 11; "New Postal Museum Opened for Shriners," *Washington Post*, June 16, 1935, 11; "A Place in the Sun," editorial, *Marconi's Monthly Stamp News*, June 1935, 8; United States Post Office Department, *Annual Report of the Postmaster-General of the United States for the Fiscal Year Ending June 30, 1937* (Washington, DC: Government Printing Office, 1937), 56.

Shaping National Identity with Commemoratives in the 1920s and 1930s

Epigraph: Thomas G. Killride, "My Stamps," in Charles J. Phillips, *Stamp Collecting, the King of Hobbies and the Hobby of Kings* (New York: H. L. Lindquist, 1936), 407–8.

1. Jack Child, *Miniature Messages: The Semiotics and Politics of Latin American Postage Stamps* (Durham: Duke University Press, 2008), 47–48. The following articles all appear in Frank L. Wilson, *The Philatelic Almanac: The Stamp Collector's Handbook* (New York: H. L. Lindquist, 1936): George B. Sloane, "A Review of the 1935 Auction Season," 27–28; C. I. Cromwell, "British Colonials in 1935," 31; and Kent B. Stiles, "Major and Minor Varieties of Postage Stamps Issued 1840–1934," 58–60.

2. 31 USC, Section 5114, RS 3576.

3. William J. Reed, "The Sun Never Sets in Philately Land," *Philatelic West* 85, no. 2 (February 1927): n.p.; Killride, "My Stamps."

4. United States Post Office Department, *Annual Report of the Postmaster-General of the United States for the Fiscal Year Ending June 30, 1936* (Washington, DC: Government Printing Office, 1936), 47; Maurice Halbwachs, *On Collective Memory*, trans. Lewis A. Coser (Chicago: University of Chicago Press, 1992); Pierre Nora, "Between Memory and History: Les Lieux de Memoire," *Representations* 26 (Spring 1989): 7–25.

5. John E. Bodnar, *Remaking America: Public Memory, Commemoration, and Patriotism in the Twentieth Century* (Princeton: Princeton University Press, 1992), 13–20, 169–85. Bodnar defines official culture as presenting the past in patriotic ways that emphasize ideals rather than complex realities. Vernacular culture represents many interests of diverse groups that reflect personal experiences in smaller communities.

6. Michael Kammen, *Mystic Chords of Memory: The Transformation of Tradition in American Culture* (New York: Knopf, 1991); Matthew Frye Jacobson, *Whiteness of a Different Color: European Immigrants and the Alchemy of Race* (Cambridge, MA: Harvard University Press, 1998); David R. Roediger, *Working toward Whiteness: How America's Immigrants Became White. The Strange Journey from Ellis Island to the Suburbs* (New York: Basic Books, 2005).

7. Katharina Hering, "'We Are All Makes of History': People and Publics in the Practice of Pennsylvania-German Family History, 1891–1966" (PhD diss., George Mason University, 2009).

8. William B. Rhoads, "The Colonial Revival and American Nationalism," *Journal of the Society of Architectural Historians* 35, no. 4 (December 1976): 239–54; Patricia West, *Domesticating History: The Political Origins of America's House Museums* (Washington, DC: Smithsonian Institution, 1999); Kammen, *Mystic Chords of Memory*.

9. Rhoads, "The Colonial Revival and American Nationalism"; West, *Domesticating History*; Kammen, *Mystic Chords of Memory*; Steven Conn, *Museums and American Intellectual Life, 1876–1926* (Chicago: University of Chicago Press, 1998); Richard Townley, Haines Halsey and Elizabeth Tower, *The Homes of Our Ancestors* (New York: Doubleday, Page, and Company, 1925); Thomas J. Schlereth, *Material Culture Studies in America* (Nashville, TN: American Association for State and Local History, 1982); Karal Ann Marling, *George Washington Slept Here: Colonial Revivals and American Culture, 1876–1986* (Cambridge, MA: Harvard University Press, 1988); Francesca Morgan, *Women and Patriotism in Jim Crow America* (Chapel Hill: University of North Carolina Press, 2005); Hamilton J. G. de Roulhac, "The Ford Museum," *American Historical Review* 36, no. 4 (July 1931): 772–75; Walter Karp, "Greenfield Village," *American Heritage Magazine* 32, no. 1 (December 1980): http://www.americanheritage.com/articles/magazine/ah/1980/1/1980_1_98.shtml; Walter Karp, "Electra Webb and Her American Past," *American Heritage Magazine* 33, no. 3 (May 1982): http://www.americanheritage.com/articles/magazine/ah/1982/3/1982_3_16.shtml; Edward Park, "My Dream and My Hope," *Colonial Williamsburg History*, n.d., http://www.history.org/Foundation/general/introhis.cfm

10. For examples of states planning activities see Benjamin Roland Lewis, *Pageantry and the Pilgrim Tercentenary Celebration (1620–1920) with Sample Pilgrim Pageants, Suggestions for Programs, Bibliographies, Etc., for the State of Utah* (Salt Lake City: University of Utah, 1920), available, from Hathi Trust: http://hdl.handle.net/2027/loc.ark:/13960/t6vx0qb15. For reporting of the events, see Chronicling America, http://chroniclingamerica.loc.gov/search/pages/results/?date1=1836&rows=20&searchType=basic&state=&date2=1922&proxtext=pilgrim+tercentenary&y=0&x=0&dateFilterType=yearRange&page=1&sort=relevance

11. Charles A. Merrill, "Urges Revival of Pilgrims' Faith," *Boston Daily Globe*, December 22, 1920, 1.

12. "Urges Bar on Aliens," *Washington Post*, February 20, 1920, 10.

13. Brody, "Pilgrim Tercentenary Issue." To view an image of the commemorative coin, see http://commons.wikimedia.org/wiki/File:Pilgrim_tercentenary_half_dollar_commemorative_obverse.jpg

14. Editor, "New Issue Notes and Chronicle," *American Philatelist* 34 (January 1921): 150.

15. Jane Kennedy, "Development of Postal Rates: 1845–1955," *Land Economics* 33, no. 2 (May 1957): 96; and Andrew K. Dart, "The History of Postage Rates in the United States since 1863," September 26, 2008 (http://www.akdart.com/postrate.html). First-class postage temporarily increased to three cents from 1917 to 1918 during American involvement in World War I.

16. One effort to circulate the Compact was by the descendants: George Ernest Bowman, *The Mayflower Compact and Its Signers, with Facsimiles and a List of the Mayflower Passengers* (Boston: Massachusetts Society of Mayflower Descendants, 1920): https://archive.org/stream/mayflowercompact00bow#page/n19/mode/2up. The five-cent "Signing of the Compact" stamp is a miniature engraving based on an Edwin White painting from 1858. William Bradford may have been the main figure in this painting, since he is pictured in the US Mint's half-dollar commemorative coin also issued for this anniversary. White specialized in American historical painting, including *Washington Resigning His Commission*, which was commissioned to hang in the Maryland State House. A copy may be seen at http://www.msa.md.gov/msa/speccol/sc1500/sc1545/e_catalog_2002/white.html

17. "Jamestown and Plymouth," *William and Mary Quarterly* 17, no. 4 (April 1909): 305–11. Interestingly, this piece ends with a nod to middle ground by specifically pointing to the "present enlightened North," which condemned the "ruinous" policies of Reconstruction, signaling that there was hope in settling these sectional disputes around the fictional "natural law" of white supremacy—made visible in many cultural articles in after Reconstruction.

18. Alton B. Parker, "The Foundations in Virginia," *William and Mary Quarterly* 1, no. 1 (January 1, 1921): 1–15.

19. "Huguenot-Walloon New Netherland Celebration," Huguenot-Walloon New Netherland Commission, 1624–1924, Program (New York, 1924).

20. Stamp Design Files, National Postal Museum (hereafter cited as Design Files), Stamps #614–616: Ruth Hawes, "Letter to Post Office Department," August 25, 1924; J. D. Riker, "Letter to Post-Master General of the United States," June 18, 1924; Lois D. Williams, "Letter to Post Office Department," July 21, 1924; Irwin Glover, "Letter to James R. Fraser," January 9, 1925; Gisle Bothne, "Letter to Postmaster General Harry S. New," December 10, 1924; Carl G. O. Hansen, "Letter to Mr. Harry S. New," December 10, 1924.

21. Roger Brody, "Huguenot-Walloon Tercentenary Issue," *Arago: People, Postage and the Post* (Washington, DC: National Postal Museum, May 16, 2006), http://www.arago.si.edu/index.asp?con=1&cmd=1&mode=1&tid=2033829&. For plaque text see photo of the monument in Shannon McCann, "Brown on White on Flickr—Photo Sharing!," *When Lost In . . .* , March 19, 2008, http://www.flickr.com/photos/whenlostin/2743408241/in/photostream

22. The Huguenot-Walloon New Netherland Commission and Antonia H. Fro-

endt, *The Huguenot-Walloon Tercentenary* (New York, 1924), available in HathiTrust: http://catalog.hathitrust.org/Record/006829950

23. Representative Kvale, Joint Resolution (H. J. Res. 270), "Authorizing Stamps to Commemorate the 100th Anniversary of the Landing of the First Norse Immigrants, 1924," *Congressional Record*, House, 68th Congress, 1st Session, 65 (May 26, 1924), 9581.

24. April Schultz, "'The Pride of the Race Had Been Touched': The 1925 Norse-American Immigration Centennial and Ethnic Identity," *Journal of American History* 77, no. 4 (March 1991): 1265–95. Whether the Norse sloop carried religious refugees or not was under some debate. One article in the *New York Times* spread those claims in the popular media: E. Armitage McCann, "Uncle Sam Honors His Norse Family," *New York Times*, October 11, 1925. A scholarly article published the same year argued against the assertion that Quakers on the sloop fled Norway because of persecution. As Henry Cadbury argued, the Norwegian government exaggerated the story of fleeing Quakers to slow the rate of Norwegian immigration to the United States in the 1840s. Norwegian officials passed a law granting religious tolerance to all of its residents in 1845. See Henry J. Cadbury, "The Norwegian Quakers of 1825," *Harvard Theological Review* 18, no. 4 (October 1925): 293–319.

25. Joint Resolution (S. J. Res. 133), "Authorizing and Requesting the Postmaster General to Design and Issue a Special Postage Stamp to Commemorate the Arrival in New York on October 9. 1825, of the Sloop Restaurationen, Bearing the First Shipload of Immigrants to the United States from Norway; and in Recognition of the Norse-American Centennial Celebration in 1925," January 3, 1925.

26. Design Files, Stamp #621.

27. Bodnar, *Remaking America*, 55–61; and Schultz, "The Pride of the Race Had Been Touched."

28. Jacobson, *Whiteness of a Different Color*, 91–117. Asians were not legally eligible for citizenship because the federal court system did not define any Asian as white, making them ineligible for naturalization.

29. Ellison DuRant Smith, April 9, 1924 *Congressional Record*, 68th Congress, 1st Session (Washington, DC: Government Printing Office, 1924).

30. Albert H. Vestal, "Coinage of 50-Cent Pieces for Anniversary of Battle of Bennington" (*Congressional Record*, 69th Congress, 2nd session (Washington, DC: Government Printing Office, 1925).

31. A large replica of the bell adorned with electric lights was built near the entrance to the Exposition and considered a highlight for visitors. The bell appeared on the stamp and on a commemorative coin. Read more about the sesquicentennial in the Encyclopedia of Greater Philadelphia, http://philadelphiaencyclopedia.org/archive/sesquicentennial-international-exposition/; Erastus Long Austin, *The Sesqui-Centennial International Exposition: A Record Based on Official Data and Departmental Reports* (Philadelphia: Current Publications, 1929); and Gordon Trotter, "Sesquicentennial Exposition Issue," *Arago: People, Postage and the Post* (Washington, DC: National Postal Museum, November 19, 2007), http://www.arago.si.edu/index.asp?con=1&cmd=1&mode=1&tid=2032940

32. "New Postage Sale Starts Saturday," *Boston Daily Globe*, March 31, 1925, A2; "Throngs at Post Office for Lexington Stamps," *Boston Daily Globe*, April 4, 1925, A3; "Elaborate Program Arranged for Lexington's Celebration," *Christian Science Monitor*, April 9, 1925, 1.

33. Roger Brody, "Lexington-Concord Issue," *Arago: People, Postage and the Post* (Washington, DC: National Postal Museum, May 16, 2006), http://www.arago.si.edu/index.asp?con=1&cmd=1&mode=1&tid=2033846

34. *Proceedings of Lexington Historical Society and Papers Relating to the History of the Town* (Lexington, MA: Lexington Historical Society, 1890), xi–xii, http://www.archive.org/details/proceedingsoflex05lexi

35. The Miriam and Ira D. Wallach Division of Art, Prints and Photographs: Print Collection, New York Public Library, "The battle of Lexington, April 19th. 1775. Plate I," New York Public Library Digital Collections. http://digitalcollections.nypl.org/items/510d47d9-7e71-a3d9-e040-e00a18064a99

36. David Hackett Fischer, *Paul Revere's Ride* (New York: Oxford University Press, 1995). For an excellent close reading of the two-cent stamp with the Amos Doolittle print, see "Why Historical Thinking Matters," interactive presentation, Center for History and New Media, George Mason University, and School of Education, Stanford University, Historical Thinking Matters, available online at http://historicalthinking matters.org/why/

37. Brody, "Lexington-Concord Issue"; Full text is available from the Poetry Foundation, http://www.poetryfoundation.org/poem/175140. Emerson's poem was sung at the dedication of another battle monument on July 4, 1837. These words were thought so moving that they were included in *The Minute Man* statue by French. Bessie Louise Pierce, *Civic Attitudes in American School Textbooks* (Chicago: University of Chicago Press, 1930), 204, https://archive.org/details/civicattitudesin00pierarch

38. Kirk Savage, *Standing Soldiers, Kneeling Slaves: Race, War, and Monument in Nineteenth-Century America* (Princeton: Princeton University Press, 1997), 162–208; Killride, in Phillips, *Stamp Collecting, the King of Hobbies and the Hobby of Kings*, 407–8. Interestingly, Daniel Chester French earned a commemorative stamp of his own when he was included in the Famous American series' artists grouping issued in 1940.

39. For an excellent examination of the culture of Washington's image, see Marling, *George Washington Slept Here.* Weems's claims have never been proven and attempts to debunk this particular myth were published in 1926 during the sesquicentennial. Mason Locke Weems, *A History of the Life and Death, Virtues and Exploits of General George Washington*, Mt Vernon edition (Philadelphia: J.B. Lippincott Company, 1918), 234; James W. Loewen, *Lies across America* (New York: Touchstone, 1999), 340. Some critiques of Washington myths were published by C. W. Woodward, *George Washington, the Image and the Man* (New York: Boni and Liveright, 1926); reviewed by James A. Woodburn, "Review: [untitled]," *American Historical Review* 32, no. 3 (April 1927): 611–14; Lorett Treese, *Valley Forge: Making and Remaking a National Symbol* (University Park: Pennsylvania State University Press, 1995).

40. Malcolm Ganser, "A Valley Forge Postage Stamp," *New York Times*, January 20, 1928, 20; "To Issue Valley Forge Stamp of Washington at Prayer," *New York Times*, May 4, 1928, 2; Harry Carr, "The Lancer," *Los Angeles Times*, May 12, 1928, a1; "Valley Forge Stamp," *Los Angeles Times*, May 27, 1928, b4.

41. Hughes writes about the struggles he encountered as Washington's biographer to discover Washington's human and more complex self that often conflicted with myths of his infallibility. Rupert Hughes, "Pitfalls of the Biographer," *Pacific Historical Review* 2, no. 1 (March 1933): 1–33; "Stamp News: About Our Commemoratives," *Youth's Companion* 102, no. 8 (August 1928): 418.

42. Marling, *George Washington Slept Here*, 1–8. In 1955, a stained-glass window with Washington kneeling was donated anonymously and installed in the Prayer Room next to the rotunda as a reminder of the religious faith of the nation during the Cold War.

43. In 1954, a definitive issue of the Statue of Liberty carried the phrase "In God We Trust" two years before it was adopted as the official motto of the United States. See Steven J. Rod, "8-Cent Statue of Liberty," *Arago: People, Postage and the Post* (Wash-

ington, DC: National Postal Museum, May 16, 2006), http://www.arago.si.edu/index.asp?con=1&cmd=1&tid=2028969

44. "Mrs. Coolidge Lays D.A.R. Stone with Old Washington Trowel," *Atlanta Constitution*, November 25, 1928, 6K.

45. Rod Juell, "2-Cent Washington," *Arago: People, Postage and the Post* (Washington, DC: National Postal Museum, May 16, 2006), http://www.arago.si.edu/index.asp?con=1&cmd=1&mode=1&tid=2033917

46. Daniel J. Kevles, *In the Name of Eugenics: Genetics and the Uses of Human Heredity* (Berkeley: University of California Press, 1985) and Jacobson, *Whiteness of a Different Color.* During a Kosciusko Day celebration in New York City, for example, the mayor referred to Poles as a separate "race." See "5,000 Hear Mayor Praise Kosciusko," *New York Times*, October 16, 1933, 19.

47. Robert H. Clancy, *Congressional Record*, 68th Congress, 1st Session (Washington, DC: Government Printing Office, 1924), 6529–32.

48. "Monuments of Two Polish Heroes to Be Unveiled in Washington May 12," *Atlanta Constitution*, May 11, 1910, 1; "Nation to Honor Polish Patriots," *Chicago Daily Tribune*, May 9, 1910, 6. For stamps that were eventually approved, such as those honoring Thaddeus Kosciuszko (Design Files, Stamp #734), see rejection letters for why petitions were denied for specific years in the stamp's design file.

49. "Savannah Exalts Pulaski's Memory," *New York Times*, October 6, 1929, N1; Telamon Culyer, "Sesqui-Centennial of Georgia's First Clash of Armies," *Atlanta Constitution*, October 6, 1929, J1; "Notable Fete Is Planned to Honor Pulaski," *Washington Post*, October 6, 1929, S5. In Design Files, Stamp #690: Bernice E. Smith, "Letter to Congressman Charles G. Edwards," April 5, 1929; Charles G. Edwards, "Letter to Honorable Walter F. Brown," April 6, 1929; American Consul Central, "Letter to Honorable Secretary of State," September 23, 1930.

50. Design Files, Stamp #690: Bernice E. Smith, "Letter to Congressman Charles G. Edwards," April 5, 1929; Charles G. Edwards, "Letter to Honorable Walter F. Brown," April 6, 1929; American Consul Central, "Letter to Honorable Secretary of State," September 23, 1930.

51. M. A. Van Wagner to Postmaster General, January 2, 1931, Design Files, Stamp #690.

52. Gary B. Nash, *Friends of Liberty: Thomas Jefferson, Tadeusz Kościuszko, and Agrippa Hull: A Tale of Three Patriots, Two Revolutions, and a Tragic Betrayal of Freedom in the New Nation* (New York: Basic Books, 2008), 207–13. Interestingly, Kosciuszko was an amateur artist who sketched Thomas Jefferson. See some examples are in the Smithsonian National Portrait Gallery collections.

53. Senator Royal S. Copeland, "Letter to Postmaster General Harry S. New," April 29, 1926, Design Files, Stamp #734.

54. Design Files, Stamp #734; Copeland to New, April 29, 1926; Senator Couzens (MI), S. J. Res. 248, "Authorizing the Issuance of a Special Postage Stamp in Honor of Brig. Gen. Thaddeus Kosciuszko," *Congressional Record*, 74 (February 6, 1931), 4121. The design file is filled with letters of support coming from individuals, politicians, businessmen, and fraternal organizations. Information Office, Post Office Department, press release, July 22, 1933.

55. "Stamp to Honor Kosciusko," *New York Times*, July 23, 1933, 13; Richard McP. Cabeen, "The Stamp Collector," *Chicago Daily Tribune*, August 13, 1933, D4; "The Stamp Album," *Washington Post*, August 20, 1933, SMA3; editorial, "Honoring Kosciusko," *Hartford Courant*, July 27, 1933.

56. An excellent telling of Kosciuszko's travails and travels can be found in Nash, *Friends of Liberty.*

57. Nash, *Friends of Liberty.* Regarding the stamp, I found some correspondence from 1986 in the design file that asked then-curator of the National Postal Museum where one could find documentary evidence of Kosciuszko's naturalization. The curator said there was no documentary evidence and attached a letter written in 1953 to the director of the Public Library of Newark stating that there was no official "naturalization, but that through his deeds and actions he became an 'American.'" See also Representative Dent (PA), H. J. Res. 771, "Joint Resolution to Confer U.S. Citizenship Upon Thaddeus Kosciusko," *Congressional Record,* 122 (January 21, 1976), 544.

58. Max G. Johl, *The United States Commemorative Stamps of the Twentieth Century* (New York: H. L. Lindquist, 1947), 268–69.

59. The first-day cover stamped in Kosciuszko, Mississippi, reads that he became a citizen by an act of Congress in 1783, perpetuating the myth of naturalization. See "734-11a 5c Kosciuszko, Kosciusko MS, 10/13/33, S, UNKN DESIGNER (Blue Env)," eBay, accessed December 31, 2013.

60. Roediger, *Working toward Whiteness*; Jacobson, *Whiteness of a Different Color,* 1998.

Representing Unity and Equality in New Deal Stamps

Epigraph: A. W. Pfeiffer, "A Postage Stamp," in Charles J. Phillips, *Stamp Collecting, the King of Hobbies and the Hobby of Kings* (New York: H. L. Lindquist, 1936), 407–8.

1. Thomas J. Alexander, "Farley's Follies," *Arago: People, Postage and the Post* (Washington, DC: National Postal Museum), http://www.arago.si.edu/index.asp?con=4&cmd=2&eid=8&slide=toc

2. Patricia West, *Domesticating History: The Political Origins of America's House Museums* (Washington, DC: Smithsonian Institution, 1999).

3. Michael Kammen, *Mystic Chords of Memory: The Transformation of Tradition in American Culture* (New York: Knopf, 1991), 411–73.

4. Patricia Raynor, "New Deal Post Office Murals," *EnRoute* (October–December 1997), http://postalmuseum.si.edu/research/articles-from-enroute/off-the-wall.html; Karal Ann Marling, *Wall-to-Wall America: Post Office Murals in the Great Depression* (Minneapolis: University of Minnesota Press, 1982).

5. Denise D. Meringolo, *Museums, Monuments, and National Parks: Toward a New Genealogy of Public History* (Amherst: University of Massachusetts Press, 2012), 95–105, 153; John E. Bodnar, *Remaking America: Public Memory, Commemoration, and Patriotism in the Twentieth Century* (Princeton: Princeton University Press, 1992), 177–81.

6. Meringolo, *Museums, Monuments, and National Parks,* 123–24.

7. "Wife Says Balked Sea Career Led to Roosevelt's Ship Hobby," *New York Times,* January 13, 1931, 34; "Stamp Collecting vs. Fishing Is Issue in Some Quarters," *Wall Street Journal,* August 3, 1932, 8; "Stamp Collecting Included among Roosevelt Hobbies," *Washington Post,* November 9, 1932, 11; C. W. B. Hurd, "Roosevelt among His Stamps," *New York Times,* September 10, 1933, sec. SM, 17; "Roosevelt Given Cup for Philately Work," *Washington Post,* April 15, 1934, 9; "Philatelic Society Honors Roosevelt," *Washington Post,* December 2, 1934, sec. SO, 11. Interestingly, Herbert Hoover applied for membership to the American Philatelic Society in 1935, something that brought a chuckle to President Roosevelt according to M. Ohlman, "President Roosevelt Talks Stamps," *Mekeel's Weekly Stamp News* (September 2, 1935): 430. FDR's inter-

est in collecting was sparked by his mother's stamp-collecting habit, and his mother gave Franklin her collection.

8. "Collected Stamps as a Boy," *Mekeel's Weekly Stamp News,* January 2, 1933, 9; Philip H. Ward Jr., "The New Administration," *Mekeel's Weekly Stamp News,* March 20, 1933, 135; Lewis Sebring Jr., "President Roosevelt Stamp Collector," *Mekeel's Weekly Stamp News,* March 20, 1933, 133, 143; Jas. Waldo Fawcett, "The Roosevelt Collection," *Mekeel's Weekly Stamp News,* December 18, 1933, 601, 612; Ohlman, "President Roosevelt Talks Stamps," 430.

9. "Roosevelt among His Stamps"; "Philatelic Society Honors Roosevelt"; The Garfield-Perry Stamp Club of Cleveland, Ohio (formed in 1890) awarded FDR the Hanford Cup, but he was not present to receive it: "Roosevelt Given Cup for Philately Work."

10. "Delivering Hope: FDR & Stamps of the Great Depression," exhibition, National Postal Museum, Washington, DC (June 9, 2009–June 6, 2010).

11. Cheryl R. Ganz, "Arago: 5-Cent Yellowstone." *Arago: People, Postage and the Post,* April 7, 2009, http://arago.si.edu/record_165005_img_1.html; "Farley Orders 'Gift Stamps' Sold to Public: Department Gives Promise Incident Will Not Be Repeated," *Washington Post,* February 6, 1935, 1. Apparently once these sheets went on sale in March 1935, value increased far beyond the stamp denominations" "Value of 'Farley Follies' Soars on New Stamp Issue: Collectors Not Happy When Experts Find Color Shades Different in Every Denomination," *Daily Boston Globe,* March 16, 1935, 1.

12. "Stamp Collectors' Mentality Praised: U.S. Official Calls Them High in Intelligence," *Washington Post,* October 21, 1934, A11.

13. The Proclamation of Peace commemorative stamp was very much about celebrating the historic site in Newburgh, New York, that served as George Washington's headquarters in the last year of the Revolutionary War. Washington stayed at Jonathan and Tryntje Hasbrouck's fieldstone farmhouse from April 1782 to August 1783, and this structure became the first publicly owned historic site in 1850. See more at http://nysparks.com/historic-sites/17/history.aspx#sthash.vaOa5HN7.dpuf. The British surrendered at Yorktown in October 1781, and soon after Washington relocated his army to New York state awaiting the final negotiations and agreement that became the Treaty of Paris. Declaring the "Cessation of Hostilities between the United States of America and the King of Great Britain," two years after the surrender was symbolic, and Washington chose the anniversary of the first battle of the war—the Battle of Lexington—to be the day when the war officially ended, April 18, 1783. George Washington, "General Orders," April 17, 1783, Letterbook 7, images 126–27, Library of Congress, Manuscripts Division, http://memory.loc.gov/cgi-bin/ampage?collId=mgw3&fileName=mgw3g/gwpage007.db&recNum=126

14. Clinton B. Eilenberger, "Speech Delivered to American Philatelic Society," *Proceeding of the 49th Annual Convention of the American Philatelic Society,* held August 27–31, 1934, Atlantic City 48, no. 1 (October 1934): 3–6.

15. United States Post Office Department, *Annual Report of the Postmaster-General of the United States for the Fiscal Year Ending June 30, 1934* (Washington, DC: Government Printing Office, 1934).

16. Harvard Sitkoff, *A New Deal for Blacks: The Emergence of Civil Rights as a National Issue* (New York: Oxford University Press, 1978); Arnold T. Hill, "An Emergency Is On!," *Opportunity, Journal of Negro Life* 11, no. 9 (September 1933): 280.

17. Frank Wilson, "To Hon. James I. Farley," September 20, 1933, Design Files, Stamp #732, http://arago.si.edu/index.asp?con=2&cmd=1&id=160708&img=6&pg=1; Third Assistant Postmaster General, "To Frank Wilson," October 2, 1933,

Design Files, Stamp #732, http://arago.si.edu/index.asp?con=2&cmd=1&id=16070 8&img=7&pg=1

18. Mary H. Lawson, "Byrd Antarctic Issue," *Arago: People, Postage and the Post* (National Postal Museum, February 1, 2007), http://www.arago.si.edu/index.asp?c on=1&cmd=1&mode=2&tid=2033020; Max G. Johl, *The United States Commemorative Stamps of the Twentieth Century* (New York: H. L. Lindquist, 1947), 261–66.

19. "Byrd Stamps Explained," *New York Times*, September 27, 1933, 16; "The Stamp Album," *Washington Post*, October 29, 1933, sec. "For the Washington Post Boys and Girls," 4; "Philatelic Notes," *Washington Post*, December 9, 1934, sec. ST, 10; Lawson, "Byrd Antarctic Issue"; Johl, *The United States Commemorative Stamps of the Twentieth Century*, 261–66.

20. Cheryl Ganz, "Amelia Earhart's Solo Transatlantic Mail," National Postal Museum, Object of the Month, May 2007, http://postalmuseum.si.edu/museum/1d_Ear hart_Mail.html; "Amelia's Plane Bears $25,000 of Stamp Fan Mail," *Chicago Daily Tribune*, July 4, 1937, sec. PART 1, 2.

21. "Amelia's Plane Bears $25,000 of Stamp Fan Mail," 2; "Gimbel's to Sell Byrd Stamps," *New York Times*, December 23, 1933, 3.

22. Eilenberger, "Speech Delivered to American Philatelic Society," 5; "Byrd Stamps Explained," 16; "The Stamp Album," 4; "Philatelic Notes," 10; Lawson, "Byrd Antarctic Issue"; Lynn Heildelbaugh, "Antarctic Post Office," National Postal Museum, November 2008, http://www.postalmuseum.si.edu/museum/1d_Antarc tic_PO.html

23. Gordon T. Trotter, "National Parks Year Issue," *Arago: People, Postage, and the Post*, November 27, 2007, http://arago.si.edu/index.asp?con=1&cmd=1&mode=1&t id=2033094

24. "National Parks Commemorative Series Sale Sets Record: Ten Varieties Are Offered in Picked Postoffices and D.C. Most Important Question Settled Is That Place an Issue Honors Is Fitting One for a First-Day Presentation," *Washington Post*, October 21, 1934, A11; United States Post Office Department, *Annual Report of the Postmaster-General of the United States for the Fiscal Year Ending June 30, 1935* (Washington, DC: Government Printing Office, 1935), 44–46.

25. Ethel McClintock Adamson, "Letter to James Farley, Postmaster General," June 22, 1934, Design Files, Stamp #784; Edith H. Hooker, "Letter to the Post Master General," February 6, 1935, Design Files, Stamp #784; Clinton B. Eilenberger, "Memorandum," June 12, 1934, Design Files, Stamp #784; Eilenberger, "Speech Delivered to American Philatelic Society," 4–6.

26. "Nation's History in New Stamps," *New York Times*, February 18, 1923.

27. John Marszalek provides excellent detail surrounding the debates of the army-navy series in "Philatelic Pugilists," in *The Ongoing Civil War New Versions of Old Stories*, ed. Herman Hattaway and Ethan Sepp Rafuse (Columbia: University of Missouri Press, 2004), 127–38.

28. Gordon Trotter, "Army and Navy Issue," *Arago: People, Postage and the Post* (Washington, DC: National Postal Museum, November 27, 2007), http://www.arago.si.edu/index.asp?con=1&cmd=1&mode=1&tid=2033175. Interestingly, the three-cent denominations pictured Union Civil War generals Grant, Sherman, and Sheridan and Admirals Porter and Farragut. Confederate generals Lee and Jackson appeared on the four-cent army stamp, while its naval counterpart featured Admirals Dewey, Sampson, and Schley, who commanded fleets during Spanish-American War battles. The five-cent represented the service academies at Annapolis and West Point. "Write Mr. Farley and Ask Him about the Stamp Issue," *Chicago Defender*, April 10, 1937.

29. Nancy F. Cott, *The Grounding of Modern Feminism* (New Haven: Yale University Press, 1987); and Alma Whitaker, "Sugar and Spice," *Los Angeles Times*, July 6, 1936, A6.

30. Monica Lynn Clements and Patricia Rosser Clements, *Cameos: Classical to Costume* (Atglen, PA: Schiffer Publishing, 1998); James David Draper, *Cameo Appearances* (New Haven: Yale University Press, 2008).

31. A series of definitives that were printed in 1938 featured profiles of presidents whose images were almost all drawn from busts. "Stamp May Bear Anthony Bust by Artist Here," *Washington Post*, July 15, 1936, X6; Gordon T. Trotter, "Susan B. Anthony Issue," *Arago: People, Postage and the Post* (Washington, DC: National Postal Museum, November 27, 2007), http://www.arago.si.edu/index.asp?con=1&cmd=1&mode=1&tid=2033174; *Encyclopedia of United States Stamps and Stamp Collecting*, "Presidential Series (1938)," *Arago: People, Postage and the Post* (Washington, DC: National Postal Museum, May 16, 2006), http://www.arago.si.edu/index.asp?con=1&cmd=1&mode=1&tid=2033221

32. "Women Honor Susan Anthony at District Fete," *Washington Post*, August 27, 1936, X13; Millicent Taylor, "For Our 'Furtherance,'" *Christian Science Monitor*, August 26, 1936, 7; "Women Join to Hail Susan B. Anthony," *New York Times*, August 27, 1936, 23; "Is Anthony Stamp a Commemorative? Philatelists Call NRA Sticker 'Orphan,'" *Christian Science Monitor*, September 15, 1936, 3; C. N. Wood, "Farley Stamps," *Washington Post*, August 9, 1936, B7. In addition to Booker T. Washington, this string of unacceptable candidates for stamps included Ruth, a Catholic baseball player; Capone, an Italian gangster, and Eleanor Holm Jarrett, an Olympic swimmer who was kicked off the team before the 1936 Berlin games for excessive drinking—the worst offender, according to Wood. Jarrett was married to a bandleader and danced on stage with the band, occasionally in her bathing suit. Later she appeared in a few films in the late 1930s.

33. John Pollock, "Letter to James A. Farley, Postmaster General," July 21, 1936, Design Files, Stamp #784; A. W. Bloss, "The Stamp Album," *Los Angeles Times*, October 20, 1940, C4; "Women Honor Susan Anthony At District Fete," X13; Taylor, "For Our 'Furtherance,'" 7; "Women Join to Hail Susan B. Anthony," 23; Cott, *The Grounding of Modern Feminism.*

34. Rodgers, H. J. Res. 153 (House of Representatives, 1935). A stamp was printed in 1948 honoring the "Five Civilized Tribes": http://arago.si.edu/index.asp?con=1&cmd=1&tid=2028812

35. Alexander T. Haimann, "Famous Americans Issue," *Arago: People, Postage and the Post* (National Postal Museum, March 20, 2006), http://www.arago.si.edu/index.asp?con=1&cmd=1&mode=1&tid=2028610

36. "By Way of Suggestion," *Chicago Defender*, May 9, 1925, A10; "How about Us?," *Chicago Defender*, June 7, 1930, 14; and Rod Juell, "1/2-Cent Hale," *Arago: People, Postage and the Post* (Washington, DC: National Postal Museum, May 16, 2006), http://arago.si.edu/flash/?s1=5|sq=nathan%20hale|sf=0. For other petitions, see Design Files, Stamps #873 and #902.

37. N. S. Noble, "The Constitution's Stamp Corner," *Atlanta Constitution*, February 10, 1935, 2K; "Write Mr. Farley and Ask Him about the Stamp Issue," 5; Arthur Whaley, "What about a Stamp?," *Chicago Defender*, December 25, 1937, 16; and Herbert A. Trenchard, "The Booker T. Washington Famous American Stamp (Scott No. 873): The Events and Ceremonies Surrounding Its Issue," *Ceremonial* 4 (n.d.): 8–11. Wright's efforts to publicly celebrate African American freedom did not end with this

stamp but included conceptualizing National Freedom Day. Ethel Valentine to President Franklin D. Roosevelt, January 25, 1938, Design Files, Stamp #902.

38. Louis Harlan, "Booker T. Washington and the Politics of Accommodation," in *Black Leaders of the Twentieth Century*, ed. John Hope Franklin and August Meier (Urbana: University of Illinois Press, 1982), 1–18.

39. Kent B. Stiles, "Releases Honor 35," *New York Times*, July 23, 1939, XX10; "Stamp Victory," *Chicago Defender*, September 16, 1939, 19; "7,000 Celebrate Issuance of Booker T. Washington Postage Stamp in Philly," *Chicago Defender*, October 7, 1939, 19.

40. Booker T. Washington, *Up from Slavery: An Autobiography* (New York: Doubleday, Page, and Company, 1919), 21; Louis R. Harlan, ed., *The Booker T. Washington Papers*, vol. 3 (Urbana: University of Illinois Press, 1974), 538–87; "7,000 Celebrate Issuance of Booker T. Washington Postage Stamp in Philly," 19.

41. "Farley at Tuskegee Same Day 'Booker T.' Stamp Goes on Sale," *Chicago Defender*, January 6, 1940, 12; "Stamps in Educators Group of Famous American Series," *New York Times*, February 8, 1940, 20; and Trenchard, "The Booker T. Washington Famous American Stamp (Scott No. 873)."

42. "3,500 Hear Postmaster Farley at Tuskegee," *Chicago Defender*, April 13, 1940, 9; "Farley Praises 'Mr. B. T.' as 'Negro Moses,'" *Atlanta Constitution*, April 8, 1940, 2; "Farley Opens 'Booker T.' Stamp at Tuskegee," *Chicago Defender*, April 13, 1940, 1; "He Couldn't Hate," *Christian Science Monitor*, April 19, 1940, 22.

43. Bloss, "The Stamp Album," C4; Special, "13TH Amendment Stamp to Be Issued," *Chicago Defender*, October 12, 1940, 4; "President Praises Negroes at Fair," *New York Times*, October 21, 1940, 20; "Emancipation Stamps Are Result of a Long Fight," *Chicago Defender*, October 26, 1940, 1.

44. Robert W. Rydell, *World of Fairs: The Century-of-Progress Expositions* (Chicago: University of Chicago Press, 1993), 157–92.

45. Bloss, "The Stamp Album," C4; "13TH Amendment Stamp to Be Issued," 4; "President Praises Negroes at Fair," 20; "Emancipation Stamps Are Result of a Long Fight," 1.

46. Kirk Savage, *Standing Soldiers, Kneeling Slaves: Race, War, and Monument in Nineteenth-Century America* (Princeton: Princeton University Press, 1997); Rydell, *World of Fairs*, 157–90.

47. Savage, *Standing Soldiers, Kneeling Slaves*, 89–128.

48. "President Praises Negroes at Fair," 20.

49. Sitkoff, *A New Deal for Blacks*; and Executive Order 8802, http://www.archives.gov/historical-docs/todays-doc/index.html?template=print&dod-date=625

50. Derek Attig, "Here Comes the Bookmobile: Public Culture and the Shape of Belonging" (PhD diss., University of Illinois, Urbana-Champaign, 2014).

51. James H. Bruns and Bureau Issues Association, *The Philatelic Truck* (Takoma Park, MD: Bureau Issues Association, 1982), 31–34. Fittingly, the Philatelic Truck parked outside of Wanamaker's original department store in Philadelphia, appearing to be an homage Wanamaker's role in the commemorative stamp program.

52. Bruns, *The Philatelic Truck*; United States Post Office Department, *Annual Report of the Postmaster-General of the United States for the Fiscal Year Ending June 30, 1939* (Washington, DC: Government Printing Office, 1939), 58; United States Post Office Department, *Annual Report of the Postmaster-General of the United States for the Fiscal Year Ending June 30, 1940* (Washington, DC: Government Printing Office, 1940), 53; United States Post Office Department, *Annual Report of the Postmaster-General of the United*

States for the Fiscal Year Ending June 30, 1942 (Washington, DC: Government Printing Office, 1942), 21; and "Philatelic Truck Starts Nation-Wide Tour," *Mekeel's Weekly Stamp News* 53, no. 20 (May 15, 1939): 240.

53. Post Office Department, *A Description of United States Postage Stamps*, Junior Edition (Washington, DC: US Government Printing Office, 1939).

54. Post Office Department, *A Description of United States Postage Stamps.*

55. Post Office Department, *A Description of United States Postage Stamps*, foreword.

56. Bruns and Bureau Issues Association, *The Philatelic Truck*; United States Post Office Department, *Annual Report of the Postmaster-General of the United States for the Fiscal Year Ending June 30, 1939* (Washington, DC: Government Printing Office, 1939), 58; United States Post Office Department, *Annual Report of the Postmaster-General of the United States for the Fiscal Year Ending June 30, 1940* (Washington, DC: Government Printing Office, 1940), 53; United States Post Office Department, *Annual Report of the Postmaster-General of the United States for the Fiscal Year Ending June 30, 1942*, 21; and "Philatelic Truck Starts Nation-Wide Tour," 240.

Afterword

1. Citizens' Stamp Advisory Committee, http://about.usps.com/who-we-are/leadership/stamp-advisory-committee.htm

2. "USPS—Citizens' Stamp Advisory Committee," http://www.usps.com/communications/organization/csac.htm

3. United States Postal Service, "Postal Reorganization," *Publication 100—The United States Postal Service—An American History 1775—2006* (Washington, DC, 2012), http://about.usps.com/publications/pub100/pub100_033.htm#ep1002835

4. Joe Burris, "Age in Which Letters Are Old-Fashioned Takes Toll on Postal Service," *Baltimore Sun*, August 7, 2009, http://www.baltimoresun.com/features/bal-md.pa.lettersaug07,0,5960461.story; "USPS—Citizens' Stamp Advisory Committee."

5. Sandeep Junnarkar, "Stamp Collecting in an E-Mail Age," New York Times Learning Network, January 20, 2005, http://www.nytimes.com/learning/teachers/featured_articles/20050120thursday.html; Justine's Stamps, A Personal Topical Stamp Collection, http://justinestamps.org/; 1847USA is now part of Stamp Smarter, http://www.stampsmarter.com/1847_landing.html. One example of the Postal Museum's social media stream is on Twitter, https://twitter.com/PostalMuseum. Many online forums exist that offer many topics for discussion, such as Stamp Community: http://www.stampcommunity.org/

6. Smithsonian National Postal Museum recently opened the William H. Gross Stamp Gallery in space newly acquired by the museum. The theme of the entire space is "Every Stamp Tells a Story": http://postalmuseum.si.edu/stampgallery/index.html; University of North Carolina, Charlotte, Africana Studies Department, *Blacks on Stamps*, 2012, online exhibition, https://blacksonstamp.omeka.net/; Brown University, students in Steven Lubar's "Museum Collecting and Collections" Fall 2015 course, *Thousands of Little Colored Windows: Brown University's Stamp Collections*, online exhibition, https://library.brown.edu/create/stamps/

References

Primary Sources

Archives and Digital Repositories

American Periodicals Series Online
American Philatelic Society Library
Duke Digital Collections, *Emergence of Advertising in America, 1850–1920.* John W. Hartman Center for Sales, Advertising & Marketing History Duke University Rare Book, Manuscript, and Special Collections Library
eBay
Library of Congress, Prints and Photographs Division
Library of Congress, *Chronicling America: Historic American Newspapers*
National Archives and Records Administration, Records of the Post Office Department, Washington, DC
New York Public Library, Print Collection, digital collections
Proquest Historical Newspapers
Readex America's Historical Newspapers
Smithsonian Institution Archives, Washington, DC
Smithsonian National Postal Museum, National Philatelic Collection and Library, Washington, DC
Smithsonian National Postal Museum, *Arago: People, Postage, and the Post,* digital collections
United States Postal Service Library and Archives, Washington, DC

Serials

A. C. Roessler's Stamp News, 1915–1921
American Journal of Philately, 1888–1898
American Philatelist, 1908–1939

American Philatelist Year Book, 1886–1907
Atlanta Constitution, 1910–1940
Boston Daily Globe, 1920–1940
Chicago Daily Tribune, 1868–1940
Chicago Defender, 1920–1940
Christian Observer, 1910
Christian Science Monitor, 1924–1940
Christian Union, 1880–1900
Collectors Club Philatelist, 1922–1932
Congressional Record, 1890–1940
Current Literature, 1888–1912
Frank Lesley's Popular Monthly, 1879
Godey's Lady's Book, 1870–1892
Harper's Weekly, 1880–1900
Hartford Courant, 1890–1933
Knickerbocker, 1844
Ladies' Home Journal, 1898–1904
Los Angeles Times, 1894–1932
Marconi's Monthly Stamp News, 1935
Mekeel's Weekly Stamp News, 1891–1940
Missionary Review of the World, 1932
The Nation, 1919
National Philatelic News, 1930
Nebraska Philatelist, 1888–1896
New England Magazine, 1896
New York Times, 1880–1940
Oliver Optic's Magazine, Our Boys and Girls, 1872
Pennsylvania Philatelist, 1890–1895
Philadelphia Stamp News, 1910
Philatelic Journal of America, 1893–1904
Philatelic West, 1896–1898
Philatelic West and Camera News, 1898–1906
Philatelic West and Collectors World, 1914–1932
Popular Mechanics, 1930–1940
Rotarian, 1930–1940
St. Nicholas, An Illustrated Magazine for Young Folks, 1875–1894
Southern Philatelist, 1890–1911
Wall Street Journal, 1927–1932
Washington Philatelist, 1890–1895
Washington Philatelic Society, 1935–1940
Washington Post, 1886–1940
Weekly Philatelic Era, 1894–1903
Youth's Companion, 1910–1928

Articles, Books, and Pamphlets

American Institute of Child Life and After School Club of America. *Young Folk's Handbook*. American Institute of Child Life, 1913.

American Institute of Child Life and William Byron Forbush. *Guide Book to Childhood:*

A Hand Book for Members of the American Institute. American Institute of Child Life, 1913.

American Philatelic Association. *Catalogue of the American Philatelic Association's Loan Exhibit of Postage Stamps to the United States Post Office Department at the World's Columbian Exposition Chicago, 1893.* Birmingham, CT: D.H. Bacon and Company, 1893.

American Philatelic Association. *List of Members of the American Philatelic Association 1889.* Ottawa, IL: American Philatelic Association, 1887.

American Philatelic Association. *Official Circular Number 1* (November 1886).

American Philatelic Society. *The Stamp Collecting Hobby.* 1934.

Armstrong, Douglas. *The Boys' Book of Stamp Collecting.* London: Grant Richards, 1913.

Averill, Lawrence Augustus. *Psychology for Normal Schools.* Boston: Houghton Mifflin, 1921.

Bacon, Edward Denny. *Catalogue of the Crawford Library of Philatelic Literature at the British Library.* Fishkill, NY: Printer's Stone in association with the British Library, 1991.

Beecher, Catharine Esther. *A Treatise on Domestic Economy: For the Use of Young Ladies at Home, and at School.* T.H. Webb & Co, 1843.

Bolles, Edwin C. "Collectors and Collecting." Privately printed essay, 1898.

Bradt, S. B., O. S. Hellwig, and R. R. Shuman. "National Organization of Philatelists." Announcement. Chicago, April 19, 1886.

Burk, Caroline F. "The Collecting Instinct." *Pedagogical Seminary* 7 (1900): 179–207.

Butler, Ellis Parker. *The Young Stamp Collector's Own Book.* Indianapolis: Bobbs-Merrill Company, 1933.

Calkins, Earnest Elmo, and Hugh Brotherton. *Care and Feeding of Hobby Horses.* New York: Leisure League of America, 1934.

Chancellor, William Estabrook. *Our Schools, Their Administration and Supervision.* Boston: D. C. Heath & Co, 1904.

Dent, John H. *Joint Resolution to Confer U.S. Citizenship upon Thaddeus Kosciusko,* 1976.

Donehoo, J. de Q. *Mekeel's Address Book of Foreign Stamp Collectors and Dealers: containing over 9000 names and addresses from 127 countries and colonies, being the most complete work of the kind ever issued.* St. Louis: C.H. Mekeel, 1897.

Field, Eugene. *The Poems of Eugene Field.* Scribner, 1919.

Fisher, Dorothy Canfield. *What Shall We Do Now? Five Hundred Games and Pastimes.* New York: F.A. Stokes Company, 1907.

Forbush, William Byron. *The Boy Problem.* Pilgrim Press, 1901.

Grant, Washington, Willard O. Wylie, and Thorn Smith. *How to Deal in Stamps: A Booklet Designed for Those Who Would Like to Engage in a Lucrative and Clean Business.* Portland, ME: Severn-Wylie-Jewett Co, 1931.

Harlan, Louis R. *The Booker T. Washington Papers.* Vol. 3. Urbana: University of Illinois Press, 1974.

Harlow, Alvin F. *Paper Chase: The Amenities of Stamp Collecting.* New York: Henry Holt and Company, 1940.

Herst, Herman. *Nassau Street; a Quarter Century of Stamp Dealing.* Vol. 1. New York: Duell, 1960.

Howe, Elizabeth. "Can the Collecting Instinct Be Utilized in Teaching?" *Elementary School Teacher* 6, no. 9 (May 1906): 466–71.

Huguenot-Walloon New Netherland Commission. *Huguenot-Walloon New Netherland Commission, 1624–1924, Program.* New York, 1924.

Humphrey, N. K. "The Biological Basis of Collecting." *Human Nature* 2, no. 2 (1979): 44–47.

"Jamestown and Plymouth." *William and Mary Quarterly* 17, no. 4 (April 1909): 305–11.

Johnston, William D. "The Acquisitive Instinct in Children as an Educational Stimulus." *Science*, new series 54, no. 1409 (December 30, 1921): 662–63.

Jouy, Etienne de. *The Paris Spectator, Or, L'hermite de la Chaussée-d'Antin, Containing Observations upon Parisian Manners and Customs at the Commencement of the Nineteenth Century*. Translated by William Jerdan. Philadelphia: M. Carey, 1816.

Lodge, Henry Cabot. *Early Memories*. New York: Charles Scribner's Sons, 1913.

Luff, John M. *What Philately Teaches: A Lecture Delivered before the Section on Philately of the Brooklyn Institute of Arts and Sciences, February 24, 1899*. New York: n.p., 1915.

McKinney, William Mark, Harold Norton Eldridge, and Edward Thompson Company. *Federal Statutes Annotated*. Northport, NY: Edward Thompson Company, 1918.

Mekeel, C. H. *Mekeel's Stamp Collectors' and Dealers' Address Book, 2nd edition, Contains over 5000 names and addresses from around the world, advertisements, hundreds of collectors*. St. Louis: C.H. Mekeel Stamp and Publishing Co, 1891.

Melville, Frederick John. *The ABC of Stamp Collecting*. London: Drane, 1903.

Mudge, E. Leigh. "Girls' Collections." *Pedagogical Seminary* 25 (1918): 319.

Nankivell, Edward J. *Stamp Collecting as a Pastime*. Stanley Gibbons Philatelic Handbooks. New York: Stanley Gibbons LTD, 1902.

National Recreation Association. *The Leisure Hours of 5,000 People; a Report of a Study of Leisure Time Activities and Desires*. New York: National Recreation Association, 1934.

Palethorpe, Arthur J. *The Study of Philately*. Bury St. Edmund's, England: Nunn, Christie & Co, 1886.

Phillips, Stanley. *The Fascination of Stamp Collecting*. London: Stanley Gibbons, 1919.

Powell, Aaron Macy, American Purity Alliance, and American Purity Alliance. *The National Purity Congress, Its Papers, Addresses, Portraits*. American Purity Alliance, 1896.

Proceedings of Lexington Historical Society and Papers Relating to the History of the Town. Lexington, MA: Lexington Historical Society, 1890.

"Recent Sales of Postage Stamps." *Chambers's Journal of Popular Literature, Science, and Art* 6 (May 4, 1889): 287–88.

Renouf, Henry. *Stamp Collecting*. New York: Leisure League of America, 1934.

Rigastamps. *Fields-Picklo Catalog of Philatelic Show Seals, Labels, and Souvenirs*. May 2005.

Rogers, Albert R. *Roger's American Philatelic Blue Book, Containing a List of Over Two Thousand Stamp Collectors and Dealers, Philatelic Papers and Societies, with Valuable Information Concerning Them, and Seven Hundred Advertisements of Collectors and Dealers*. New York: Albert R. Rogers, 1893.

A Stamp Collector's Souvenir. St. Louis: C.H. Mekeel Stamp and Publishing Co, 1893.

Thorp, Prescott Holden. *Stamp Collecting*. New York: Boy Scouts of America, 1931.

United States Department of the Treasury. *Laws of the United States Relating to Loans and the Currency, Since 1860*. Washington, DC: Government Printing Office, 1878.

United States Post Office Department. *Annual Report of the Postmaster-General of the United States*. Washington, DC: Government Printing Office, 1890–1944.

United States Post Office Department. Division of Stamps. *A Description of United States Postage Stamps: Historical and Commemorative Issues from 1893–1938*. Washington, DC: Government Print Office, 1939.

Washington, Booker T. *Up from Slavery: An Autobiography*. New York: Doubleday, Page, and Company, 1919.

Whitley, M. T. "Children's Interest in Collecting." *Journal of Educational Psychology* 20 (1929): 249–61.

Wierenga, Theron. *Postal Laws and Regulations of the United States of America 1847*. Holland, MI: n.p., 1980.

Wilson, Frank L. *The Philatelic Almanac: The Stamp Collector's Handbook*. New York: H.L. Lindquist, 1936.

Witty, Paul A., and Harvey C. Lehman. "The Collecting Interests of Town Children and Country Children." *Journal of Educational Psychology* 24 (1933): 170–84.

Witty, Paul A., and Harvey C. Lehman. "Further Studies of Children's Interest in Collecting." *Journal of Educational Psychology* 21 (1930): 112–27.

Witty, Paul A., and Harvey C. Lehman. "The Present Status of the Tendency to Collect and Hoard." *Psychological Review* 34 (1927): 48–56.

Witty, Paul A., and Harvey C. Lehman. "Sex Differences: Collecting Interests." *Journal of Educational Psychology* 22 (1931): 221–28.

Wylie, Willard O. *The Charm of Stamp Collecting*. Portland, ME: Severn-Wylie-Jewett Co, 1915.

Yoxall, J. H. *The ABC about Collecting*. Vol. 2. London: S. Paul, 1910.

Yoxall, J. H. *More about Collecting*. London: S. Paul, 1913.

Secondary Sources

Articles

Abelson, Elaine S. "The Invention of Kleptomania." *Signs* 15, no. 1 (Autumn 1989): 123–43.

Abrahams, Ethel Ewert, and Rachel K. Pannabecker. "'Better Choose Me': Addictions to Tobacco, Collecting, and Quilting, 1880–1920." *Uncoverings* 21 (2000): 79–105.

Breckenridge, Carol A. "The Aesthetics and Politics of Colonial Collecting: India at World Fairs." *Comparative Studies in Society and History* 31, no. 2 (April 1989): 195–216.

Briggs, Michael. "The Story of Stanley Gibbons." *Gibbons Stamp Monthly*, July 2006.

Buten, Harry M. "The Philosophy of Collecting." *National Philatelic Museum* 5, no. 1 (1953): 7–16.

Cadbury, Henry J. "The Norwegian Quakers of 1825." *Harvard Theological Review* 18, no. 4 (October 1925): 293–319.

Carpenter, Daniel P. "State Building through Reputation Building: Coalitions of Esteem and Program Innovation in the National Postal System, 1883–1913." *Studies in American Political Development* 14 (Fall 2000): 121–55.

Case, Donald O. "Serial Collecting as Leisure, and Coin Collecting in Particular." *Library Trends* 57, no. 4 (2009): 729–52.

Cusack, Igor. "Nationalism and the Colonial Imprint: The Stamps of Portugal and Lusophone Africa and Asia." *Nations and Nationalism* 11, no. 4 (October 2005): 591–612.

Dotson, Floyd. "Patterns of Voluntary Association among Urban Working-Class Families." *American Sociological Review* 16, no. 5 (October 1951): 687–93.

Fuller, Wayne E. "The Populists and the Post Office." *Agricultural History* 65, no. 1 (Winter 1991): 1–16.

Fuller, Wayne E. "The South and the Rural Free Delivery of Mail." *Journal of Southern History* 25, no. 4 (November 1959): 499–521.

Gatchell, L. B. "Philosophy of Collecting." *National Philatelic Museum* 5, no. 1 (1953): 35, 103.

Gelber, Steven M. "Free Market Metaphor: The Historical Dynamics of Stamp Collecting." *Comparative Studies in Society and History* 34, no. 4 (October 1992): 742–69.

Gelber, Steven M. "A Job You Can't Lose: Work and Hobbies in the Great Depression." *Journal of Social History* 24, no. 4 (Summer 1991): 741–66.

Glassberg, David. "Public History and the Study of Memory." *Public Historian* 18, no. 2 (Spring 1996): 7–23.

Goy, Naidene. "Pen Pals in Foreign Lands." *English Journal* 37, no. 6 (June 1948): 320–21.

Grant, Jonathan. "The Socialist Construction of Philately in the Early Soviet Era." *Comparative Studies in Society and History* 37, no. 3 (July 1995): 476–93.

Grier, Katherine C. *Culture & Comfort: Parlor Making and Middle-Class Identity, 1850–1930.* Washington, DC: Smithsonian Institution Press, 1997.

Guglielmo, Thomas A. "Fighting for Caucasian Rights: Mexicans, Mexican Americans, and the Transnational Struggle for Civil Rights in World War II Texas." *Journal of American History* 92, no. 4 (March 2006): 1212–37.

Gura, Philip F. "How I Met and Dated Miss Emily Dickinson: An Adventure on eBay." *Common-Place* 4, no. 2 (January 2004). http://common-place.org/book/how-i-met-and-dated-miss-emily-dickinson-an-adventure-on-ebay/

Hackett, David G. "The Prince Hall Masons and the African American Church: The Labors of Grand Master and Bishop James Walker Hood, 1831–1918." *Church History* 69, no. 4 (December 2000): 770–802.

Harbert, Earl N. "Review of Dorothy Canfield Fisher: A Biography by Ida H. Washington." *New England Quarterly* 56, no. 2 (June 1983): 309–11.

Harris, Neil. "American Poster Collecting: A Fitful History." *American Art* 12, no. 1 (Spring 1998): 10–39.

Hastie, Amelie. "History in Miniature: Colleen Moore's Dollhouse and Historical Recollection." *Camera Obscura* 16, no. 3 (2001): 113–57.

Hoganson, Kristin L. "Cosmopolitan Domesticity: Importing the American Dream, 1865–1920." *American Historical Review* 107, no. 1 (February 2002): 55–83.

Hook, Bailey van. "From the Lyrical to the Epic: Images of Women in American Murals at the Turn of the Century." *Winterthur Portfolio* 26, no. 1 (Spring 1991): 63–80.

Horowitz, Helen Lefkowitz. "Victoria Woodhull, Anthony Comstock, and Conflict over Sex in the United States in the 1870s." *Journal of American History* 87, no. 2 (September 1, 2000): 403–34.

Izenman, Alan J., and Charles J. Sommer. "Philatelic Mixtures and Multimodal Densities." *Journal of the American Statistical Association* 83, no. 404 (December 1, 1988): 941–53.

Karp, Walter. "Electra Webb and Her American Past." *American Heritage Magazine* 33, no. 3 (May 1982): online archives.

Karp, Walter. "A Fascination with the Common Place." *American Heritage Magazine* 37, no. 5 (September 1986): online archives.

Karp, Walter. "Greenfield Village." *American Heritage Magazine* 32, no. 1 (December 1980): online archives.

Kennedy, Jane. "Development of Postal Rates: 1845–1955." *Land Economics* 33, no. 2 (May 1957): 93–112.

Kielbowicz, Richard B. "Postal Subsidies for the Press and the Business of Mass Culture, 1880–1920." *Business History Review* 64, no. 3 (Autumn 1990): 451–88.

Klein, Kerwin Lee. "On the Emergence of Memory in Historical Discourse." *Representations* 69 (Winter 2000): 27–150.

Komarovsky, Mirra. "The Voluntary Associations of Urban Dwellers." *American Sociological Review* 11, no. 6 (December 1946): 686–98.

Lankton, Larry. "Something Old, Something New: The Reexhibition of the Henry Ford Museum's Hall of Technology." *Technology and Culture* 21, no. 4 (October 1980): 594–613.

Lindgren, James M. "'Virginia Needs Living Heroes': Historic Preservation in the Progressive Era." *Public Historian* 13, no. 1 (Winter 1991): 9–24.

Lucier, Paul. "The Professional and the Scientist in Nineteenth-Century America." *Isis* 100, no. 4 (December 1, 2009): 699–732.

Mackay, James A. "The Universal Postal Union Collection of Postage Stamps." *British Museum Quarterly* 31, nos. 1–2 (October 1, 1966): 4–8.

Marquis, Alice Goldfarb. "Written on the Wind: The Impact of Radio during the 1930s." *Journal of Contemporary History* 19, no. 3 (July 1984): 385–415.

Martin, Ann Smart. "Material Things and Cultural Meanings: Notes on the Study of Early American Material Culture." *William and Mary Quarterly* 53, no. 1 (January 1996): 5–12.

Mather, William G. "Income and Social Participation." *American Sociological Review* 6, no. 3 (June 1941): 380–83.

McCarthy, Molly. "Consuming History?" *Common-Place* 1, no. 2 (January 2001). http://common-place.org/book/consuming-history/

Melchionne, Kevin. "Collecting as an Art." *Philosophy and Literature* 23, no. 1 (April 1999): 148–56.

Nora, Pierre. "Between Memory and History: Les Lieux de Memoire." *Representations* 26 (Spring 1989): 7–25.

Nuessel, Frank, and Caterina Cicogna. "Postage Stamps as Pedagogical Instruments in the Italian Curriculum." *Italica* 69, no. 2 (Summer 1992): 210–27.

Nygren, Edward J. "The Almighty Dollar: Money as a Theme in American Painting." *Winterthur Portfolio* 23, nos. 2–3 (Summer–Autumn 1988): 129–50.

Olmstead, A. D. "Hobbies and Serious Leisure." *World Leisure and Recreation* 35, no. 1 (1993): 27–32.

O'Malley, Michael. "Specie and Species: Race and the Money Question in Nineteenth-Century America." *American Historical Review* 99, no. 2 (April 1994): 369–95.

Park, Edward. "My Dream and My Hope." *Colonial Williamsburg*, website. http://www.history.org/Foundation/general/introhis.cfm

Parker, Alton B. "The Foundations in Virginia." *William and Mary Quarterly* 1, no. 1 (January 1, 1921): 1–15.

Payne, Raymond. "An Approach to the Study of Relative Prestige of Formal Organizations." *Social Forces* 32, no. 3 (March 1954): 244–47.

Priest, George L. "The History of the Postal Monopoly in the United States." *Journal of Law and Economics* 18, no. 1 (April 1975): 33–80.

Reid, Donald M. "The Symbolism of Postage Stamps: A Source for the Historian." *Journal of Contemporary History* 19, no. 2 (April 1984): 223–49.

Raynor, Patricia. "New Deal Post Office Murals." *EnRoute*, December 1997. http://postalmuseum.si.edu/research/articles-from-enroute/off-the-wall.html

Rhoads, William B. "The Colonial Revival and American Nationalism." *Journal of the Society of Architectural Historians* 35, no. 4 (December 1976): 239–54.

Roulhac, Hamilton J. G. de. "The Ford Museum." *American Historical Review* 36, no. 4 (July 1931): 772–75.

Savage, Kirk. "Molding Emancipation: John Quincy Adams Ward's 'The Freedman' and the Meaning of the Civil War." *Art Institute of Chicago Museum Studies* 27, no. 1 (2001): 26–101.

Schnitzel, Paul. "A Note on the Philatelic Demand for Postage Stamps." *Southern Economic Journal* 45, no. 4 (April 1979): 1261–65.

Schultz, April. "'The Pride of the Race Had Been Touched': The 1925 Norse-American Immigration Centennial and Ethnic Identity." *Journal of American History* 77, no. 4 (March 1991): 1265–95.

Schwartz, Barry, and Howard Schuman. "History, Commemoration, and Belief: Abraham Lincoln in American Memory, 1945–2001." *American Sociological Review* 70, no. 2 (April 2005): 183–203.

Stammers, Tom. "The Bric-a-Brac of the Old Regime: Collecting and Cultural History in Post-Revolutionary France." *French History* 22 (September 2008): 295–315.

Swiencicki, Mark A. "Consuming Brotherhood: Men's Culture, Style and Recreation as Consumer Culture, 1880–1930." *Journal of Social History* 31, no. 4 (Summer 1998): 773–808.

Thelen, David. "Memory and American History." *Journal of American History* 75, no. 4 (March 1989): 1117–29.

Trenchard, Herbert A. "The Booker T. Washington Famous American Stamp (Scott No. 873): The Events and Ceremonies Surrounding Its Issue." *Ceremonial* 4 (n.d.): 8–11.

Walker, Frederick. "My Philosophy of Collecting." *National Philatelic Museum* 5, no. 1 (1953): 31–32.

Whiting, Cécile. "Trompe L'œil Painting and the Counterfeit Civil War." *Art Bulletin* 79, no. 2 (June 1, 1997): 251–68.

Winter, Jay. "The Memory Boom in Contemporary Historical Studies." *Raritan* 21, no. 1 (Summer 2001): 52–66.

Woodburn, James A. "Review." *American Historical Review* 32, no. 3 (April 1927): 611–14.

Wosh, Peter J. "Going Postal." *American Archivist* 61, no. 1 (April 1, 1998): 220–39.

Books, Dissertations, Theses

Alejandro, Reynaldo. *Classic Menu Design: From the Collection of the New York Public Library.* Glen Cove, NY: PBC International, 1988.

Altman, Dennis. *Paper Ambassadors: The Politics of Stamps.* North Ryde, NSW, Australia: Angus & Robertson, 1991.

Anderson, Benedict R. *Imagined Communities: Reflections on the Origin and Spread of Nationalism.* Revised ed. London: Verso, 2006.

Appadurai, Arjun. *Modernity at Large: Cultural Dimensions of Globalization.* Minneapolis: University of Minnesota Press, 1996.

Appleby, Joyce Oldham. *Telling the Truth about History.* New York: Norton, 1994.

Attig, Derek. "Here Comes the Bookmobile: Public Culture and the Shape of Belonging." PhD dissertation, University of Illinois, Urbana-Champaign, 2014.

Austin, Erastus Long. *The Sesqui-Centennial International Exposition: A Record Based on Official Data and Departmental Reports.* Philadelphia: Current Publications, 1929.

Axelrod, Steven Gould, Camille Roman, and Thomas J. Travisano, eds. *The New Anthology of American Poetry.* Vol. 1. Piscataway, NJ: Rutgers University Press, 2003.

Badger, Anthony J. *The New Deal: The Depression Years, 1933–1940.* New York: Farrar, Straus & Giroux, 1989.

Bal, Mieke, ed. *Acts of Memory: Cultural Recall in the Present.* Hanover, NH: University Press of New England, 1999.

Belk, Russell W. *Collecting in a Consumer Society.* New York: Routledge, 1995.

Bennett, Tony. *The Birth of the Museum: History, Theory, Politics.* London: Routledge, 1995.

Bierman, Stanley M. *More of the World's Greatest Stamp Collectors.* Sidney, OH: Linn's Stamp News, 1990.

Bierman, Stanley M. *The World's Greatest Stamp Collectors.* New York: Frederick Fell Publishers, 1981.

Blom, Philipp. *To Have and to Hold: An Intimate History of Collectors and Collecting.* Woodstock, NY: Overlook Press, 2003.

Bodnar, John E. *Remaking America: Public Memory, Commemoration, and Patriotism in the Twentieth Century.* Princeton, NJ: Princeton University Press, 1992.

Bogart, Ernest Ludlow. *War Costs and Their Financing, a Study of the Financing of the War and the After-War Problems of Debt and Taxation.* New York: D. Appleton and Company, 1921.

Boggs, Winthrop S. *The Foundations of Philately.* Princeton, NJ: D. Van Nostrand, 1955.

Brennan, Sheila Ann. "'Do Your Children Play—or Go to the Movies?': Constructions of Childhood and Class in Progressive Reform Rhetoric from the Silent Era." Master's thesis, University of Notre Dame, 1996.

Brinkley, Alan. *The End of Reform: New Deal Liberalism in Recession and War.* New York: Alfred A. Knopf, 1995.

Bronner, Simon J., ed. *American Material Culture and Folklife.* Logan: Utah State University Press, 1992.

Bronner, Simon J., ed. *Consuming Visions: Accumulation and Display of Goods in America, 1880–1920.* New York: Norton / Winterthur Museum, 1989.

Bruns, James H., and Bureau Issues Association. *The Philatelic Truck.* Takoma Park, MD: Bureau Issues Association, 1982.

Carrick, Alice Van Leer. *Collector's Luck; or, A Repository of Pleasant and Profitable Discourses Descriptive of the Household Furniture and Ornaments of Olden Time.* Boston: Atlantic Monthly Press, 1919.

Child, Jack. *Miniature Messages: The Semiotics and Politics of Latin American Postage Stamps.* Durham: Duke University Press, 2008.

Christ, Edwin. "The Adult Stamp Collector." PhD dissertation, University of Missouri, Sociology, 1957.

Clements, Monica Lynn, and Patricia Rosser Clements. *Cameos: Classical to Costume.* Atglen, PA: Schiffer Publishing, 1998.

Cohen, Lizabeth. *A Consumer's Republic: The Politics of Mass Consumption in Postwar America.* New York: Knopf, 2003.

Cohen, Lizabeth. *Making the New Deal, Industrial Workers in Chicago, 1919–1939.* Cambridge: Cambridge University Press, 1990.

Collins, A. Frederick. *Collecting Stamps for Fun and Profit.* New York: Appleton-Century Co., 1936.

Combs, W. V. *U.S. Departmental Specimen Stamps.* N.p.: American Philatelic Society, 1965.

Conn, Steven. *Museums and American Intellectual Life, 1876–1926.* Chicago: University of Chicago Press, 1998.

Cott, Nancy F. *The Grounding of Modern Feminism.* New Haven: Yale University Press, 1987.

Crane, Susan A. *Collecting and Historical Consciousness in Early Nineteenth-Century Germany.* Ithaca: Cornell University Press, 2000.

Crummett, Polly De Steiguer. *Button Collecting.* Chicago: Lightner Publishing, 1939.

Cushing, Marshall. *Story of Our Post Office: The Greatest Government Department in All its Phases.* Boston: A.M. Thayer, 1893.

Deane, Ethel. *Byways of Collecting.* London, New York: Cassell, 1908.

Dewey, John. *The School and Society: Being Three Lectures.* Chicago: University of Chicago Press, 1899.

Dexter, George Blake. *The Lure of Amateur Collecting.* Boston: Little, Brown, and Company, 1923.

Dilworth, Leah, ed. *Acts of Possession: Collecting in America.* New Brunswick, NJ: Rutgers University Press, 2003.

Diner, Steven J. *A Very Different Age: Americans of the Progressive Era.* New York: Hill and Wang, 1998.

Douglas, Susan J. *Inventing American Broadcasting, 1899–1922.* Baltimore: Johns Hopkins University Press, 1987.

Draper, James David. *Cameo Appearances.* New Haven: Yale University Press, 2008.

Dubin, Steven C. *Displays of Power: Memory and Amnesia in the American Museum.* New York: New York University Press, 1999.

Dumenil, Lynn. *The Modern Temper: American Culture and Society in the 1920s.* New York: Hill and Wang, 1995.

Durost, W. *Children's Collecting Activity Related to Social Factors.* New York: Bureau of Publications, Teachers' College, Columbia University, 1932.

Elsner, John, and Roger Cardinal, eds. *The Cultures of Collecting.* Cambridge, MA: Harvard University Press, 1994.

Fischer, David Hackett. *Paul Revere's Ride.* New York: Oxford University Press, 1995.

Foucault, Michel. *The Archaeology of Knowledge.* Translated by A. M. Sheridan Smith. New York: Pantheon Books, 1972.

Foy, Jessica H., and Thomas J. Schlereth, eds. *American Home Life, 1880–1930: A Social History of Spaces and Services.* Knoxville: University of Tennessee Press, 1992.

Franklin, John Hope, and August Meier. *Black Leaders of the Twentieth Century.* Urbana: University of Illinois Press, 1982.

Freud, Sigmund. *The Standard Edition of the Complete Psychological Works of Sigmund Freud.* Translated by James Strachey. London: Hogarth Press, 1948.

Fuller, Wayne E. *The American Mail: Enlarger of the Common Life.* Chicago: University of Chicago Press, 1972.

Fuller, Wayne E. *Morality and the Mail in Nineteenth Century America.* Urbana: University of Illinois Press, 2003.

Gamwell, Lynn, and Richard Wells, eds. *Sigmund Freud and Art: His Personal Collection of Antiquities.* Binghamton: State University of New York Press, 1989.

Garvey, Ellen Gruber. *The Adman in the Parlor: Magazines and the Gendering of Consumer Culture, 1880s to 1910s.* New York: Oxford University Press, 1996.

Gelber, Steven M. *Hobbies: Leisure and the Culture of Work in America.* New York: Columbia University Press, 1999.

Gerstle, Gary. *American Crucible: Race and Nation in the Twentieth Century*. Princeton: Princeton University Press, 2001.

Gibbons, Herbert Adams. *John Wanamaker*. Port Washington, NY: Kennikat Press, 1971.

Gilje, Paul A, ed. *Wages of Independence: Capitalism in the Early American Republic*. Madison, WI: Madison House, 1997.

Gillis, John A. *Commemorations: The Politics of National Identity*. Princeton: Princeton University Press, 1994.

Glickman, Lawrence B., ed. *Consumer Society in American History: A Reader*. Ithaca: Cornell University Press, 1999.

Goldstein, Carolyn M. *Do It Yourself: Home Improvement in 20th-Century America*. Princeton, NJ: Princeton Architectural Press, 1998.

Halbwachs, Maurice. *On Collective Memory*. Translated by Lewis A. Coser. Chicago: University of Chicago Press, 1992.

Hallgren, Mauritz. *All About Stamps: Their History and the Art of Collecting Them*. New York: Alfred A. Knopf, 1940.

Halsey, Richard, Townley Haines, and Elizabeth Tower. *The Homes of Our Ancestors*. New York: Doubleday, Page, and Company, 1925.

Hardin, Wes. *An American Invention: The Story of the Henry Ford Museum and Greenfield Village*. Dearborn: Henry Ford Museum and Greenfield Village, 1999.

Haring, Kristen. *Ham Radio's Technical Culture*. Cambridge, MA: MIT Press, 2007.

Hass, Kristin Ann. *Carried to the Wall: American Memory and the Vietnam Veterans Memorial*. Berkeley: University of California Press, 1998.

Hattaway, Herman, and Ethan Sepp Rafuse, eds. *The Ongoing Civil War: New Versions of Old Stories*. Columbia: University of Missouri Press, 2004.

Hazlitt, William Carew. *The Coin Collector*. London: G. Redway, 1896.

Henkin, David M. *The Postal Age: The Emergence of Modern Communications in Nineteenth-Century America*. Chicago: University of Chicago Press, 2006.

Hering, Katharina. "'We Are All Makers of History': People and Publics in the Practice of Pennsylvania-German Family History, 1891–1966." PhD dissertation, George Mason University, 2009.

Hoganson, Kristin L. *Consumers' Imperium: The Global Production of American Domesticity, 1865–1920*. Chapel Hill: University of North Carolina Press, 2007.

Hoganson, Kristin L. *Fighting for American Manhood: How Gender Politics Provoked the Spanish-American and Philippine-American Wars*. New Haven: Yale University Press, 1998.

Horowitz, Daniel. *The Morality of Spending: Attitudes toward the Consumer Society in America, 1875–1940*. Baltimore: Johns Hopkins University Press, 1985.

Horowitz, Roger, and Arwen Mohun. *His and Hers: Gender, Consumption, and Technology*. Charlottesville: University of Virginia Press, 1998.

Jacobson, Lisa. *Raising Consumers: Children and the American Mass Market in the Early Twentieth Century*. New York: Columbia University Press, 2004.

Jacobson, Matthew Frye. *Roots Too: White Ethnic Revival in Post-Civil Rights America*. Cambridge, MA: Harvard University Press, 2006.

Jacobson, Matthew Frye. *Whiteness of a Different Color: European Immigrants and the Alchemy of Race*. Cambridge, MA: Harvard University Press, 1998.

Johl, Max G. *The United States Commemorative Stamps of the Twentieth Century*. New York: H.L. Lindquist, 1947.

John, Richard R. *Spreading the News: The American Postal System from Franklin to Morse.* Cambridge, MA: Harvard University Press, 1998.

Judt, Matthias, Charles McGovern, and Susan Strasser. *Getting and Spending: European and American Consumer Societies in the Twentieth Century.* Washington, DC: German Historical Institute, 1998.

Kalb, Charles F., Jr. *Background to United States Philately, Handbook# 1: The Junior Philatelic Society of America.* Dubuque, IA: Economy Mail Service, 1966.

Kammen, Michael. *Mystic Chords of Memory: The Transformation of Tradition in American Culture.* New York: Knopf, 1991.

Kaplan, Amy, and Donald E. Pease, eds. *Cultures of United States Imperialism.* Durham: Duke University Press, 1993.

Karp, Ivan, and Christine Mullen Kreamer, eds. *Museums and Communities: The Politics of Public Culture.* Washington, DC: Smithsonian Institution Press, 1992.

Karp, Ivan, and Steven D. Lavine, eds. *Exhibiting Cultures: The Poetics and Politics of Museum Display.* Washington, DC: Smithsonian Institution Press, 1991.

Kevles, Daniel J. *In the Name of Eugenics: Genetics and the Uses of Human Heredity.* Berkeley: University of California Press, 1985.

Ketchum, William C. *The Collections of the Margaret Woodbury Strong Museum.* Rochester, NY: Margaret Woodbury Strong Museum, 1982.

Kett, Joseph F. *The Pursuit of Knowledge under Difficulties: From Self-improvement to Adult.* Palo Alto, CA: Stanford University Press, 1994.

Kingery, W. David. *Learning from Things: Method and Theory of Material Culture Studies.* Washington, DC: Smithsonian Institution Press, 1996.

Kraut, Alan M. *Silent Travelers: Germs, Genes, and the "Immigrant Menace".* New York: Basic Books, 1994.

Laird, Pamela Walker. *Advertising Progress: American Business and the Rise of Consumer Marketing.* Baltimore: Johns Hopkins University Press, 1998.

Lampland, Ruth, ed. *Hobbies for Everybody.* New York: Harper & Brothers, 1934.

Landsberg, Alison. *Prosthetic Memory: The Transformation of American Remembrance in the Age of Mass Culture.* New York: Columbia University Press, 2004.

Leach, William. *Land of Desire: Merchants, Power, and the Rise of a New American Culture.* New York: Pantheon Books, 1993.

Leon, Warren, and Roy Rosenzweig, eds. *History Museums in the United States: A Critical Assessment.* Urbana: University of Illinois Press, 1989.

Levine, Lawrence W. *Highbrow/Lowbrow: The Emergence of Cultural Hierarchy in America.* Cambridge, MA: Harvard University Press, 1988.

Lindsay, Vachel. *Adventures While Preaching the Gospel of Beauty.* New York: Mitchell Kennerley, 1914.

Lipman, Jean, ed. *The Collector in America.* New York: Viking Press, 1970.

Lowenthal, David. *The Past Is a Foreign Country.* Cambridge: Cambridge University Press, 1985.

Lubar, Steven D., Kathleen M. Kendrick, and National Museum of American History. *Legacies: Collecting America's History at the Smithsonian.* Washington, DC: Smithsonian Institution Press, 2001.

Lubar, Steven D., and W. D. Kingery, eds. *History from Thing: Essays on Material Culture.* Washington, DC: Smithsonian Institution Press, 1993.

Lundberg, Ferdinand. *America's 60 Families.* New York: Vanguard Press, 1937.

Lynch, Bohun. *Collecting; An Essay.* New York: Harper & Brothers, 1928.

Macleod, David. *Building Character in the American Boy: The Boy Scouts, YMCA, and Their Forerunners.* Madison: University of Wisconsin Press, 2004.

Marling, Karal Ann. *George Washington Slept Here: Colonial Revivals and American Culture, 1876–1986.* Cambridge, MA: Harvard University Press, 1988.

Marling, Karal Ann. *Wall-to-Wall America: Post Office Murals in the Great Depression.* Minneapolis: University of Minnesota Press, 1982.

Marquis, Albert Nelson. *The Book of Detroiters: A Biographical Dictionary of Leading Living Men of the City of Detroit.* Chicago: A.N. Marquis & Company, 1908.

Marquis, Albert Nelson *The Book of Detroiters: A Biographical Dictionary of Leading Living Men of the City of Detroit.* Chicago: A.N. Marquis & Company, 1914.

Martinez, Katherine, and Kenneth L. Ames, eds. *Material Culture of Gender / Gender of Material Culture.* Ann Arbor: University of Michigan Press, 1992.

McCracken, Grant. *Culture and Consumption: New Approaches to the Symbolic Character of Consumer Goods and Activities.* Bloomington: Indiana University Press, 1990.

McDannell, Colleen. *Material Christianity: Religion and Popular Culture in America.* New Haven: Yale University Press, 1995.

McGovern, Charles. *Sold American: Consumption and Citizenship, 1890–1945.* Chapel Hill: University of North Carolina Press, 2006.

McMillen, Wheeler. *The Young Collector.* New York: D. Appleton, 1928.

Mebane, John. *The Coming Collecting Boom.* South Brunswick, NJ: A. S. Barnes, 1968.

Moore, R. Laurence. *Selling God: American Religion in the Marketplace of Culture.* New York: Oxford University Press, 1994.

Morgan, Francesca. *Women and Patriotism in Jim Crow America.* Chapel Hill: University of North Carolina Press, 2005.

Muensterberger, Werner. *Collecting: An Unruly Passion: Psychological Perspectives.* Princeton: Princeton University Press, 1994.

Nasaw, David. *Going Out: The Rise and Fall of Public Amusements.* Cambridge, MA: Harvard University Press, 1999.

Nash, Gary B. *Friends of Liberty: Thomas Jefferson, Tadeusz Kościuszko, and Agrippa Hull: A Tale of Three Patriots, Two Revolutions, and a Tragic Betrayal of Freedom in the New Nation.* New York: Basic Books, 2008.

National Recreation Association. *The Leisure Hours of 5,000 People; a Report of a Study of Leisure Time Activities and Desires.* New York: National Recreation Association, 1934.

New-York Historical Society. *Guide to the American Art-Union Print Collection, 1840–1851.* New York: New-York Historical Society, 2002.

Newman, Peter T., and Lowell S. Rohrbach. *American Issue: The U.S. Postage Stamp, 1842–1869.* Washington, DC: Smithsonian Institution Press, 1984.

Ororsz, Joel J. *Curators and Culture: The Museum Movement in America, 1740–1870.* Tuscaloosa: University of Alabama Press, 1990.

Pakenham, Thomas. *The Scramble for Africa: White Man's Conquest of the Dark Continent from 1876 to 1912.* New York: Avon Books, 1992.

Pearce, Susan M. *Interpreting Objects and Collections.* London: Routledge, 1994.

Pearce, Susan M. *Museums, Objects, and Collections.* Leicester: Leicester University Press, 1992.

Pearce, Susan M. *On Collecting: An Investigation into Collecting in the European Tradition.* London: Routledge, 1995.

Pearce, Susan M., Alexandra Bounia, and Paul Martin. *The Collector's Voice: Critical Readings in the Practice of Collecting.* Burlington, VT: Ashgate, 2000.

Peiss, Kathy Lee. *Cheap Amusements: Working Women and Leisure in Turn-of-the-Century New York.* Philadelphia: Temple University Press, 1986.

Pierce, Bessie Louise. *Civic Attitudes in American School Textbooks.* Chicago: University of Chicago Press, 1930.

Pitney-Bowes and Research Dept. *The Stamp Racket: A Survey Covering the Traffic in Counterfeit, Stolen and Washed Postage Stamps.* Stamford, CT: The Company, 1938.

Prown, Jules David. *Art as Evidence: Writings on Art and Material Culture.* New Haven: Yale University Press, 2001.

Pynchon, Thomas. *The Crying of Lot 49.* New York: J.B. Lippincott, 1965.

Radway, Janice A. *A Feeling for Books: The Book-of-the-Month Club, Literary Taste, and Middle-Class Desire.* Chapel Hill: University of North Carolina Press, 1997.

Reebel, Patrick A. *United States Post Office: Current Issues and Historical Background.* New York: Nova Science Publishers, 2003.

Rigby, Douglas, and Elizabeth Rigby. *Lock, Stock, and Barrel: The Story of Collecting.* Philadelphia: Lippincott, 1949.

Robie, Virginia Huntington. *By-paths in Collecting.* New York: Century Company, 1912.

Robie, Virginia Huntington. *The Quest of the Quaint.* Boston: Little, Brown, 1916.

Roediger, David R. *Working toward Whiteness: How America's Immigrants Became White. The Strange Journey from Ellis Island to the Suburbs.* New York: Basic Books, 2005.

Rosenzweig, Roy. *Eight Hours for What We Will: Workers and Leisure in an Industrial City, 1870–1920.* Cambridge: Cambridge University Press, 1985.

Rosenzweig, Roy, and David Thelen. *The Presence of the Past: Popular Uses of History in American Life.* New York: Columbia University Press, 1998.

Ross, Dorothy. *The Origins of American Social Science.* Cambridge: Cambridge University Press, 1991.

Rowed, Charles. *Collecting as a Pastime.* New York: Cassell, 1920.

Ruutz-Rees, Janet E. *Home Occupations.* New York: D. Appleton, 1883.

Rydell, Robert W. *All the World's a Fair: Visions of Empire at American International Expositions, 1876–1916.* Chicago: University of Chicago Press, 1984.

Rydell, Robert W. *World of Fairs: The Century-of-Progress Expositions.* Chicago: University of Chicago Press, 1993.

Said, Edward W. *Orientalism.* New York: Pantheon Books, 1978.

Sandler, Carol. *Margaret Woodbury Strong: Collector.* Rochester, NY: Strong Museum, 1989.

Sandweiss, Martha A. *Photography in Nineteenth-Century America.* New York: Harry N. Abrams, 1991.

Savage, Kirk. *Standing Soldiers, Kneeling Slaves: Race, War, and Monument in Nineteenth-Century America.* Princeton: Princeton University Press, 1997.

Scales, T. Laine. *All That Fits a Woman: Training Southern Baptist Women for Charity and Mission, 1907–1926.* Macon, GA: Mercer University Press, 2000.

Schlereth, Thomas J. *Cultural History and Material Culture: Everyday Life, Landscapes, Museums.* Ann Arbor, MI: UMI Research Press, 1990.

Schlereth, Thomas J. *Material Culture Studies in America.* Nashville, TN: American Association for State and Local History, 1982.

Scott, David H. T. *European Stamp Design: A Semiotic Approach to Designing Messages.* London: Academy Editions, 1995.

Scranton, Philip, ed. *Beauty and Business: Commerce, Gender, and Culture in Modern America.* New York: Routledge, 2001.

Sheehan, Susan, and Howard B. Means. *The Banana Sculptor, the Purple Lady, and*

the All-Night Swimmer: Hobbies, Collecting, and Other Passionate Pursuits. New York: Simon & Schuster, 2002.
Simonds, William Adams. *Henry Ford and Greenfield Village.* New York: Frederick A. Stokes, 1938.
Sinnette, Elinor Des Verney, W. Paul Coates, and Thomas C. Battle, eds. *Black Bibliophiles and Collectors: Preservers of Black History.* Washington, DC: Howard University Press, 1990.
Sitkoff, Harvard. *A New Deal for Blacks: The Emergence of Civil Rights as a National Issue.* New York: Oxford University Press, 1978.
Skocpol, Theda. *Diminished Democracy: From Membership to Management in American Civic Life.* Norman: University of Oklahoma Press, 2003.
Slawson, Douglas J. *The Department of Education Battle, 1918–1932: Public Schools, Catholic Schools, and the Social Order.* Notre Dame: University of Notre Dame Press, 2005.
Smith, Leonard H., Jr. *Philately and Postal History, an Introduction.* Clearwater, FL: N.H. Smith, 1970.
Smithsonian Institution Libraries and Robert W. Rydell. *The Books of the Fairs: Materials about World's Fairs, 1834–1916, in the Smithsonian Institution Libraries.* Chicago: American Library Association, 1992.
Smulyan, Susan. *Selling Radio: The Commercialization of American Broadcasting, 1920–1934.* Washington, DC: Smithsonian Institution Press, 1994.
Stebbins, R. A. *Amateurs, Professionals, and Serious Leisure.* Montreal: McGill-Queens University Press, 1992.
Stewart, Susan. *On Longing: Narratives of the Miniature, the Gigantic, the Souvenir, the Collection.* Baltimore: John Hopkins University Press, 1984.
Strange, Edward Fairbrother. *The Collector.* London, 1927.
Sturken, Marita. *Tangled Memories: The Vietnam War, the AIDS Epidemic, and the Politics of Remembering.* Berkeley: University of California Press, 1997.
Sturken, Marita. *Tourists of History: Memory, Kitsch, and Consumerism from Oklahoma City to Ground Zero.* Durham: Duke University Press, 2007.
Taussig, Charles William, and Theodore Arthur Meyer. *The Book of Hobbies; or, A Guide to Happiness.* New York: Minton, 1924.
Taylor, Joshua Charles. *America as Art.* Washington, DC: Smithsonian Institution Press, 1976.
Teall, Gardner Callahan. *The Pleasures of Collecting.* New York: Century, 1920.
Townsend, Robert. *History's Babel: Scholarship, Professionalization, and the Historical Enterprise in the United States, 1880–1940.* Chicago: University of Chicago Press, 2013.
Trachtenberg, Alan. *Brooklyn Bridge: Fact and Symbol.* New York: Oxford University Press, 1965.
Trachtenberg, Alan. *The Incorporation of America: Culture and Society in the Gilded Age.* New York: Hill and Wang, 1982.
Treese, Lorett. *Valley Forge: Making and Remaking a National Symbol.* University Park: Pennsylvania State University Press, 1995.
Trumbull, Charles Galludet. *Anthony Comstock, Fighter: Some Impressions of a Lifetime of Adventure in Conflict with the Powers of Evil.* Vol. 2. New York: Fleming H. Revell, 1913.
Tucker, Susan, Katherine Ott, and Patricia Buckler, eds. *The Scrapbook in American Life.* Philadelphia: Temple University Press, 2006.
United States Bureau of Engraving and Printing. *History of the Bureau of Engraving and Printing, 1862–1962.* Reprint. New York: Sanford J. Durst, 1978.

United States Postal Service. *Publication 100—The United States Postal Service—An American History 1775–2006.* Washington, DC: USPS, 2012.

Veblen, Thorstein. *The Theory of the Leisure Class: An Economic Study of Institutions.* New York: Mentor, 1899.

Vors, Frederic. *Bibelots and Curios: A Manual for Collectors, with a Glossary of Technical Terms.* New York: D. Appleton, 1879.

Wadham, Charles King. *Some Reminiscences and Reflections on Collecting Autographs.* Dalton, MA: Privately printed (New Haven: Printing Office of the Yale University Press), 1931.

Weeks, William R. *History of the American Numismatic and Archeological Society.* New York: American Numismatic and Archeological Society, 1892.

Weems, Mason Locke. *A History of the Life and Death, Virtues and Exploits of General George Washington.* Mt Vernon edition. Philadelphia: J.B. Lippincott Company, 1918.

Weisberg, Gabriel P., DeCourcy E. McIntosh, Alison McQueen, and Frick Art and Historical Center. *Collecting in the Gilded Age: Art Patronage in Pittsburgh, 1890–1910.* Pittsburgh: Frick Art and Historical Center; distributed by University Press of New England, 1997.

West, Elliot, and Paula Petrik, eds. *Small Worlds: Children and Adolescents in America, 1850–1950.* Lawrence: University Press of Kansas, 1992.

West, Patricia. *Domesticating History: The Political Origins of America's House Museums.* Washington, DC: Smithsonian Institution, 1999.

Wiebe, Robert H. *The Search for Order, 1877–1920.* New York: Hill and Wang, 1967.

Williams, Henry T., and C. S. Jones. *Beautiful Homes. Or, Hints in House Furnishing.* New York: H. T. Williams, 1878.

Williamson, George Charles. *The Amateur Collector; Everybody's Book on Collecting.* New York: R.M. McBride, 1924.

Williamson, George Charles. *The Miniature Collector: A Guide for the Amateur Collector of Portrait Miniatures.* London: H. Jenkins, 1921.

Wood, Kenneth A. *Post Dates: A Chronology of Intriguing Events in the Mails and Philately.* Albany, OR: Van Dahl Publications, 1985.

Wooddy, Carroll Hill. *The Growth of the Federal Government, 1915–1932.* New York: McGraw-Hill, 1934.

Wright, John L., and Henry Ford Museum and Greenfield Village. *Possible Dreams: Enthusiasm for Technology in America.* Dearborn, MI: Henry Ford Museum and Greenfield Village, 1992.

Young, James E. *The Texture of Memory: Holocaust Memorials and Meaning.* New Haven: Yale University Press, 1993.

Index

Note: Page numbers in italics refer to illustrations.